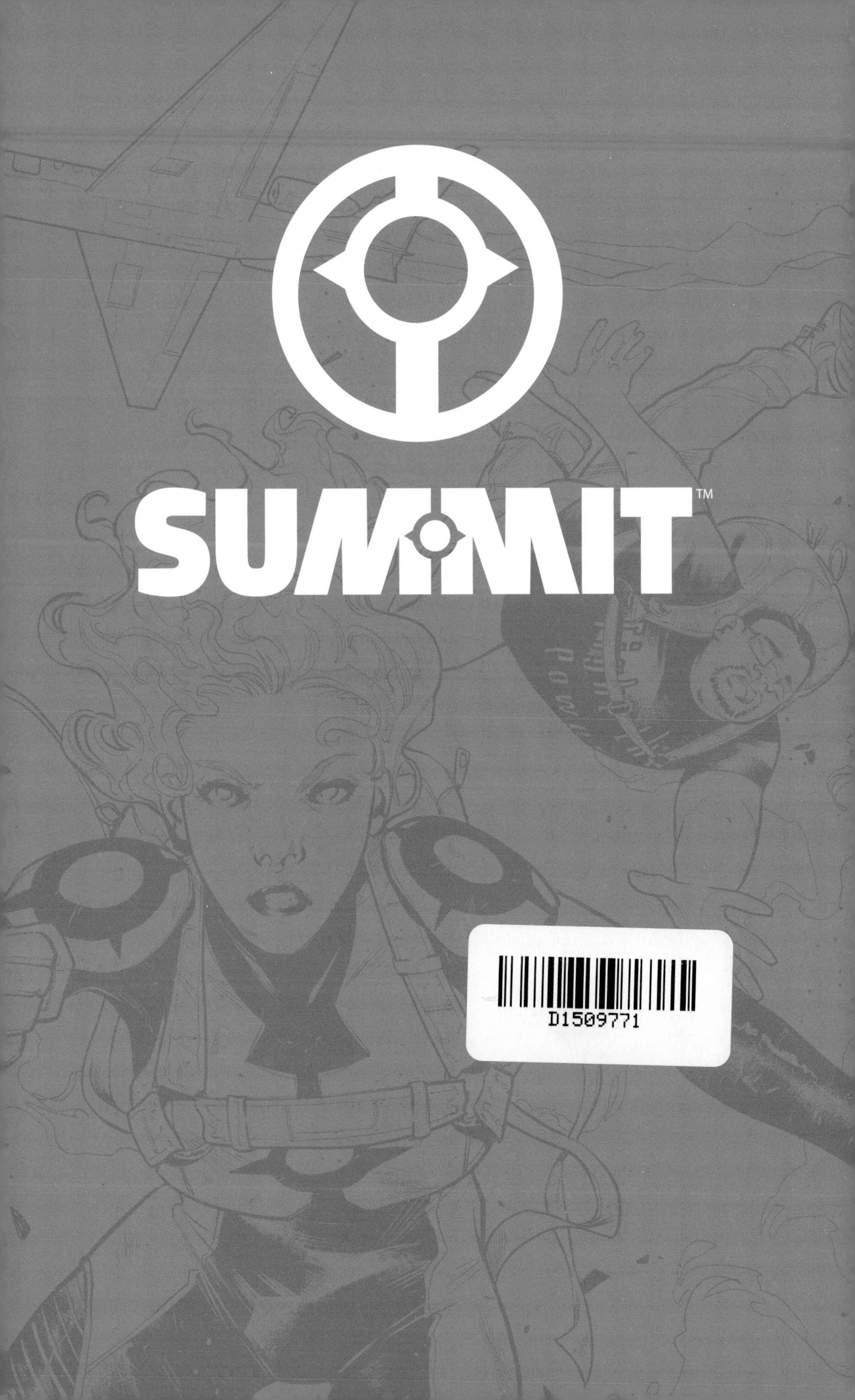

SUMMIT™

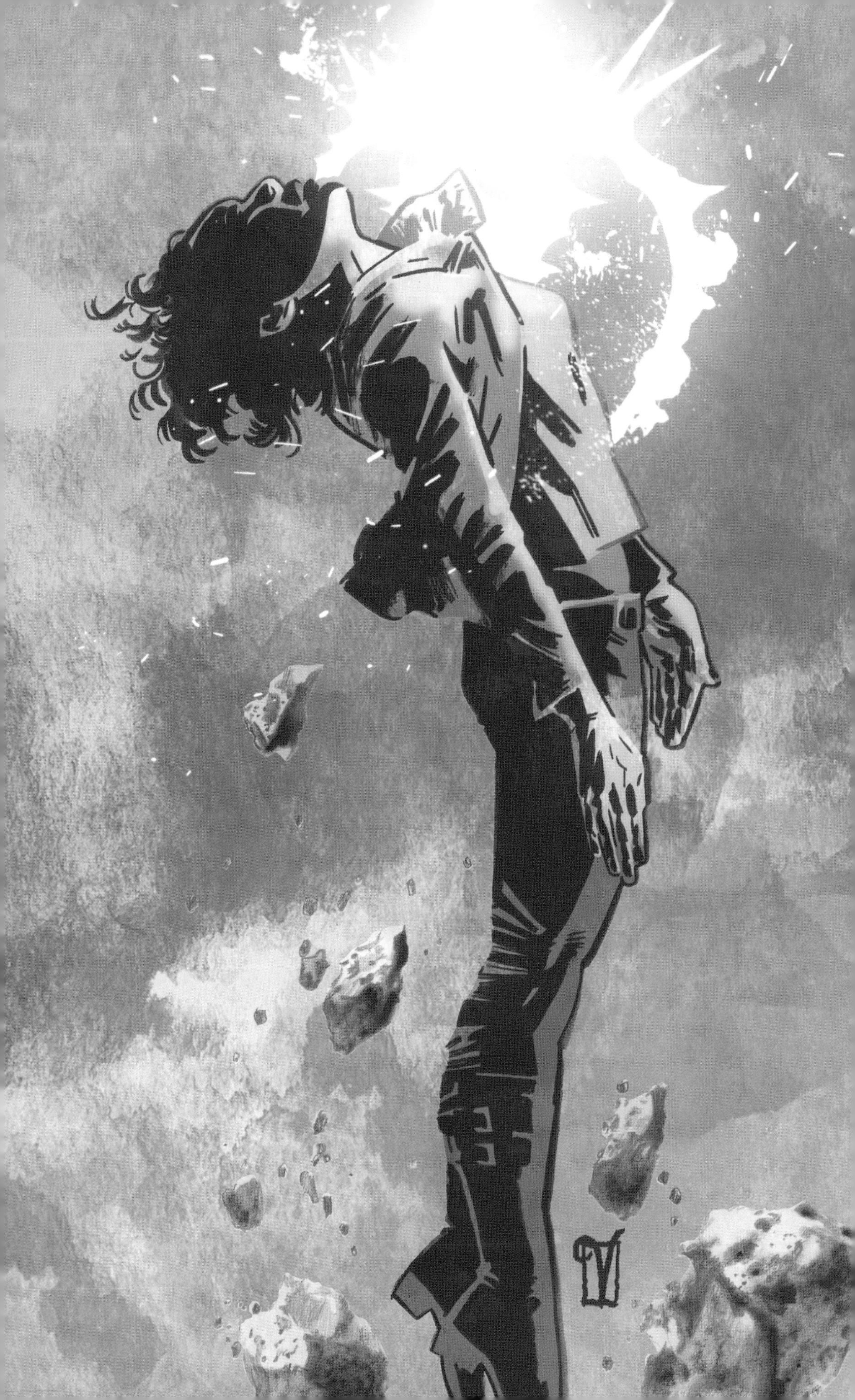

CATALYST™ PRIME

SUMMIT™

PRICE OF POWER

written by **AMY CHU**
illustrated by **FEDERICO DALLOCHIO, WILL ROSADO,** and **MARIKA CRESTA**
lettered by **DERON BENNETT** and **AW'S DC HOPKINS**
colored by **SOTOCOLOR**

JOSEPH ILLIDGE • senior editor
DESIREE RODRIGUEZ • editor
KAT VENDETTI and **AXEL BORDELON** • editorial assistant
cover by **VALENTINE DE LANDRO**

LION™ FORGE

ISBN: 978-1-5493-0285-5

Library of Congress Control Number: 2018941616

10 9 8 7 6 5 4 3 2 1

CHAPTER
ONE

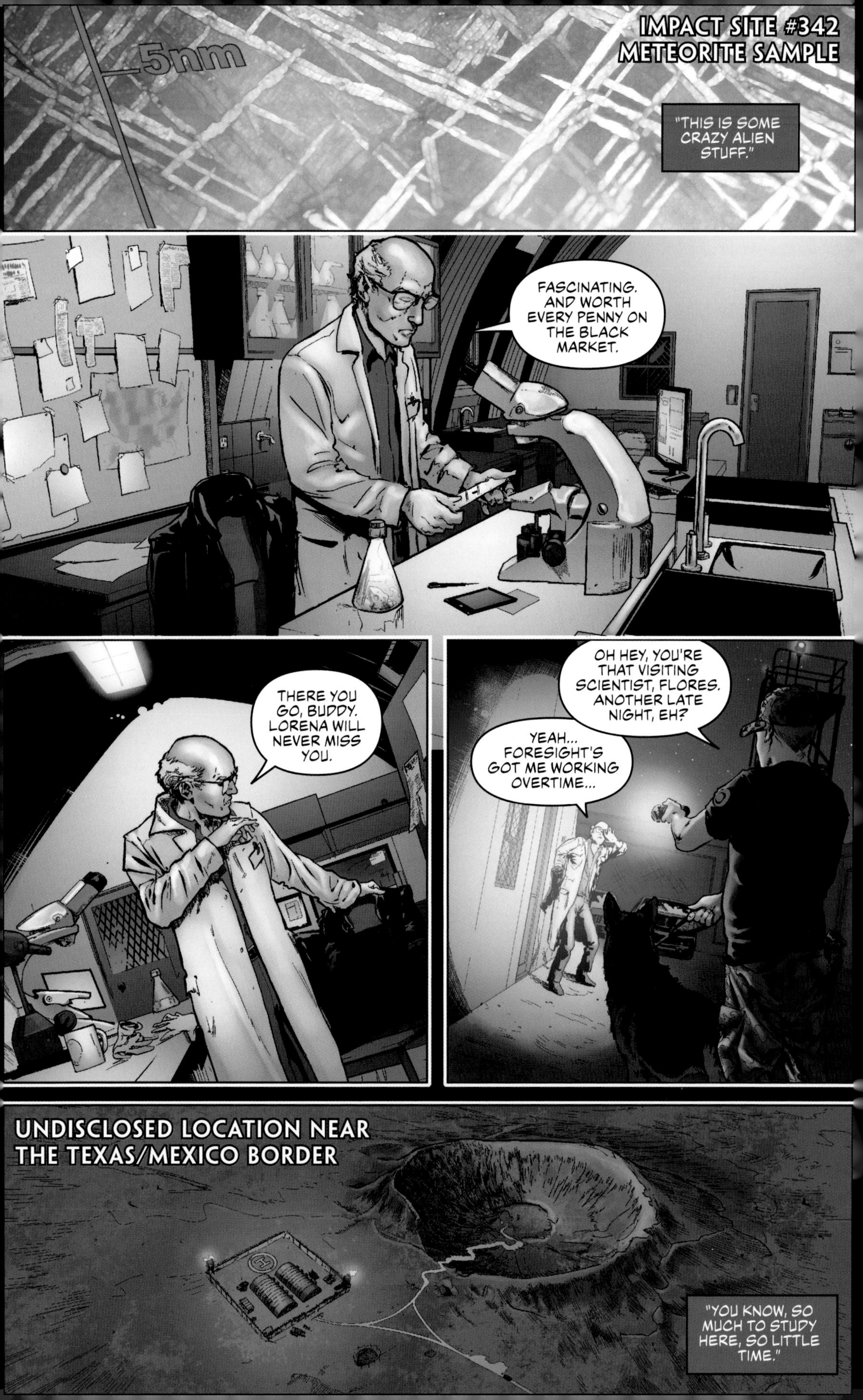

5nm
IMPACT SITE #342
METEORITE SAMPLE
"THIS IS SOME CRAZY ALIEN STUFF."
FASCINATING. AND WORTH EVERY PENNY ON THE BLACK MARKET.
THERE YOU GO, BUDDY. LORENA WILL NEVER MISS YOU.
OH HEY, YOU'RE THAT VISITING SCIENTIST, FLORES. ANOTHER LATE NIGHT, EH?
YEAH... FORESIGHT'S GOT ME WORKING OVERTIME...
UNDISCLOSED LOCATION NEAR THE TEXAS/MEXICO BORDER
"YOU KNOW, SO MUCH TO STUDY HERE, SO LITTLE TIME."

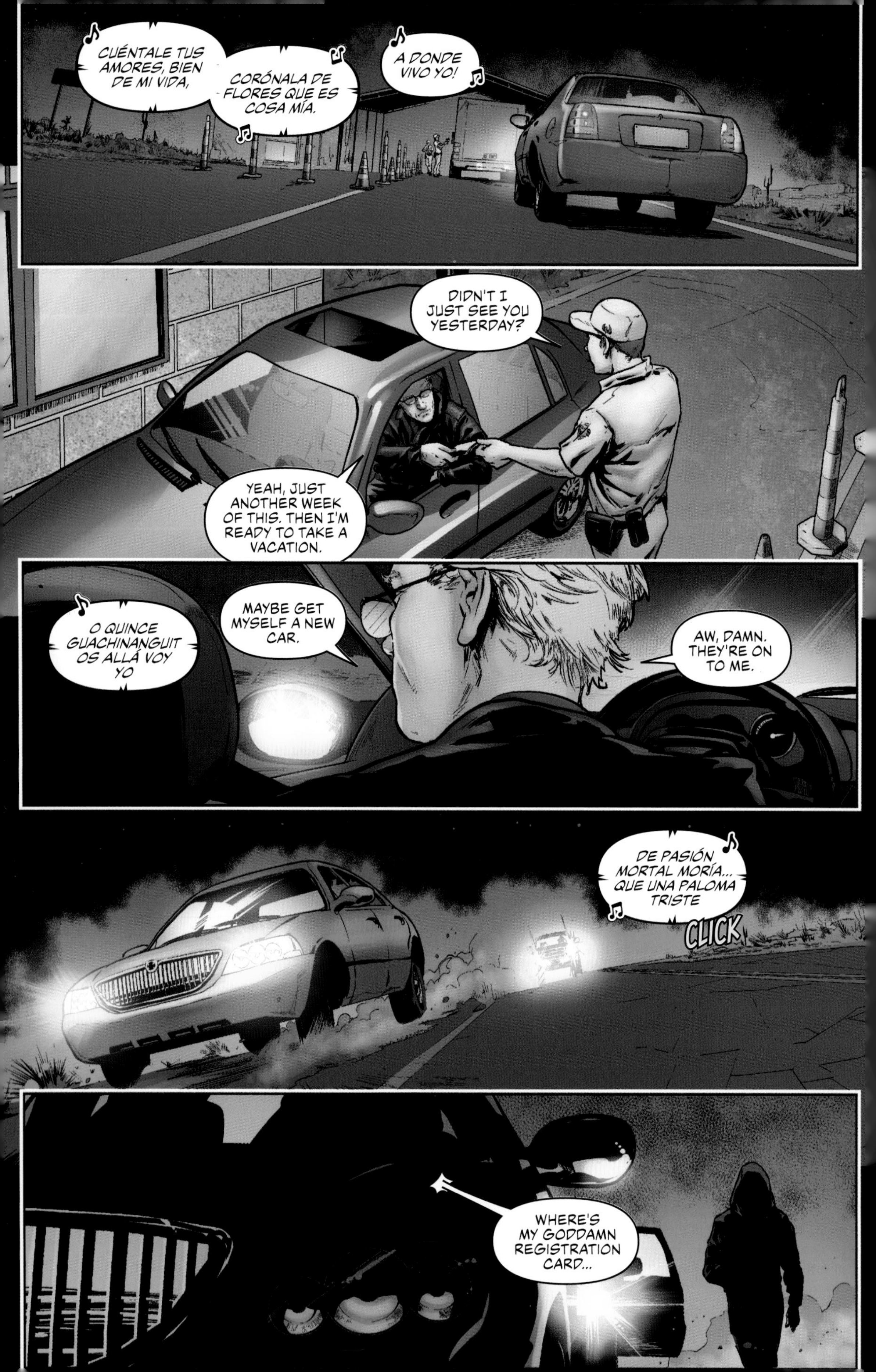
CUÉNTALE TUS AMORES, BIEN DE MI VIDA,
CORÓNALA DE FLORES QUE ES COSA MÍA.
A DONDE VIVO YO!
DIDN'T I JUST SEE YOU YESTERDAY?
YEAH, JUST ANOTHER WEEK OF THIS. THEN I'M READY TO TAKE A VACATION.
O QUINCE GUACHINANGUIT OS ALLÁ VOY YO
MAYBE GET MYSELF A NEW CAR.
AW, DAMN. THEY'RE ON TO ME.
DE PASIÓN MORTAL MORÍA... QUE UNA PALOMA TRISTE
CLICK
WHERE'S MY GODDAMN REGISTRATION CARD...

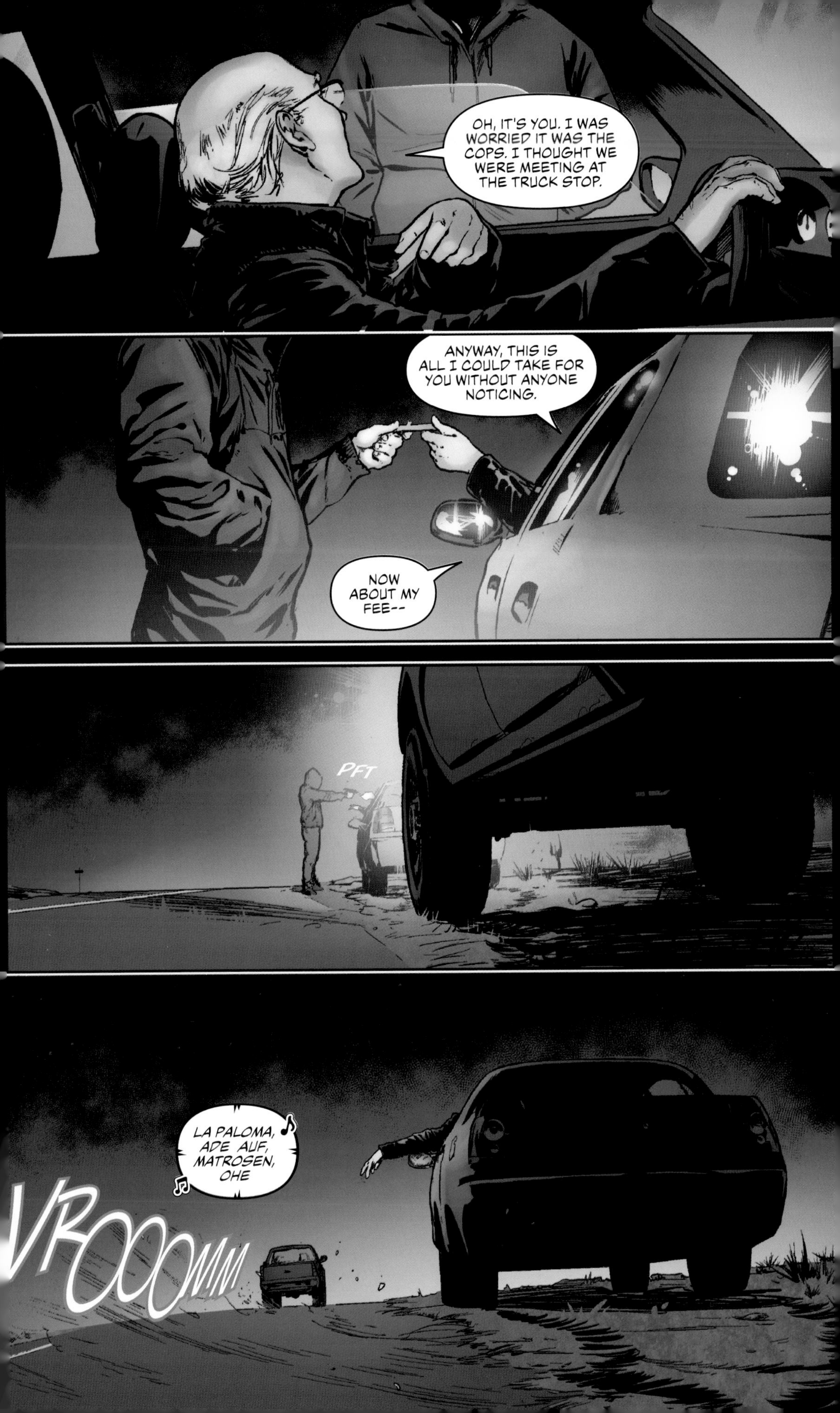
OH, IT'S YOU. I WAS WORRIED IT WAS THE COPS. I THOUGHT WE WERE MEETING AT THE TRUCK STOP.
ANYWAY, THIS IS ALL I COULD TAKE FOR YOU WITHOUT ANYONE NOTICING.
NOW ABOUT MY FEE--
PFT
LA PALOMA, ADE AUF, MATROSEN, OHE
VROOOMM

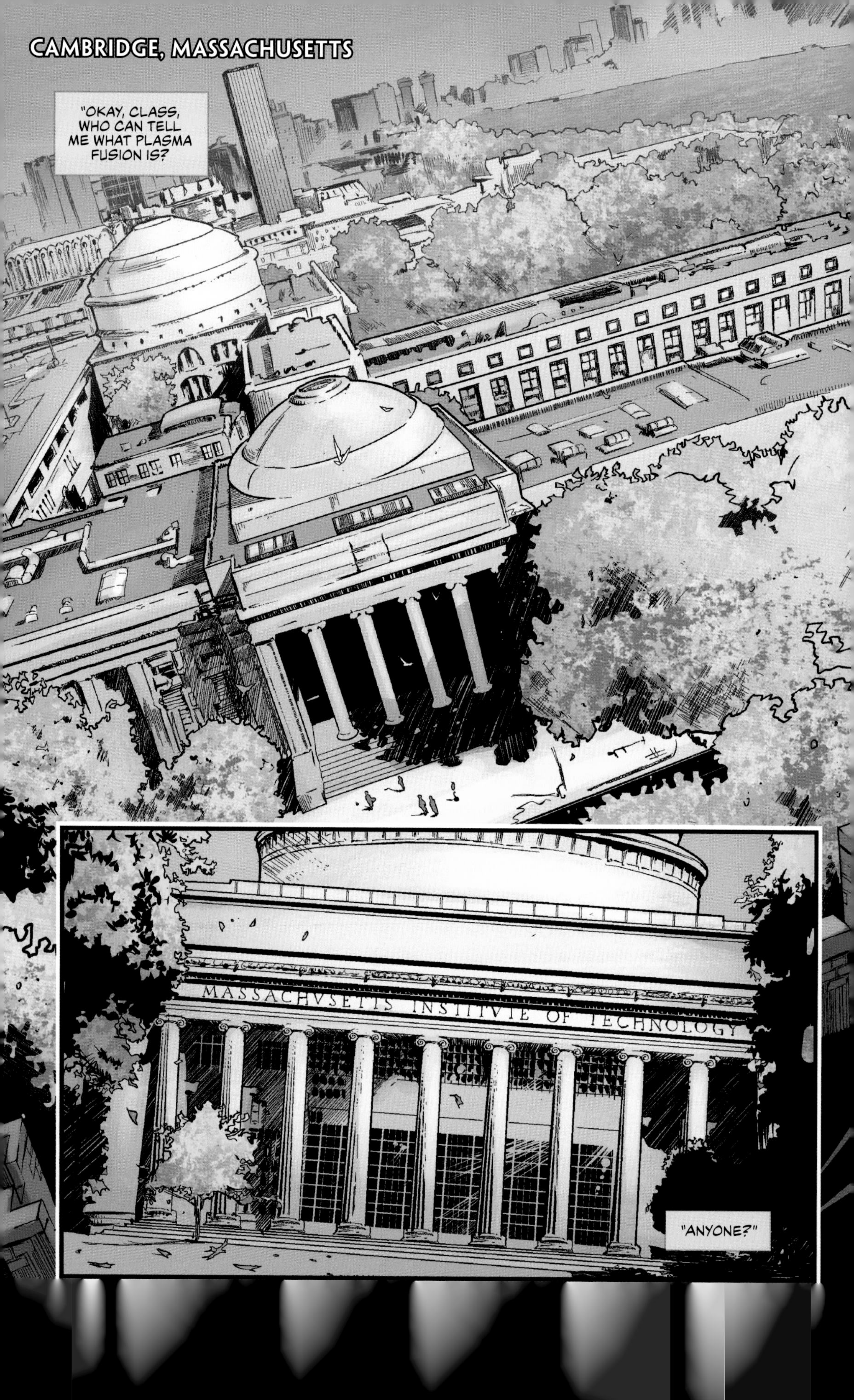
CAMBRIDGE, MASSACHUSETTS
"OKAY, CLASS, WHO CAN TELL ME WHAT PLASMA FUSION IS?
MASSACHVSETTS INSTITVTE OF TECHNOLOGY
"ANYONE?"

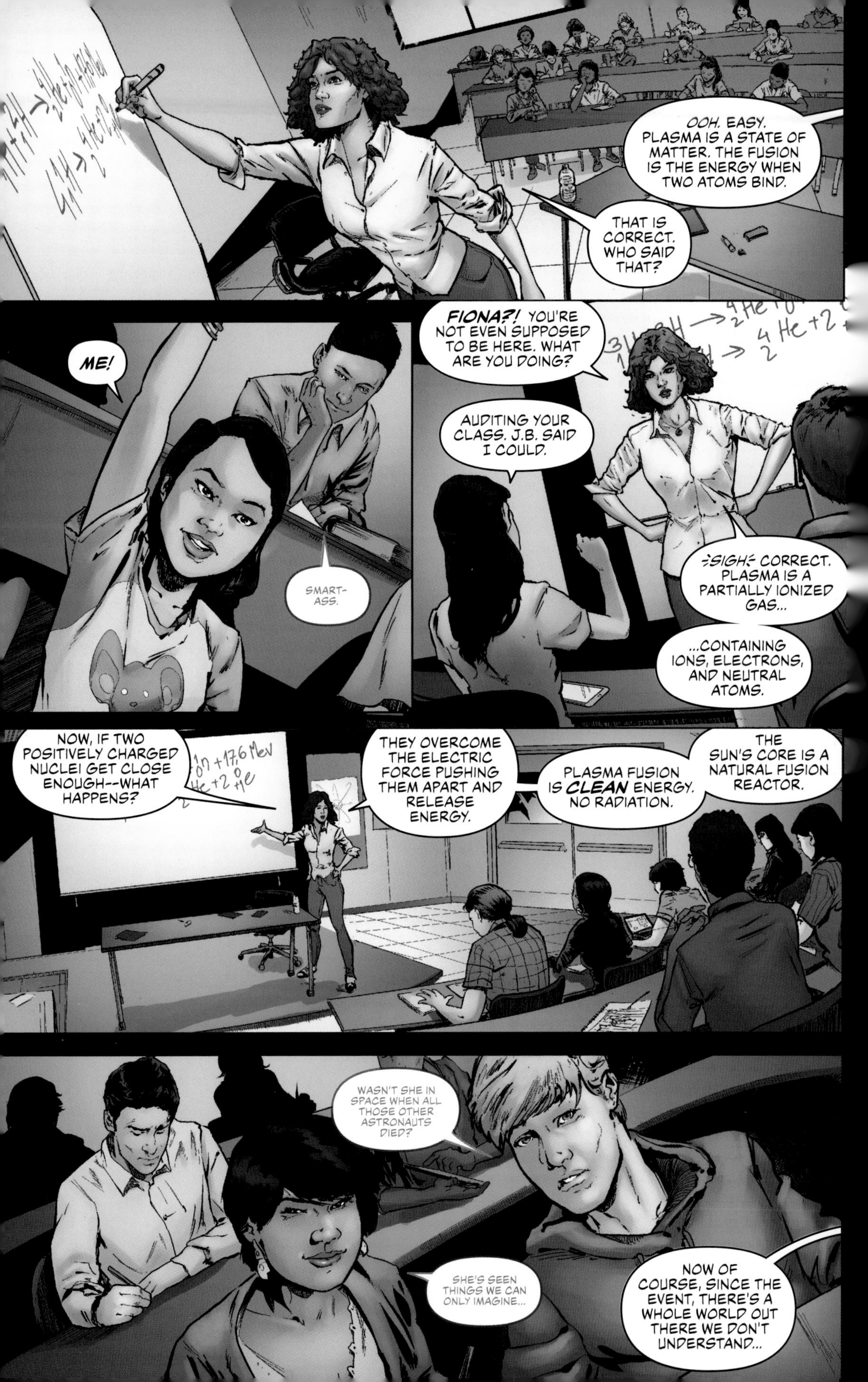
OOH. EASY. PLASMA IS A STATE OF MATTER. THE FUSION IS THE ENERGY WHEN TWO ATOMS BIND.
THAT IS CORRECT. WHO SAID THAT?
ME!
SMART-ASS.
FIONA?! YOU'RE NOT EVEN SUPPOSED TO BE HERE. WHAT ARE YOU DOING?
AUDITING YOUR CLASS. J.B. SAID I COULD.
-SIGH- CORRECT. PLASMA IS A PARTIALLY IONIZED GAS...
...CONTAINING IONS, ELECTRONS, AND NEUTRAL ATOMS.
NOW, IF TWO POSITIVELY CHARGED NUCLEI GET CLOSE ENOUGH--WHAT HAPPENS?
THEY OVERCOME THE ELECTRIC FORCE PUSHING THEM APART AND RELEASE ENERGY.
PLASMA FUSION IS CLEAN ENERGY. NO RADIATION.
THE SUN'S CORE IS A NATURAL FUSION REACTOR.
WASN'T SHE IN SPACE WHEN ALL THOSE OTHER ASTRONAUTS DIED?
SHE'S SEEN THINGS WE CAN ONLY IMAGINE...
NOW OF COURSE, SINCE THE EVENT, THERE'S A WHOLE WORLD OUT THERE WE DON'T UNDERSTAND...

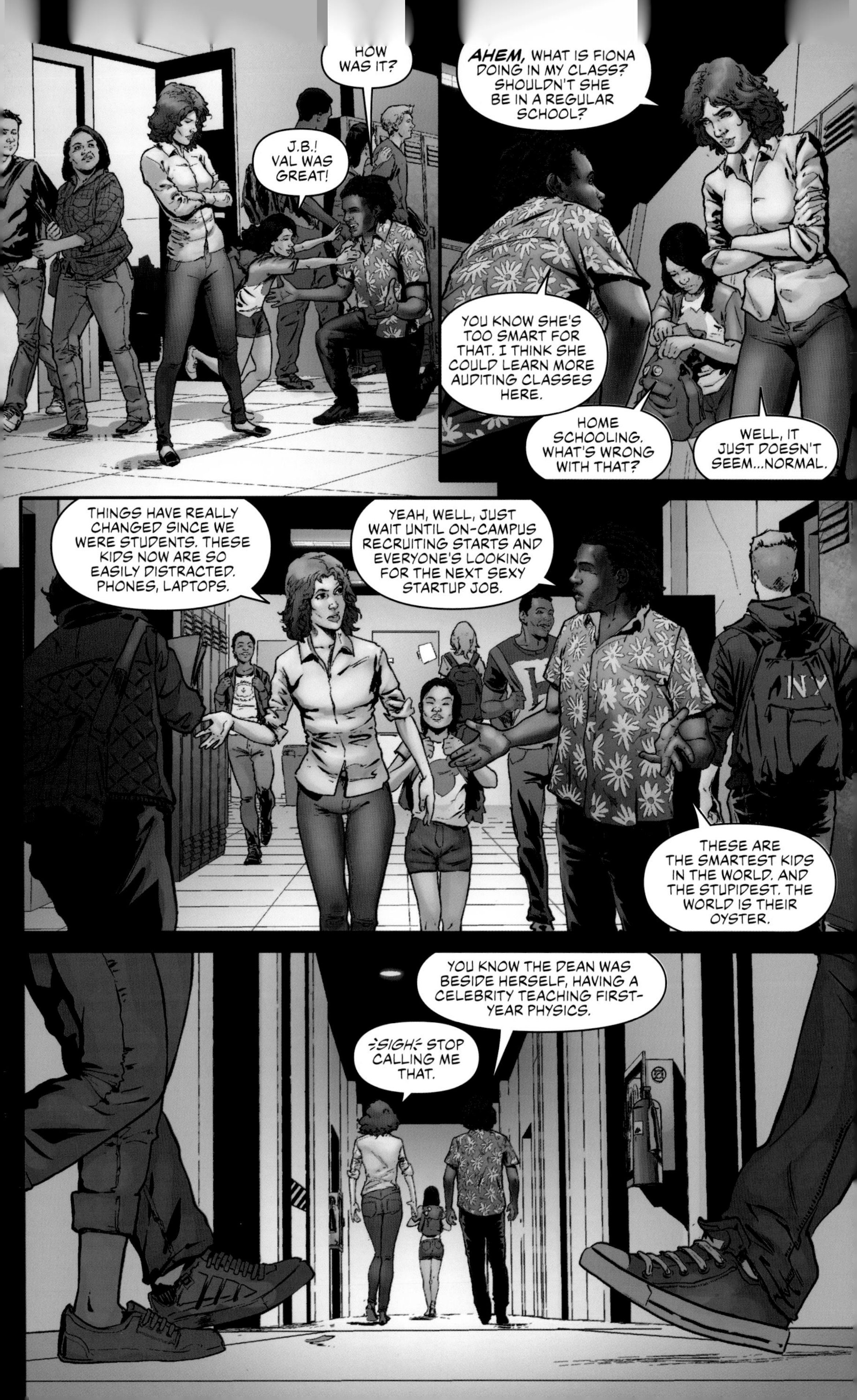
HOW WAS IT?
J.B.! VAL WAS GREAT!
AHEM, WHAT IS FIONA DOING IN MY CLASS? SHOULDN'T SHE BE IN A REGULAR SCHOOL?
YOU KNOW SHE'S TOO SMART FOR THAT. I THINK SHE COULD LEARN MORE AUDITING CLASSES HERE.
HOME SCHOOLING. WHAT'S WRONG WITH THAT?
WELL, IT JUST DOESN'T SEEM...NORMAL.
THINGS HAVE REALLY CHANGED SINCE WE WERE STUDENTS. THESE KIDS NOW ARE SO EASILY DISTRACTED. PHONES, LAPTOPS.
YEAH, WELL, JUST WAIT UNTIL ON-CAMPUS RECRUITING STARTS AND EVERYONE'S LOOKING FOR THE NEXT SEXY STARTUP JOB.
THESE ARE THE SMARTEST KIDS IN THE WORLD. AND THE STUPIDEST. THE WORLD IS THEIR OYSTER.
YOU KNOW THE DEAN WAS BESIDE HERSELF, HAVING A CELEBRITY TEACHING FIRST-YEAR PHYSICS.
-SIGH- STOP CALLING ME THAT.

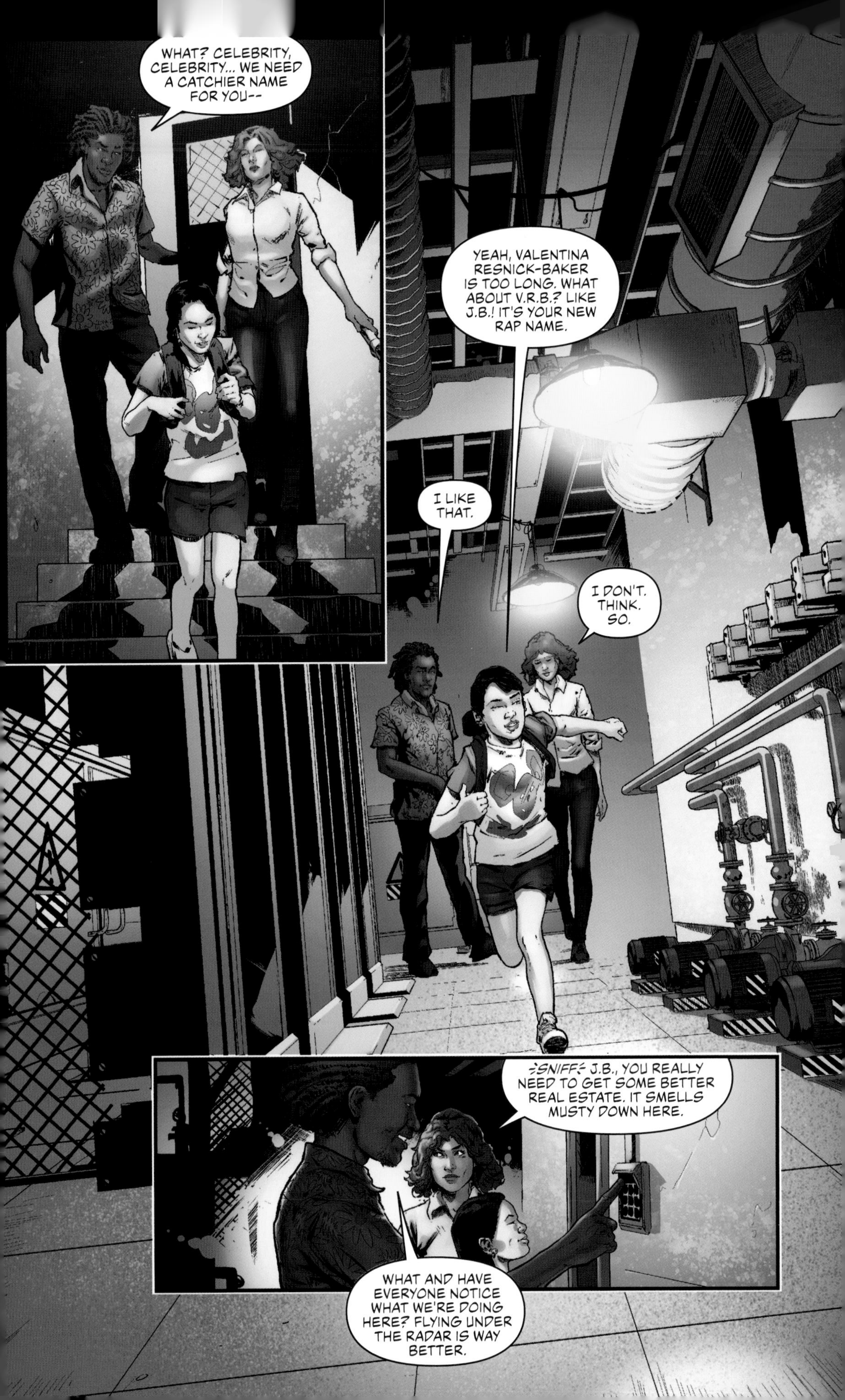
WHAT? CELEBRITY, CELEBRITY... WE NEED A CATCHIER NAME FOR YOU--
YEAH, VALENTINA RESNICK-BAKER IS TOO LONG. WHAT ABOUT V.R.B.? LIKE J.B.! IT'S YOUR NEW RAP NAME.
I LIKE THAT.
I DON'T. THINK. SO.
SNIFF J.B., YOU REALLY NEED TO GET SOME BETTER REAL ESTATE. IT SMELLS MUSTY DOWN HERE.
WHAT AND HAVE EVERYONE NOTICE WHAT WE'RE DOING HERE? FLYING UNDER THE RADAR IS WAY BETTER.

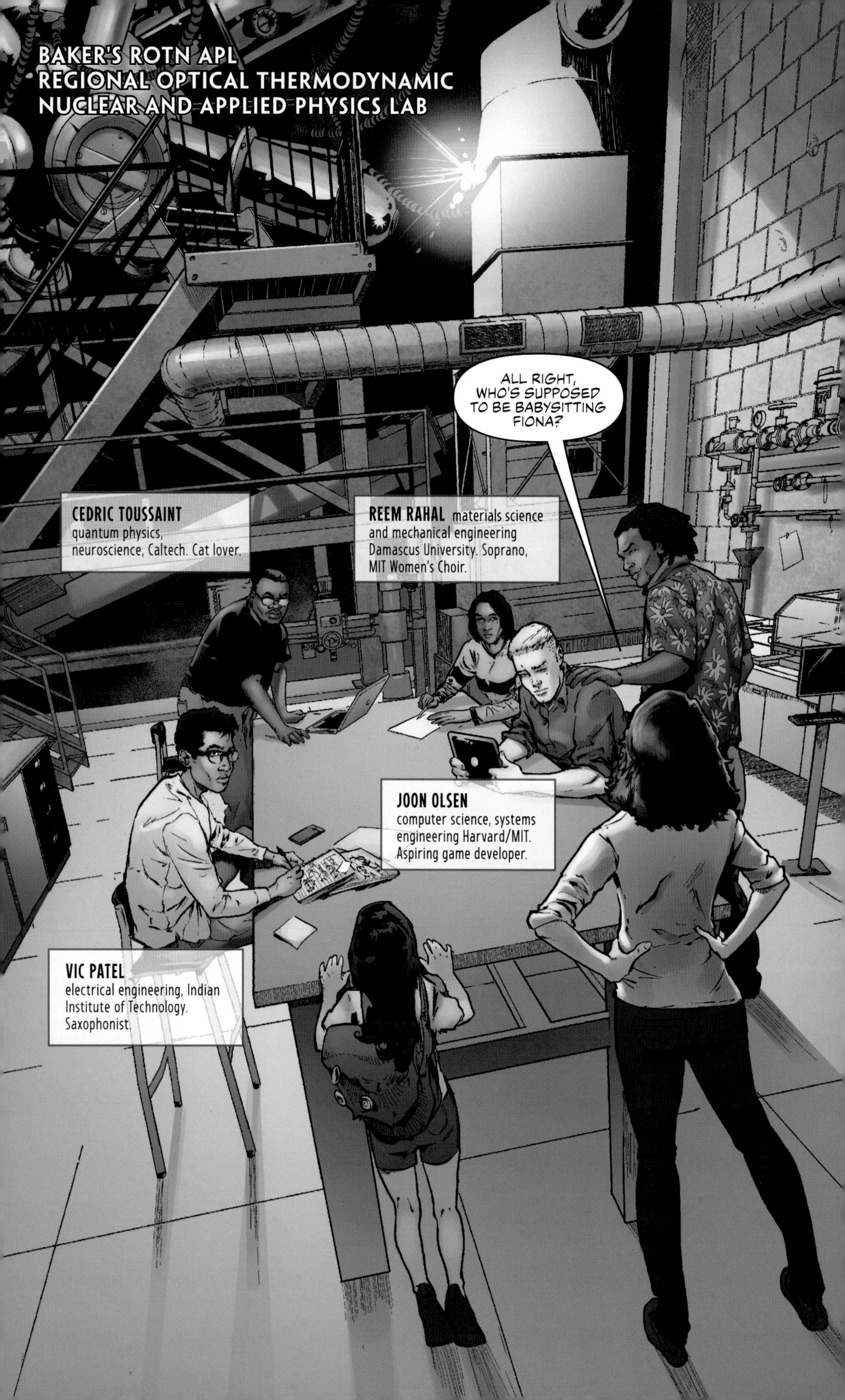
BAKER'S ROTN APL
REGIONAL OPTICAL THERMODYNAMIC
NUCLEAR AND APPLIED PHYSICS LAB
ALL RIGHT, WHO'S SUPPOSED TO BE BABYSITTING FIONA?
CEDRIC TOUSSAINT quantum physics, neuroscience, Caltech. Cat lover.
REEM RAHAL materials science and mechanical engineering Damascus University. Soprano, MIT Women's Choir.
JOON OLSEN computer science, systems engineering Harvard/MIT. Aspiring game developer.
VIC PATEL electrical engineering, Indian Institute of Technology. Saxophonist.

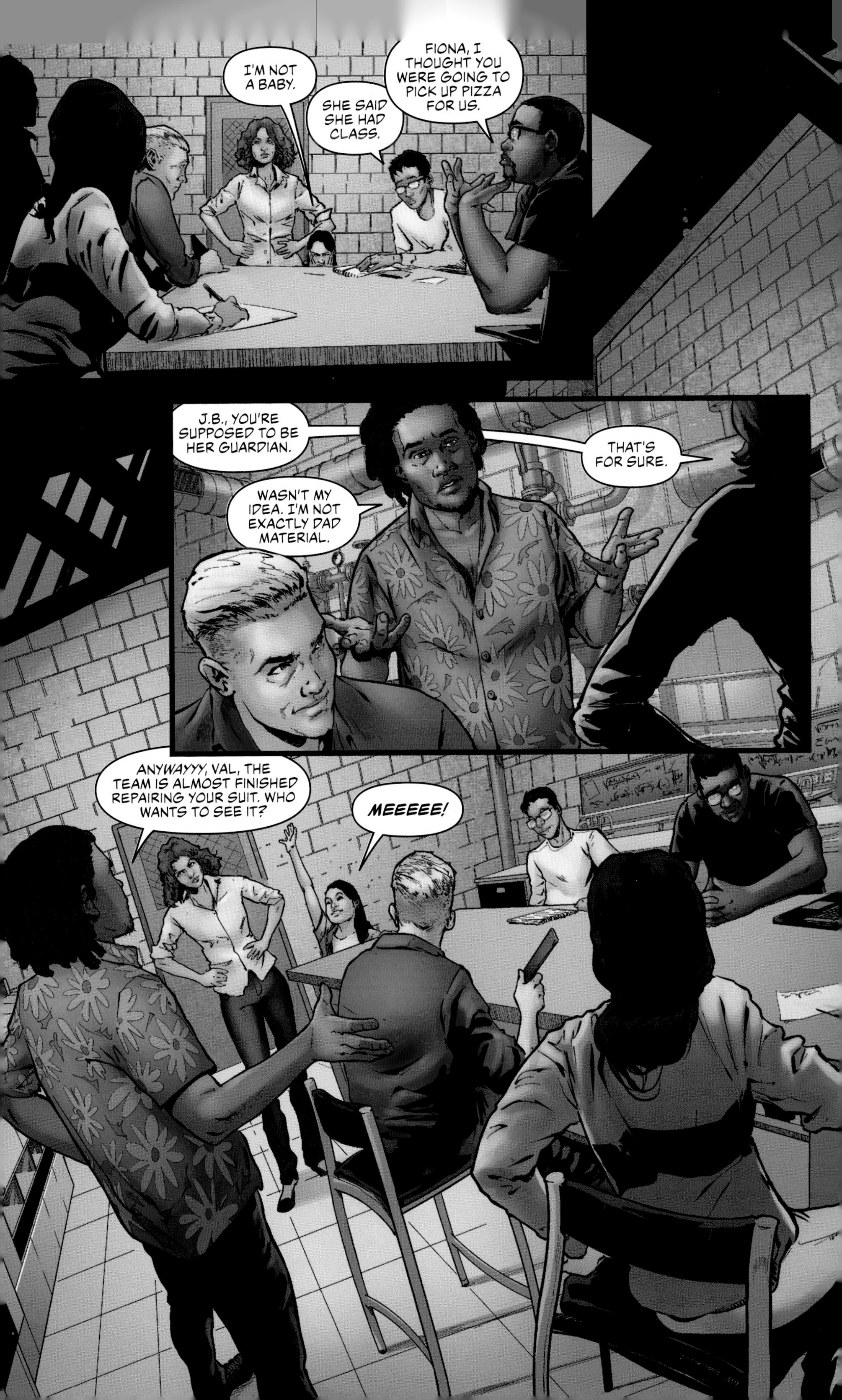
I'M NOT A BABY.
SHE SAID SHE HAD CLASS.
FIONA, I THOUGHT YOU WERE GOING TO PICK UP PIZZA FOR US.
J.B., YOU'RE SUPPOSED TO BE HER GUARDIAN.
THAT'S FOR SURE.
WASN'T MY IDEA. I'M NOT EXACTLY DAD MATERIAL.
ANYWAYYY, VAL, THE TEAM IS ALMOST FINISHED REPAIRING YOUR SUIT. WHO WANTS TO SEE IT?
MEEEEE!

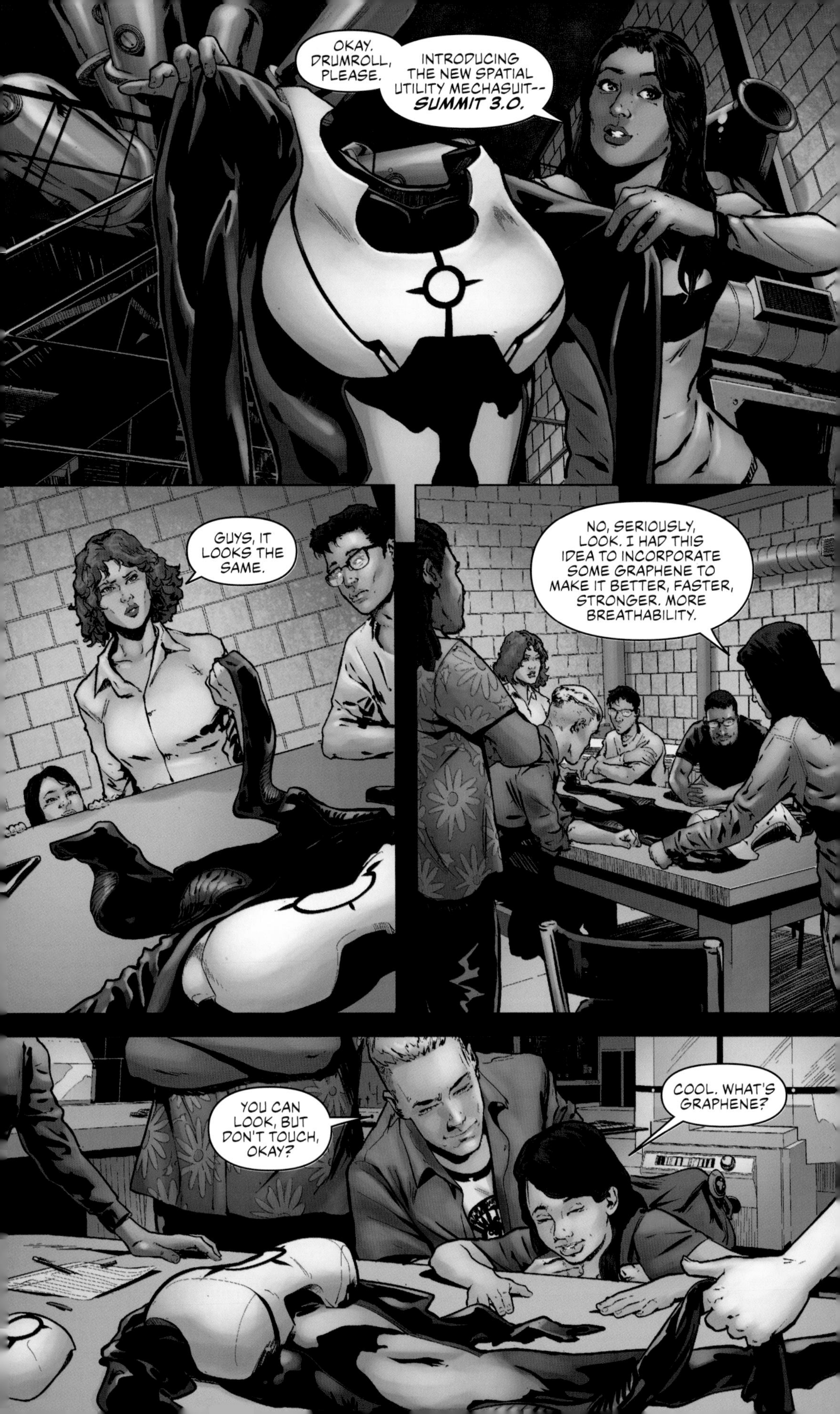
OKAY. DRUMROLL, PLEASE.
INTRODUCING THE NEW SPATIAL UTILITY MECHASUIT-- SUMMIT 3.0.
GUYS, IT LOOKS THE SAME.
NO, SERIOUSLY, LOOK. I HAD THIS IDEA TO INCORPORATE SOME GRAPHENE TO MAKE IT BETTER, FASTER, STRONGER. MORE BREATHABILITY.
YOU CAN LOOK, BUT DON'T TOUCH, OKAY?
COOL. WHAT'S GRAPHENE?

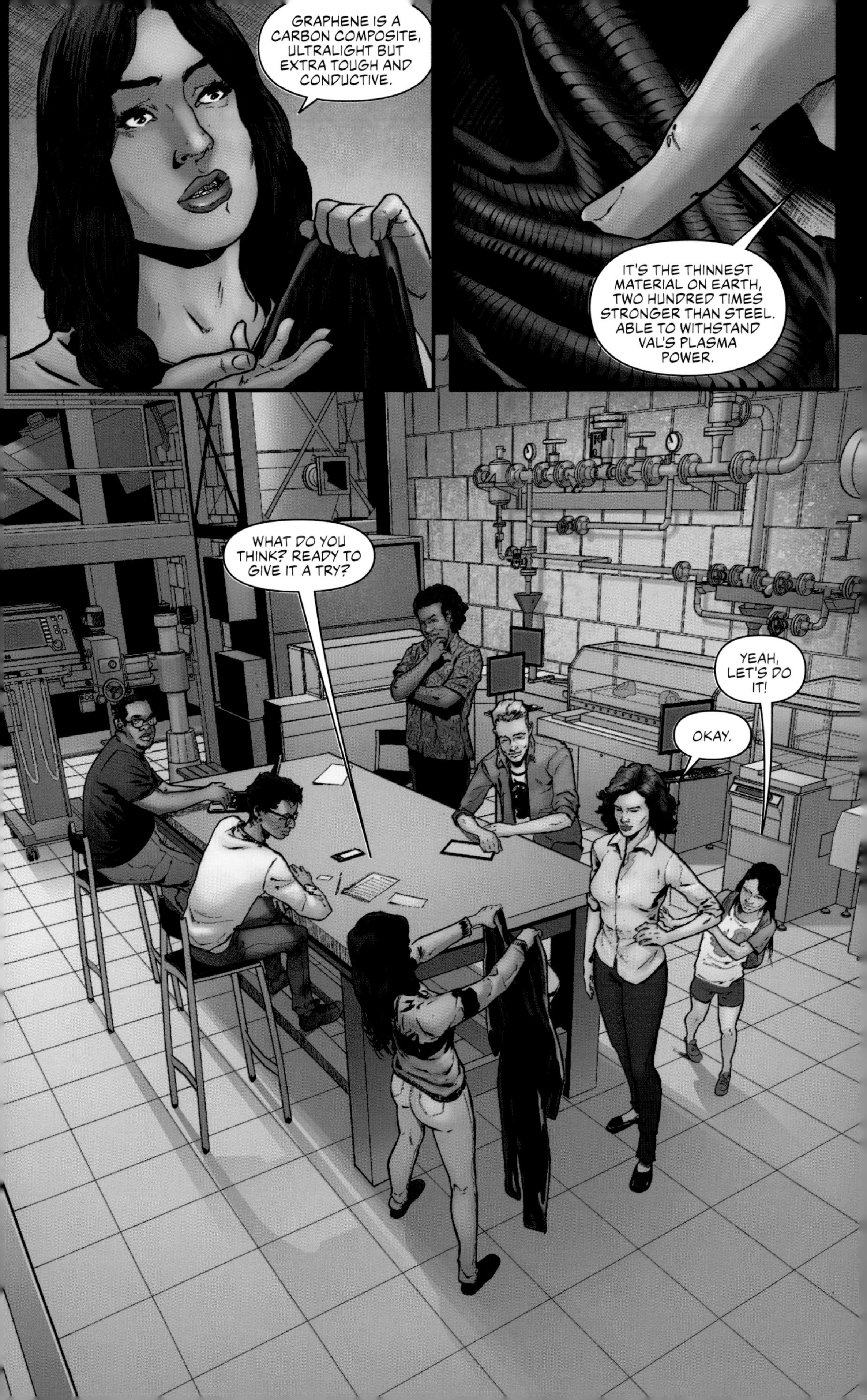
GRAPHENE IS A CARBON COMPOSITE, ULTRALIGHT BUT EXTRA TOUGH AND CONDUCTIVE.
IT'S THE THINNEST MATERIAL ON EARTH, TWO HUNDRED TIMES STRONGER THAN STEEL. ABLE TO WITHSTAND VAL'S PLASMA POWER.
WHAT DO YOU THINK? READY TO GIVE IT A TRY?
YEAH, LET'S DO IT!
OKAY.

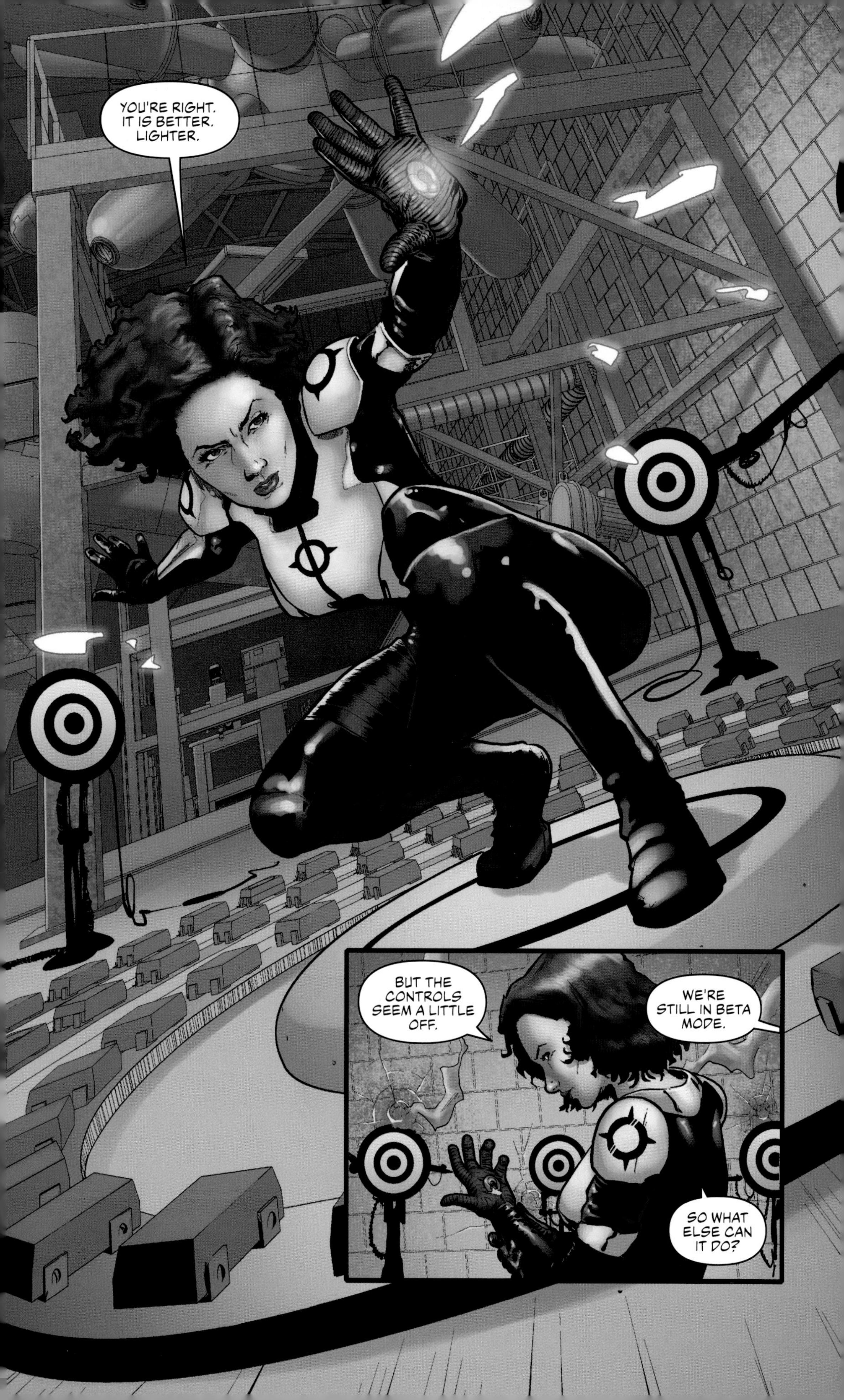
YOU'RE RIGHT. IT IS BETTER. LIGHTER.
BUT THE CONTROLS SEEM A LITTLE OFF.
WE'RE STILL IN BETA MODE.
SO WHAT ELSE CAN IT DO?

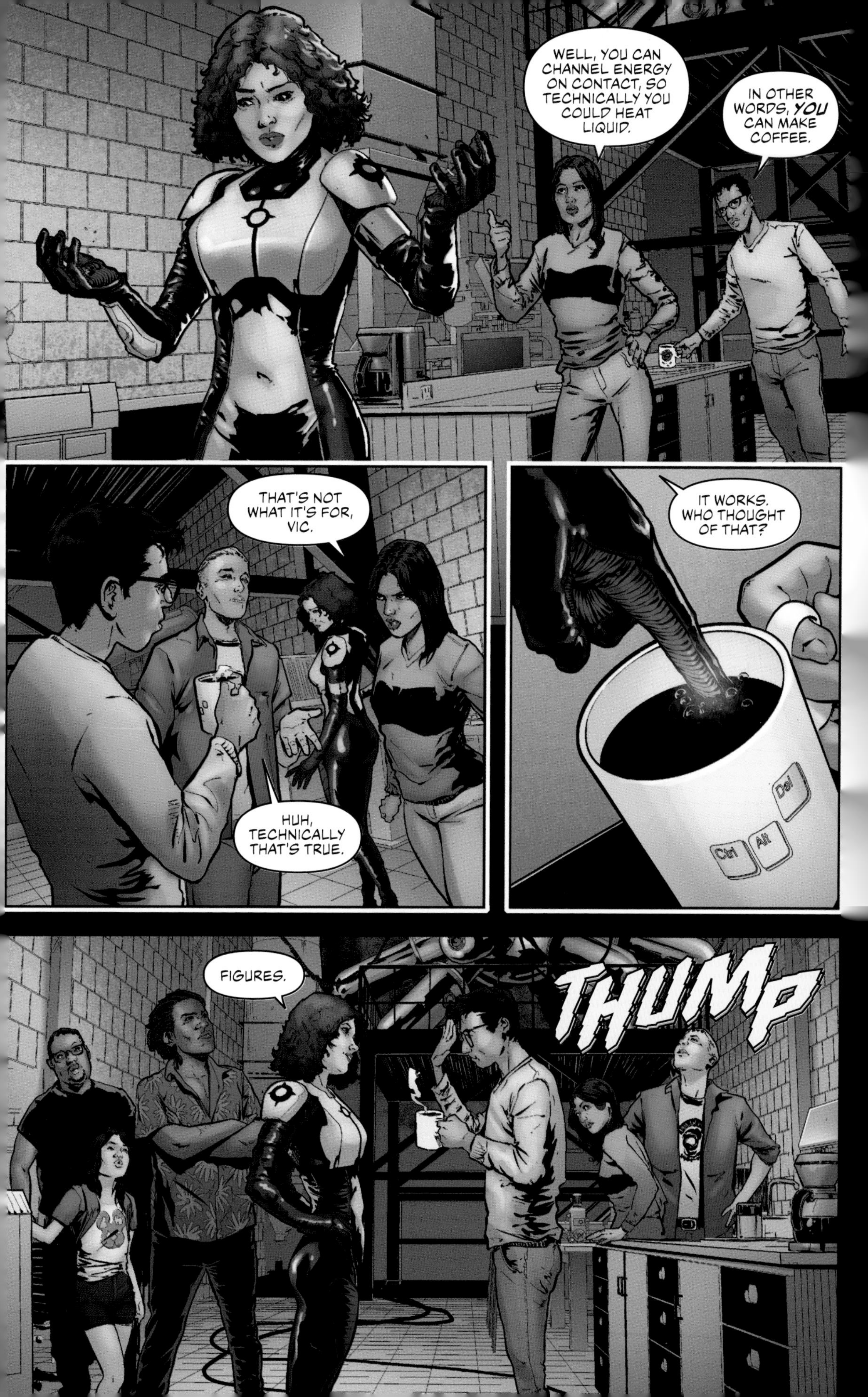
WELL, YOU CAN CHANNEL ENERGY ON CONTACT, SO TECHNICALLY YOU COULD HEAT LIQUID.
IN OTHER WORDS, YOU CAN MAKE COFFEE.
THAT'S NOT WHAT IT'S FOR, VIC.
HUH, TECHNICALLY THAT'S TRUE.
IT WORKS. WHO THOUGHT OF THAT?
Ctrl Alt Del
FIGURES.
THUMP

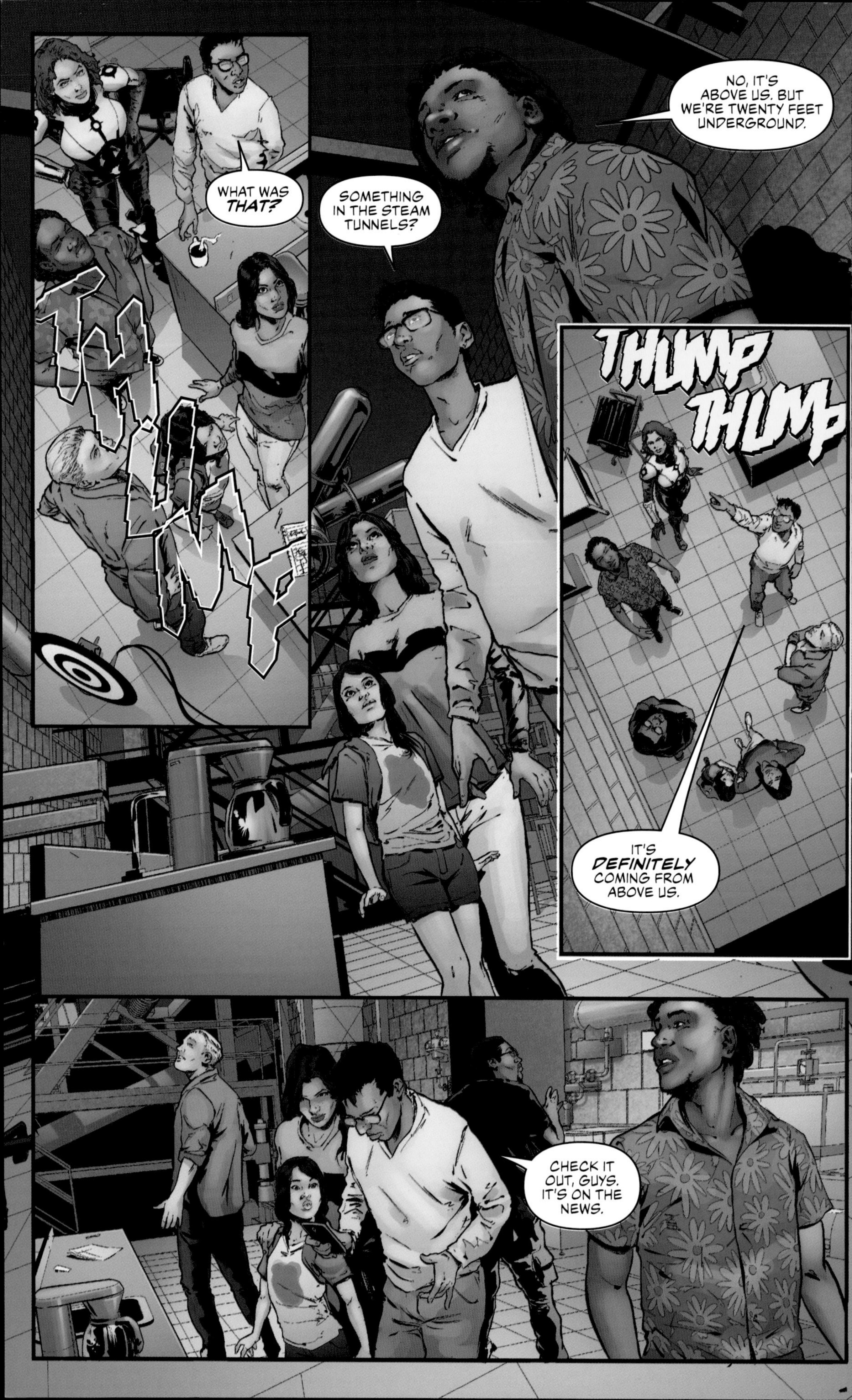
WHAT WAS *THAT?*
THUMP
SOMETHING IN THE STEAM TUNNELS?
NO, IT'S ABOVE US. BUT WE'RE TWENTY FEET UNDERGROUND.
THUMP THUMP
IT'S *DEFINITELY* COMING FROM ABOVE US.
CHECK IT OUT, GUYS. IT'S ON THE NEWS.

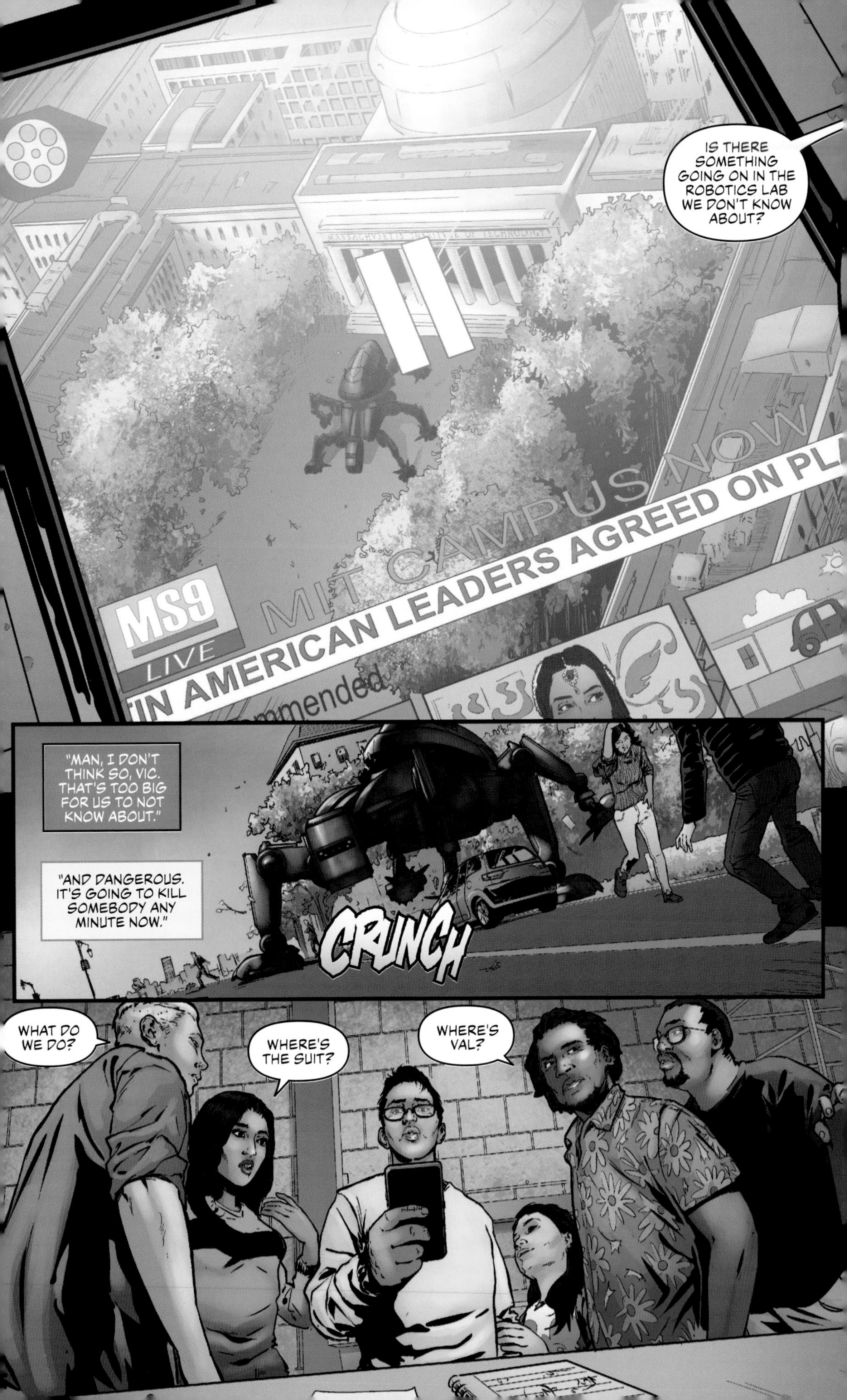

IS THERE SOMETHING GOING ON IN THE ROBOTICS LAB WE DON'T KNOW ABOUT?
MS9
LIVE
MIT CAMPUS NOW
IN AMERICAN LEADERS AGREED ON PL
mmended
"MAN, I DON'T THINK SO, VIC. THAT'S TOO BIG FOR US TO NOT KNOW ABOUT."
"AND DANGEROUS. IT'S GOING TO KILL SOMEBODY ANY MINUTE NOW."
CRUNCH
WHAT DO WE DO?
WHERE'S THE SUIT?
WHERE'S VAL?

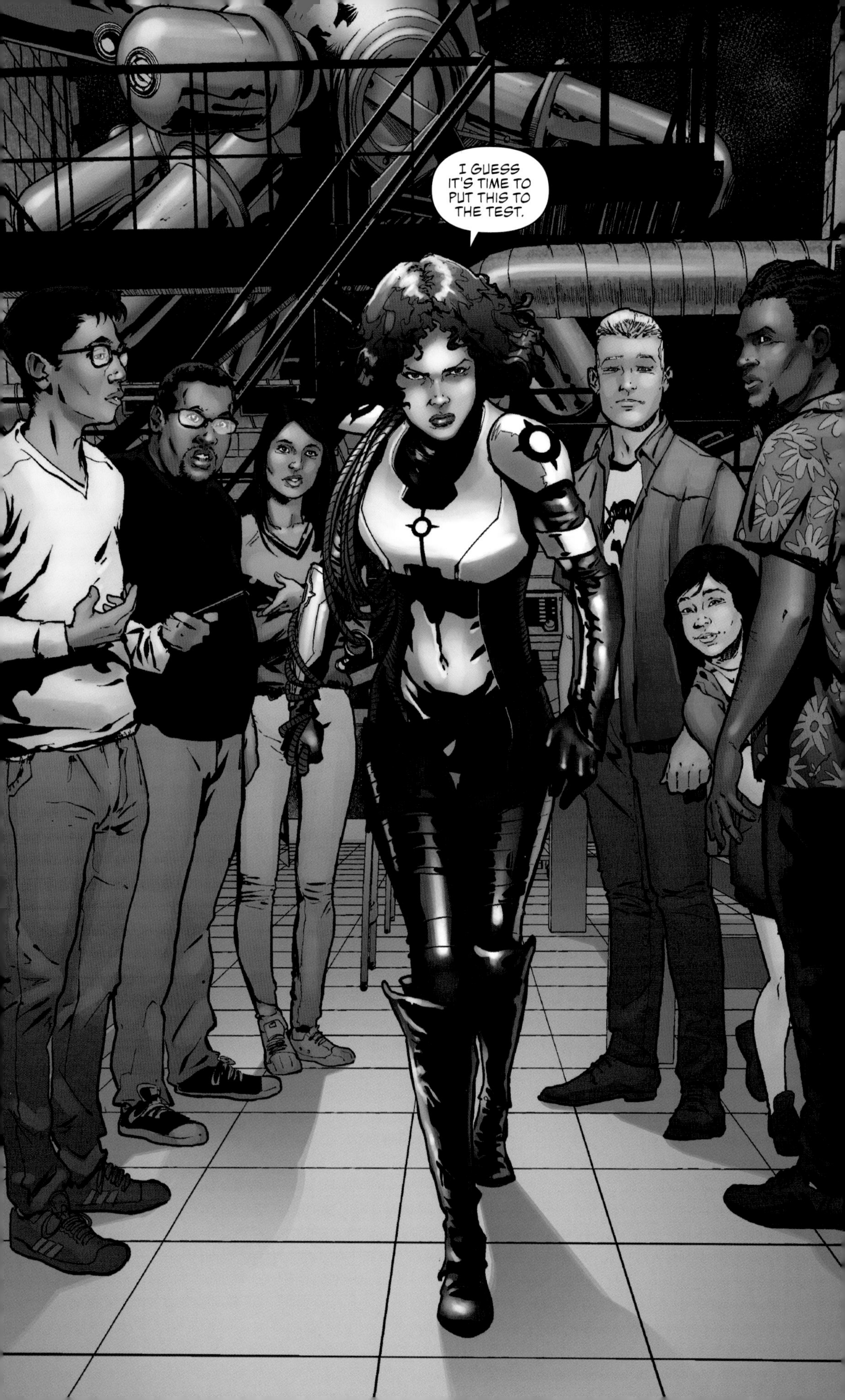
I GUESS IT'S TIME TO PUT THIS TO THE TEST.

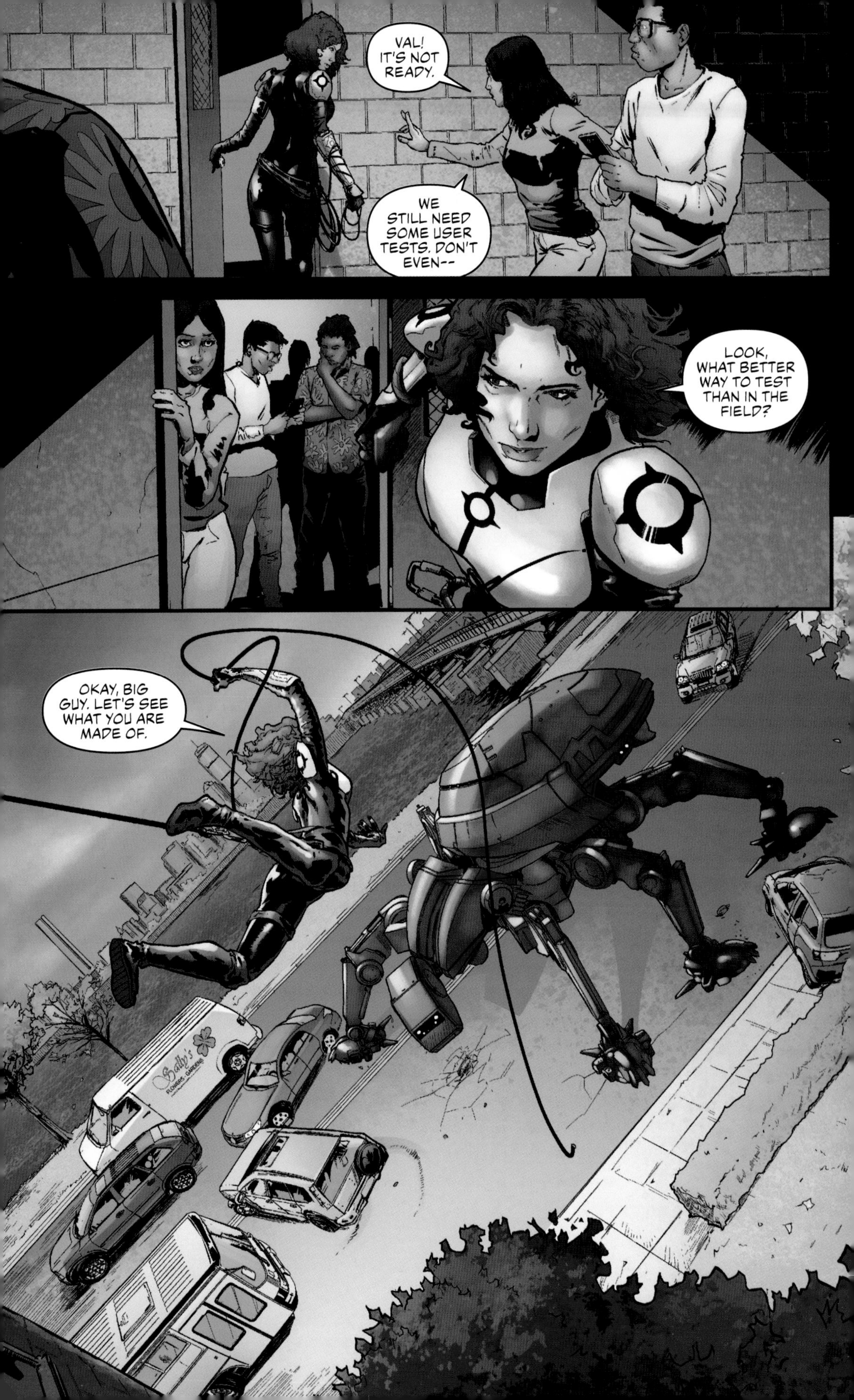
VAL! IT'S NOT READY.
WE STILL NEED SOME USER TESTS. DON'T EVEN--
LOOK, WHAT BETTER WAY TO TEST THAN IN THE FIELD?
OKAY, BIG GUY. LET'S SEE WHAT YOU ARE MADE OF.
Sally's FLOWERS & GARDENS

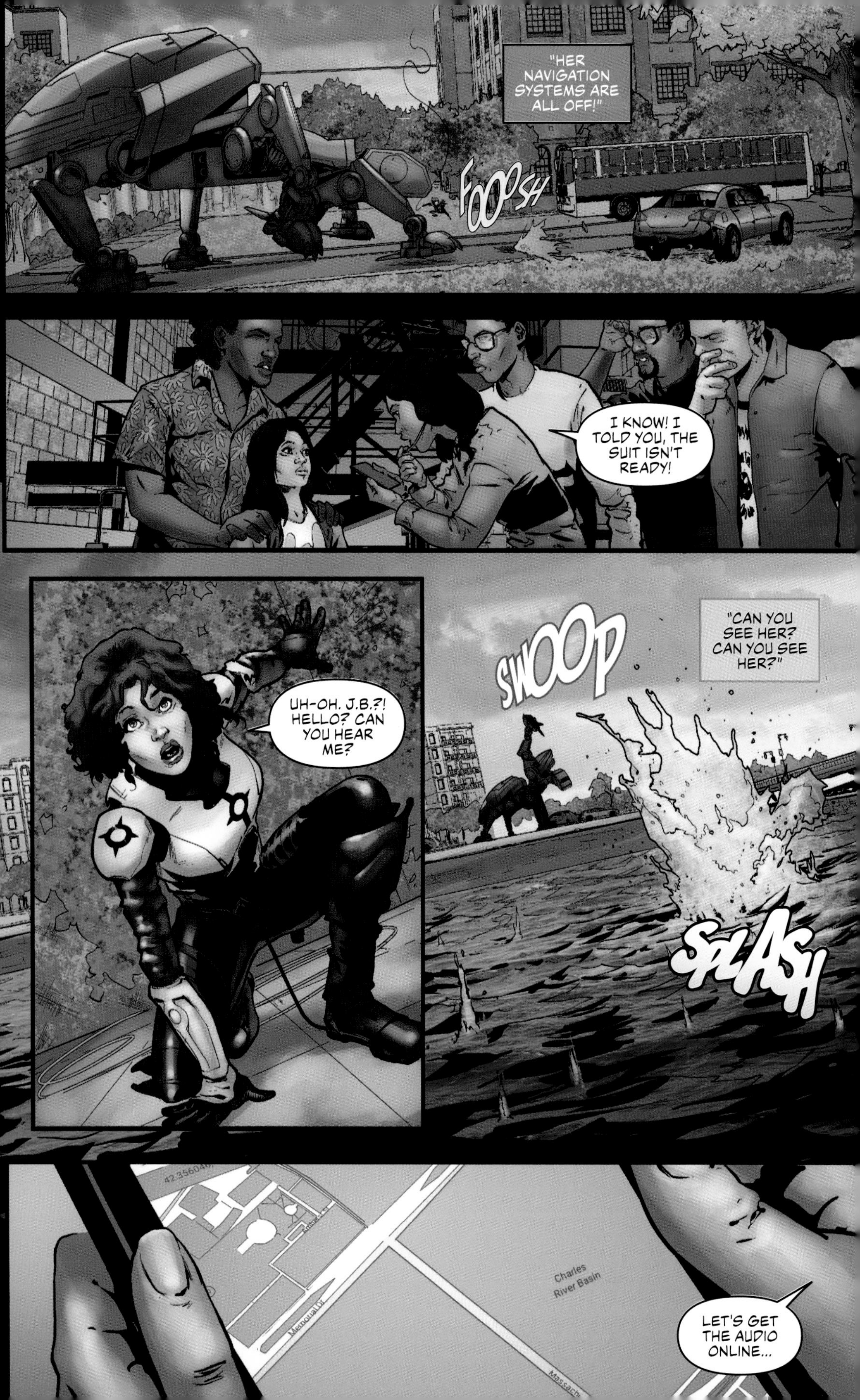
"HER NAVIGATION SYSTEMS ARE ALL OFF!"
FOOOSH
I KNOW! I TOLD YOU, THE SUIT ISN'T READY!
UH-OH. J.B.?! HELLO? CAN YOU HEAR ME?
SWOOP
"CAN YOU SEE HER? CAN YOU SEE HER?"
SPLASH
Charles River Basin
Memorial Dr
LET'S GET THE AUDIO ONLINE...

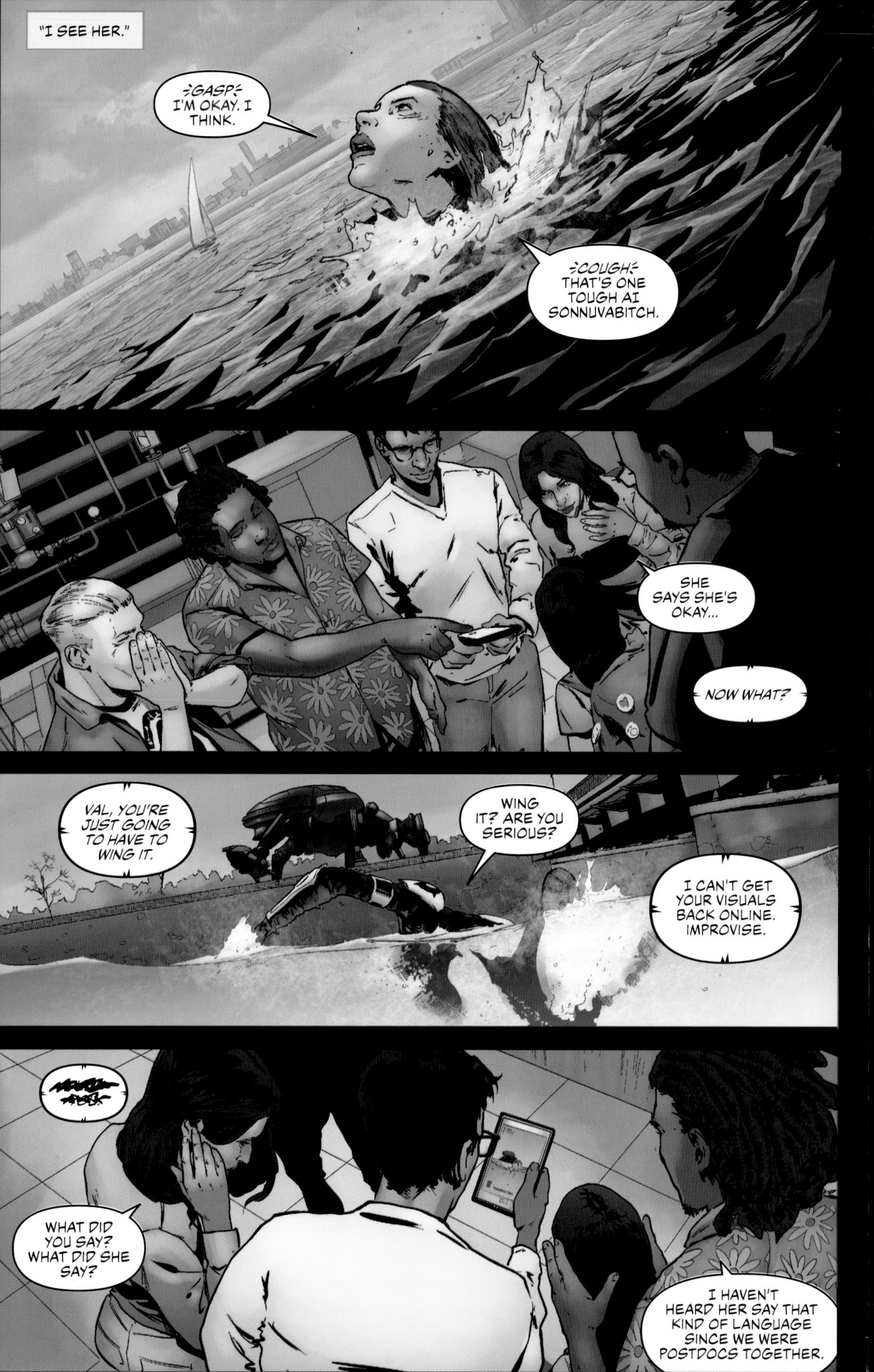
"I SEE HER."
GASP I'M OKAY. I THINK.
COUGH THAT'S ONE TOUGH AI SONNUVABITCH.
SHE SAYS SHE'S OKAY...
NOW WHAT?
VAL, YOU'RE JUST GOING TO HAVE TO WING IT.
WING IT? ARE YOU SERIOUS?
I CAN'T GET YOUR VISUALS BACK ONLINE. IMPROVISE.
WHAT DID YOU SAY? WHAT DID SHE SAY?
I HAVEN'T HEARD HER SAY THAT KIND OF LANGUAGE SINCE WE WERE POSTDOCS TOGETHER.

SOMEONE MADE THIS THING. SOMEONE WITH AN ADVANCED KNOWLEDGE OF ROBOTICS. THIS IS PRETTY HI-TECH TECH.

THE MATERIAL SEEMS FAIRLY INDESTRUCTIBLE. SOME KIND OF UNKNOWN ALLOY. I'M GOING TO NEED TO FIGURE OUT ANOTHER WAY.

IT'S GOT TO HAVE A POWER SOURCE AND SOME NAVIGATIONAL TRANSPONDER SYSTEM.

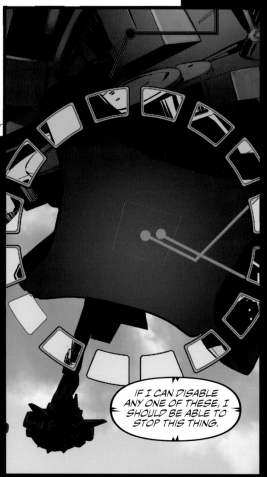

IF I CAN DISABLE ANY ONE OF THESE, I SHOULD BE ABLE TO STOP THIS THING.

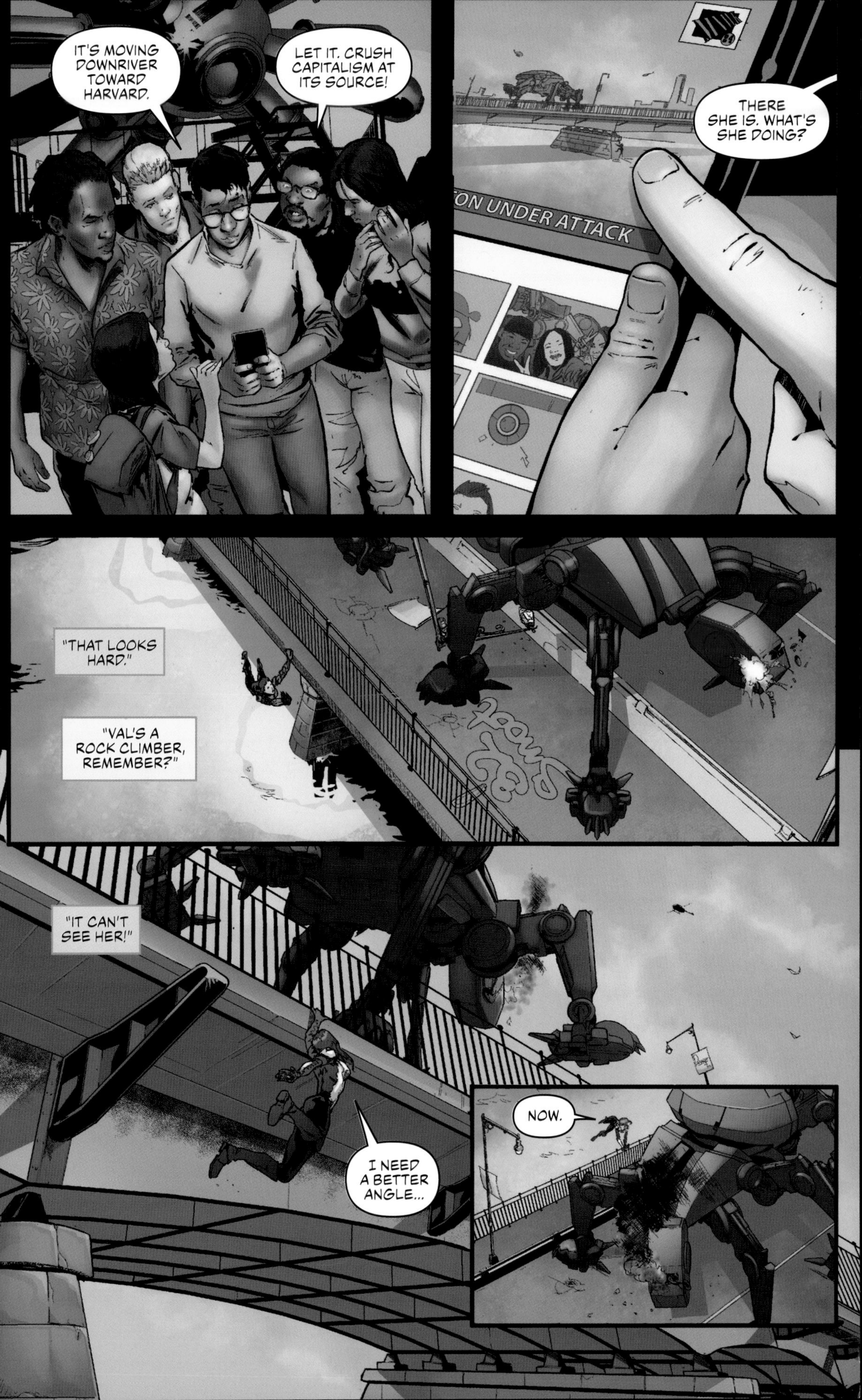
IT'S MOVING DOWNRIVER TOWARD HARVARD.
LET IT. CRUSH CAPITALISM AT ITS SOURCE!
THERE SHE IS. WHAT'S SHE DOING?
...TON UNDER ATTACK
"THAT LOOKS HARD."
"VAL'S A ROCK CLIMBER, REMEMBER?"
"IT CAN'T SEE HER!"
I NEED A BETTER ANGLE...
NOW.

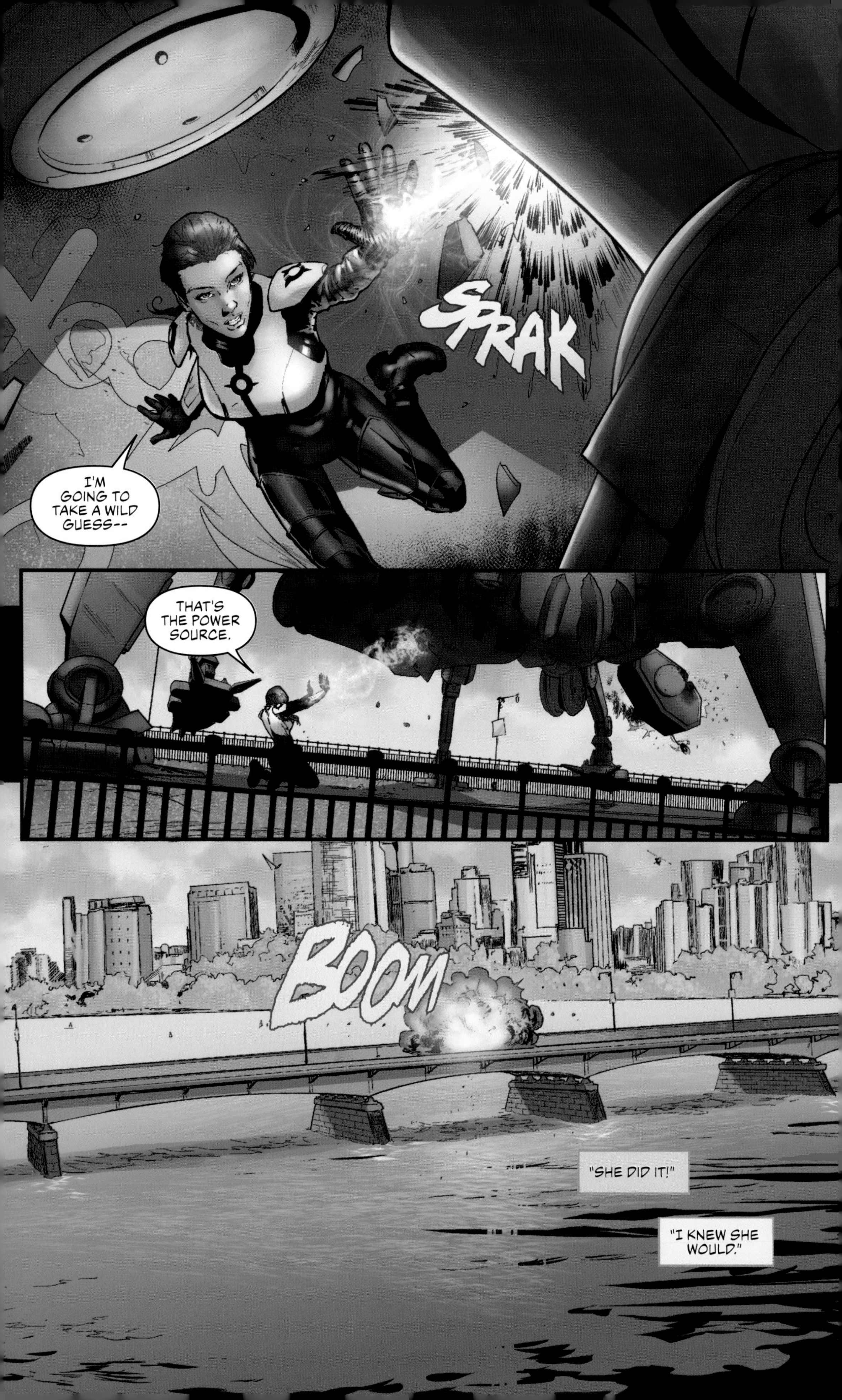
SPRAK
I'M GOING TO TAKE A WILD GUESS--
THAT'S THE POWER SOURCE.
BOOM
"SHE DID IT!"
"I KNEW SHE WOULD."

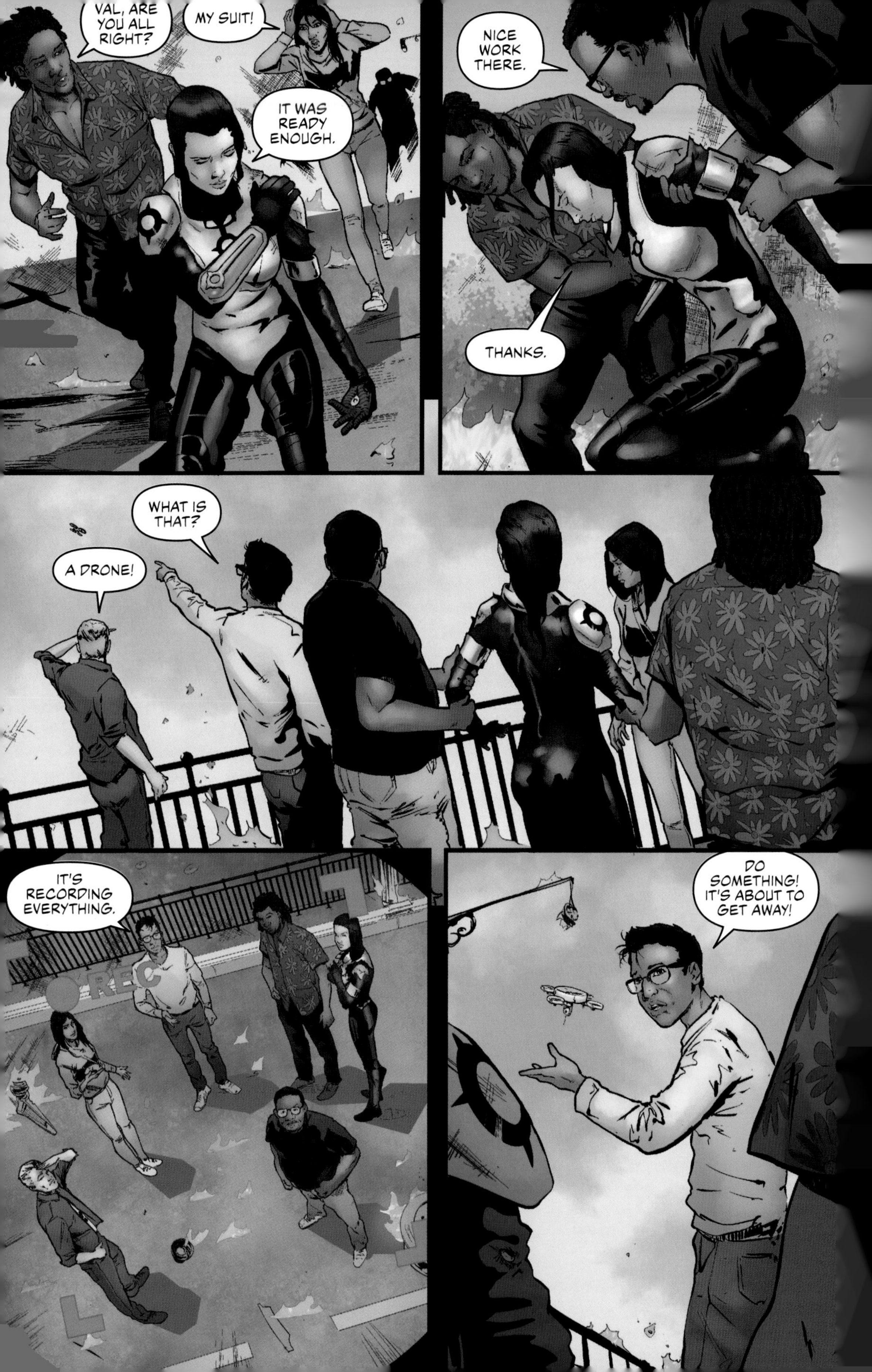
VAL, ARE YOU ALL RIGHT?
MY SUIT!
IT WAS READY ENOUGH.
NICE WORK THERE.
THANKS.
WHAT IS THAT?
A DRONE!
IT'S RECORDING EVERYTHING.
DO SOMETHING! IT'S ABOUT TO GET AWAY!

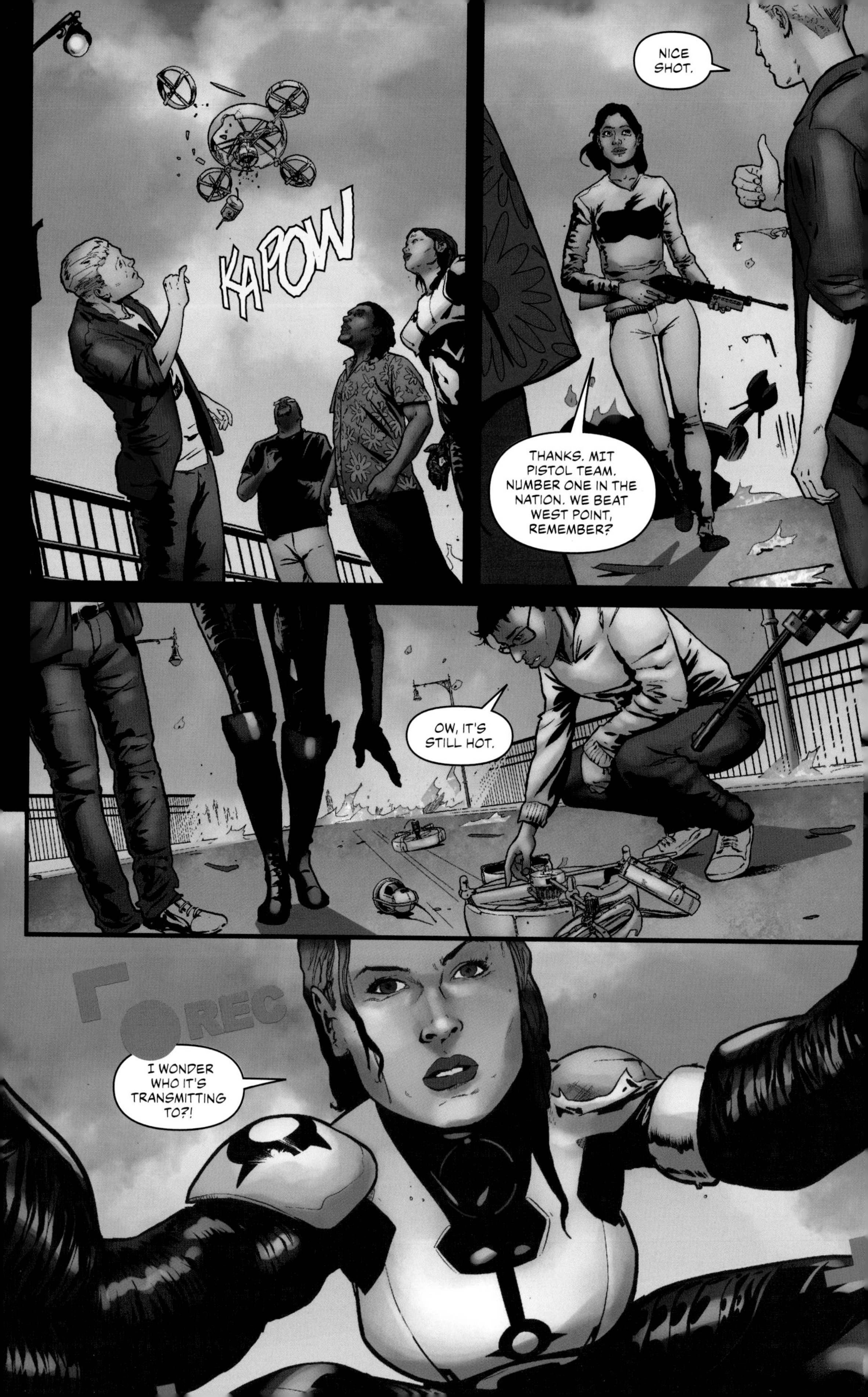
KAPOW
NICE SHOT.
THANKS. MIT PISTOL TEAM. NUMBER ONE IN THE NATION. WE BEAT WEST POINT, REMEMBER?
OW, IT'S STILL HOT.
REC
I WONDER WHO IT'S TRANSMITTING TO?!

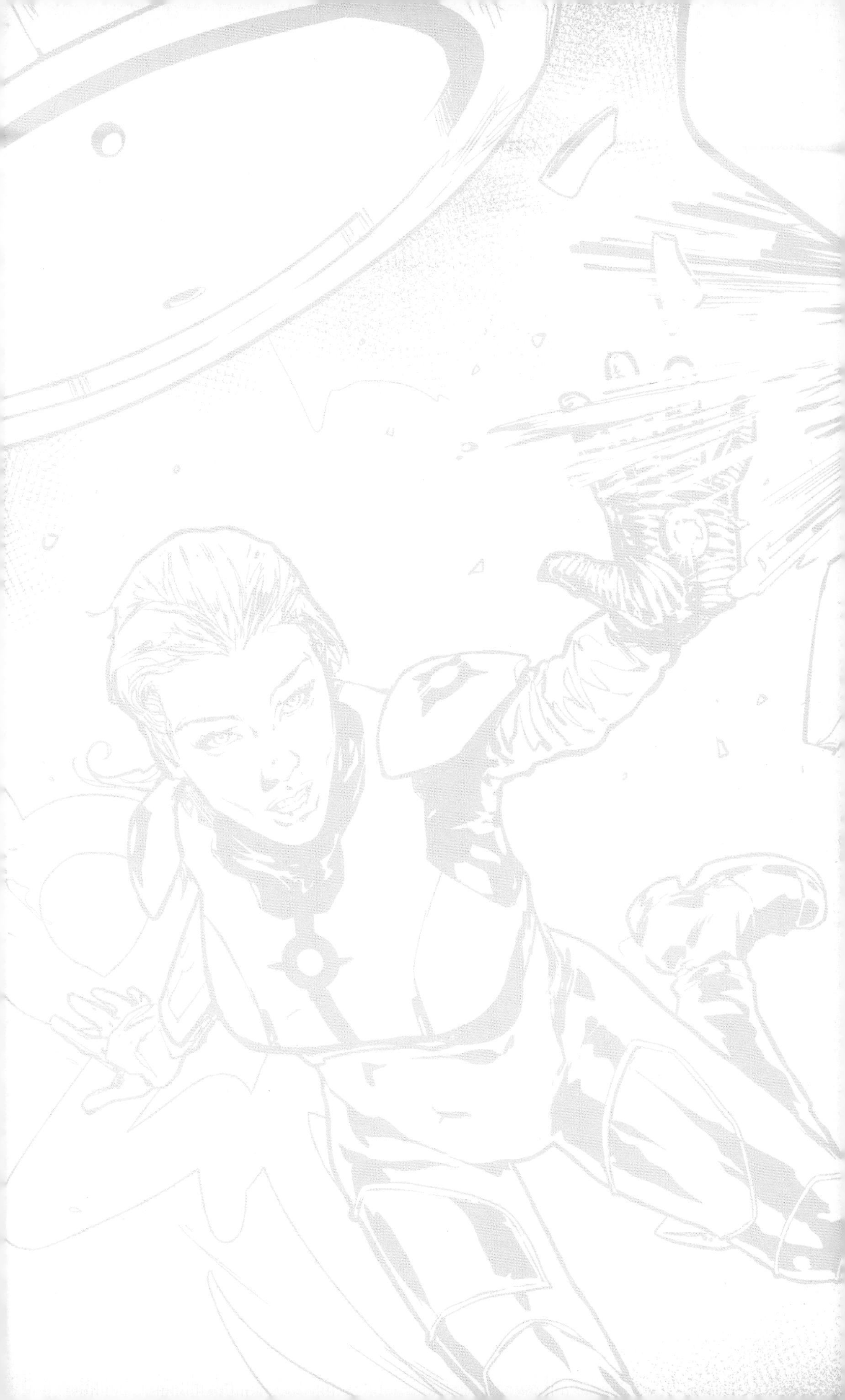

CHAPTER TWO

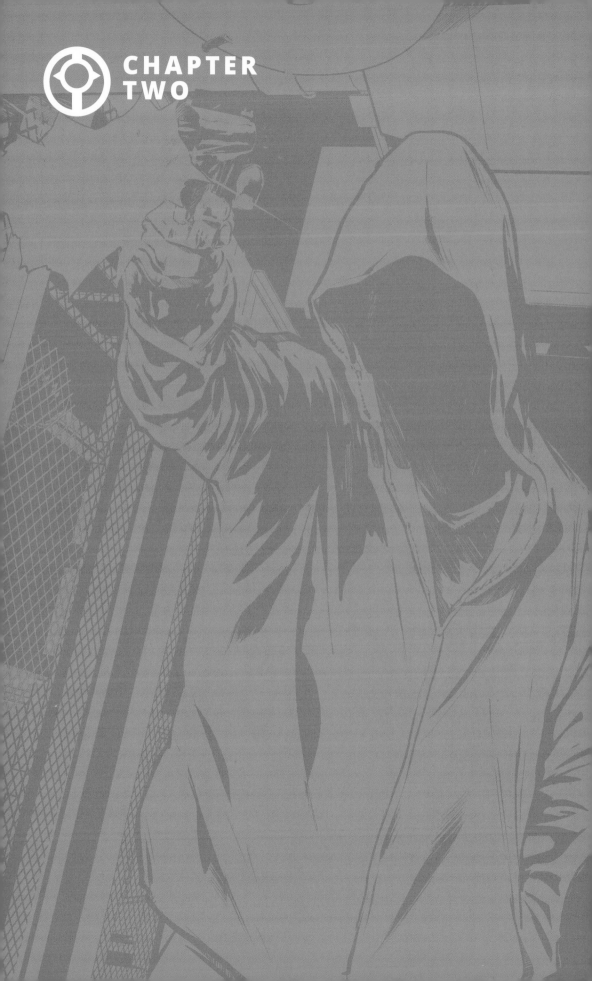

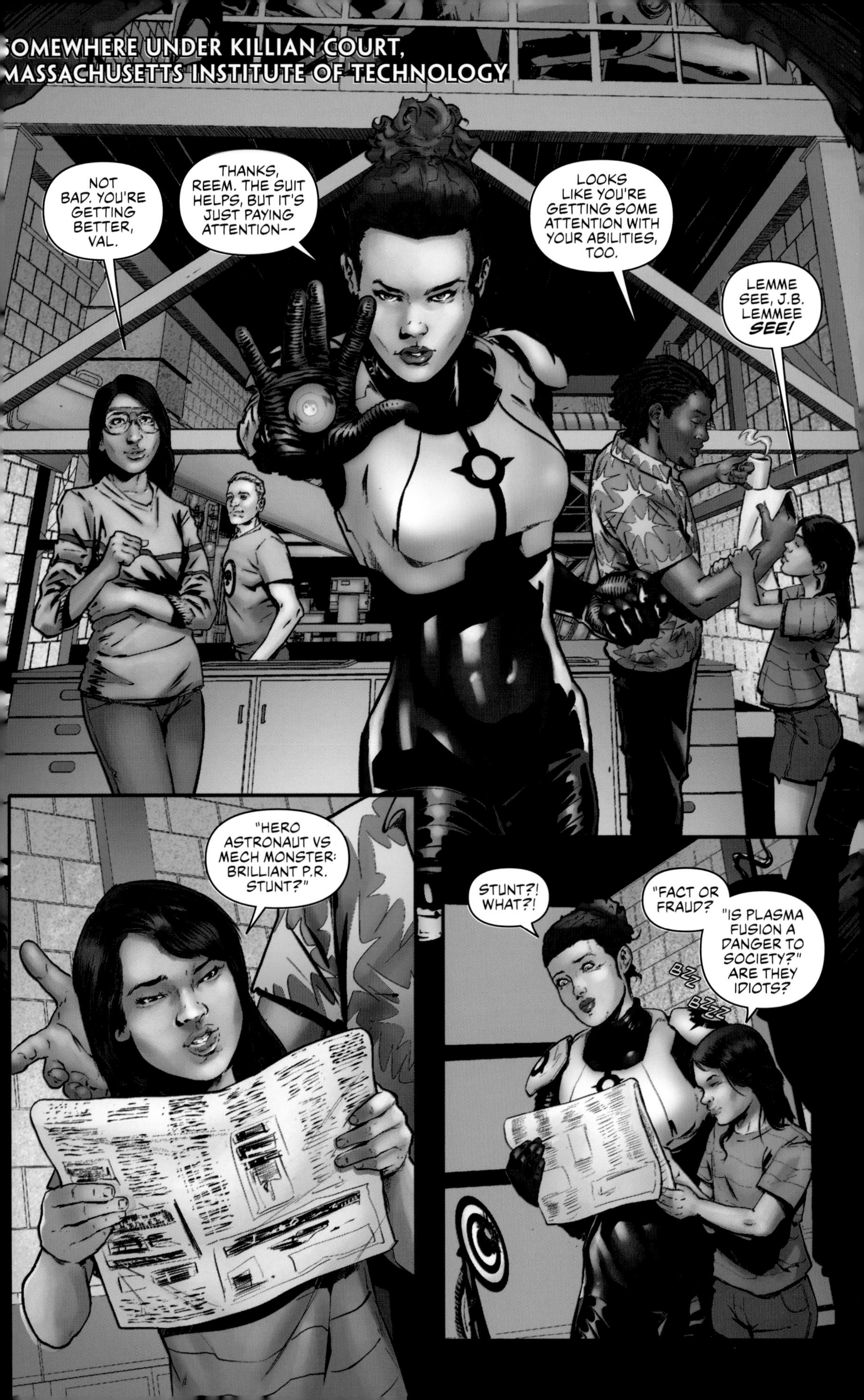
SOMEWHERE UNDER KILLIAN COURT,
MASSACHUSETTS INSTITUTE OF TECHNOLOGY
NOT BAD. YOU'RE GETTING BETTER, VAL.
THANKS, REEM. THE SUIT HELPS, BUT IT'S JUST PAYING ATTENTION--
LOOKS LIKE YOU'RE GETTING SOME ATTENTION WITH YOUR ABILITIES, TOO.
LEMME SEE, J.B. LEMMEE ***SEE!***
"HERO ASTRONAUT VS MECH MONSTER: BRILLIANT P.R. STUNT?"
STUNT?! WHAT?!
"FACT OR FRAUD?
"IS PLASMA FUSION A DANGER TO SOCIETY?" ARE THEY IDIOTS?
BZZ
BZZZ

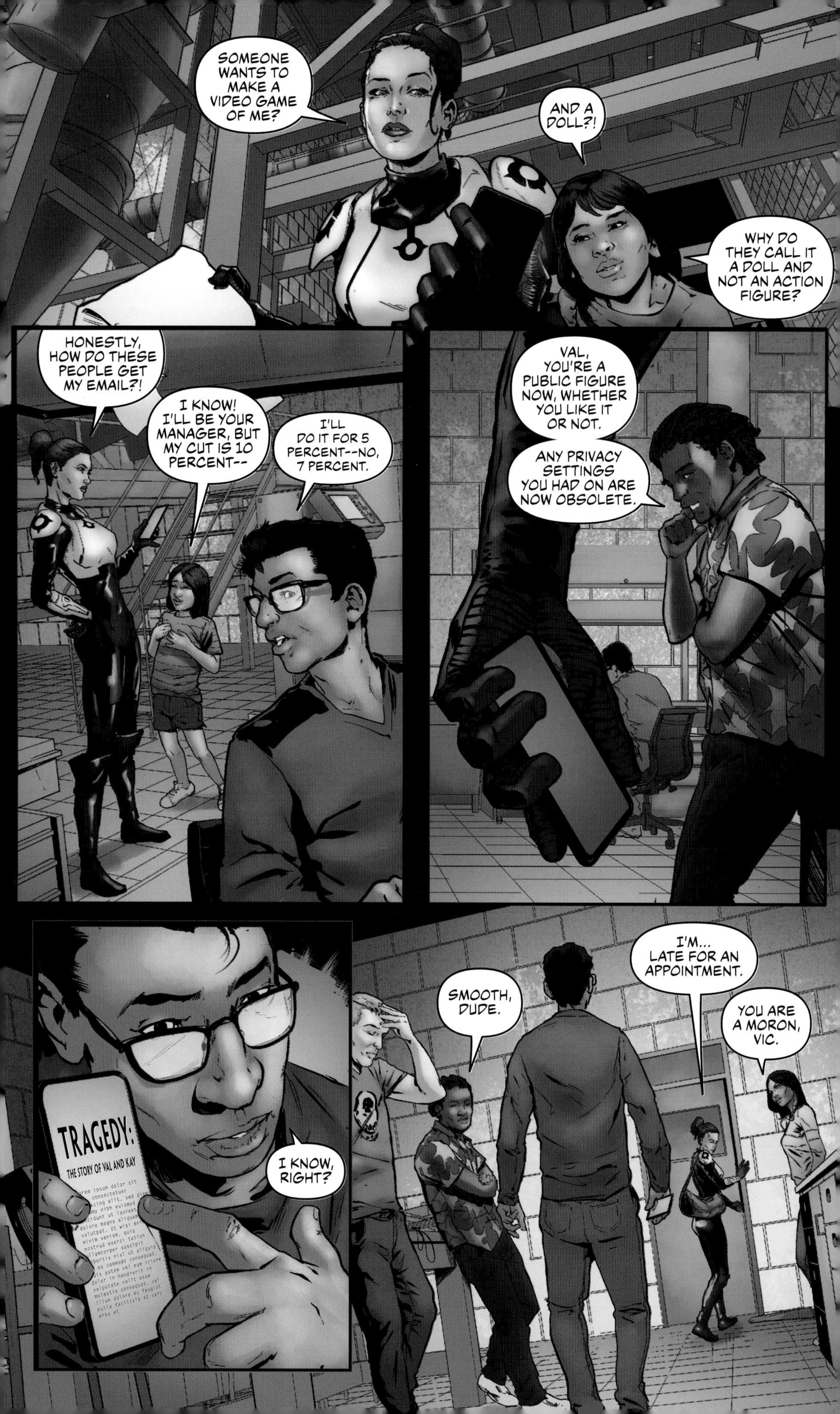
SOMEONE WANTS TO MAKE A VIDEO GAME OF ME?
AND A DOLL?!
WHY DO THEY CALL IT A DOLL AND NOT AN ACTION FIGURE?
HONESTLY, HOW DO THESE PEOPLE GET MY EMAIL?!
I KNOW! I'LL BE YOUR MANAGER, BUT MY CUT IS 10 PERCENT--
I'LL DO IT FOR 5 PERCENT--NO, 7 PERCENT.
VAL, YOU'RE A PUBLIC FIGURE NOW, WHETHER YOU LIKE IT OR NOT.
ANY PRIVACY SETTINGS YOU HAD ON ARE NOW OBSOLETE.
TRAGEDY:
THE STORY OF VAL AND KAY
I KNOW, RIGHT?
SMOOTH, DUDE.
I'M... LATE FOR AN APPOINTMENT.
YOU ARE A MORON, VIC.

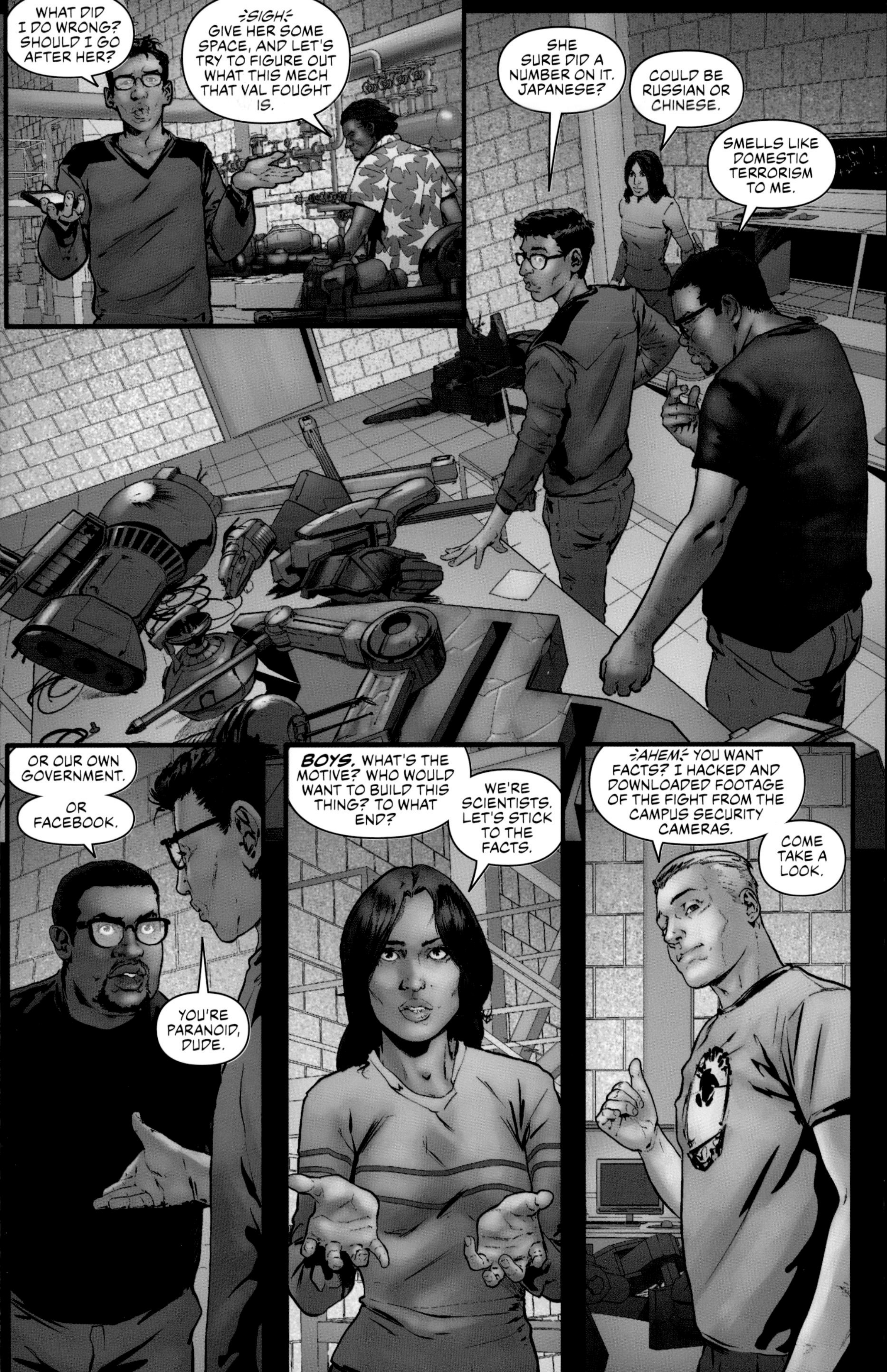
WHAT DID I DO WRONG? SHOULD I GO AFTER HER?
-SIGH- GIVE HER SOME SPACE, AND LET'S TRY TO FIGURE OUT WHAT THIS MECH THAT VAL FOUGHT IS.
SHE SURE DID A NUMBER ON IT. JAPANESE?
COULD BE RUSSIAN OR CHINESE.
SMELLS LIKE DOMESTIC TERRORISM TO ME.
OR OUR OWN GOVERNMENT.
OR FACEBOOK.
YOU'RE PARANOID, DUDE.
BOYS. WHAT'S THE MOTIVE? WHO WOULD WANT TO BUILD THIS THING? TO WHAT END?
WE'RE SCIENTISTS. LET'S STICK TO THE FACTS.
-AHEM- YOU WANT FACTS? I HACKED AND DOWNLOADED FOOTAGE OF THE FIGHT FROM THE CAMPUS SECURITY CAMERAS.
COME TAKE A LOOK.

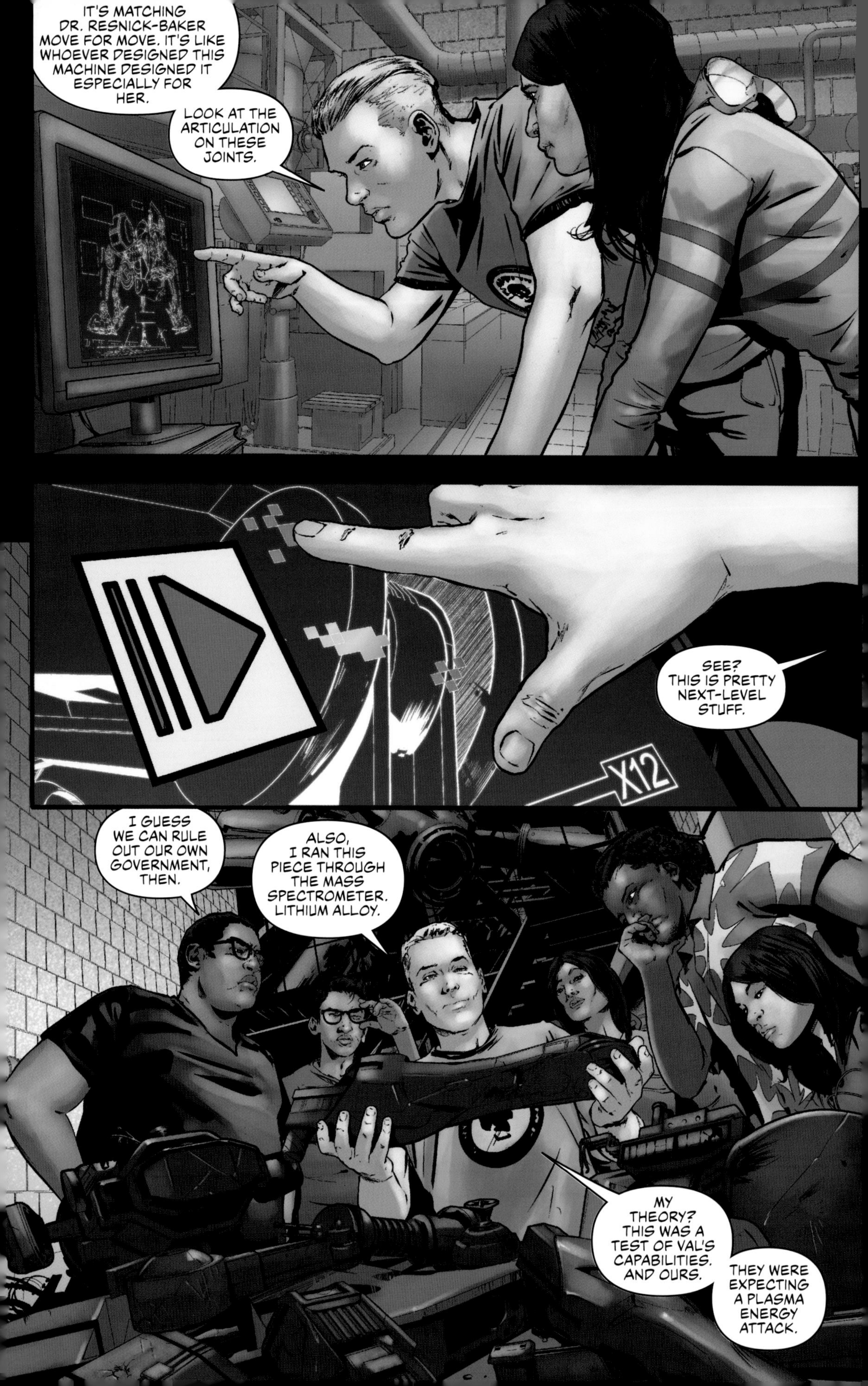
IT'S MATCHING DR. RESNICK-BAKER MOVE FOR MOVE. IT'S LIKE WHOEVER DESIGNED THIS MACHINE DESIGNED IT ESPECIALLY FOR HER.
LOOK AT THE ARTICULATION ON THESE JOINTS.
SEE? THIS IS PRETTY NEXT-LEVEL STUFF.
X12
I GUESS WE CAN RULE OUT OUR OWN GOVERNMENT, THEN.
ALSO, I RAN THIS PIECE THROUGH THE MASS SPECTROMETER. LITHIUM ALLOY.
MY THEORY? THIS WAS A TEST OF VAL'S CAPABILITIES. AND OURS.
THEY WERE EXPECTING A PLASMA ENERGY ATTACK.

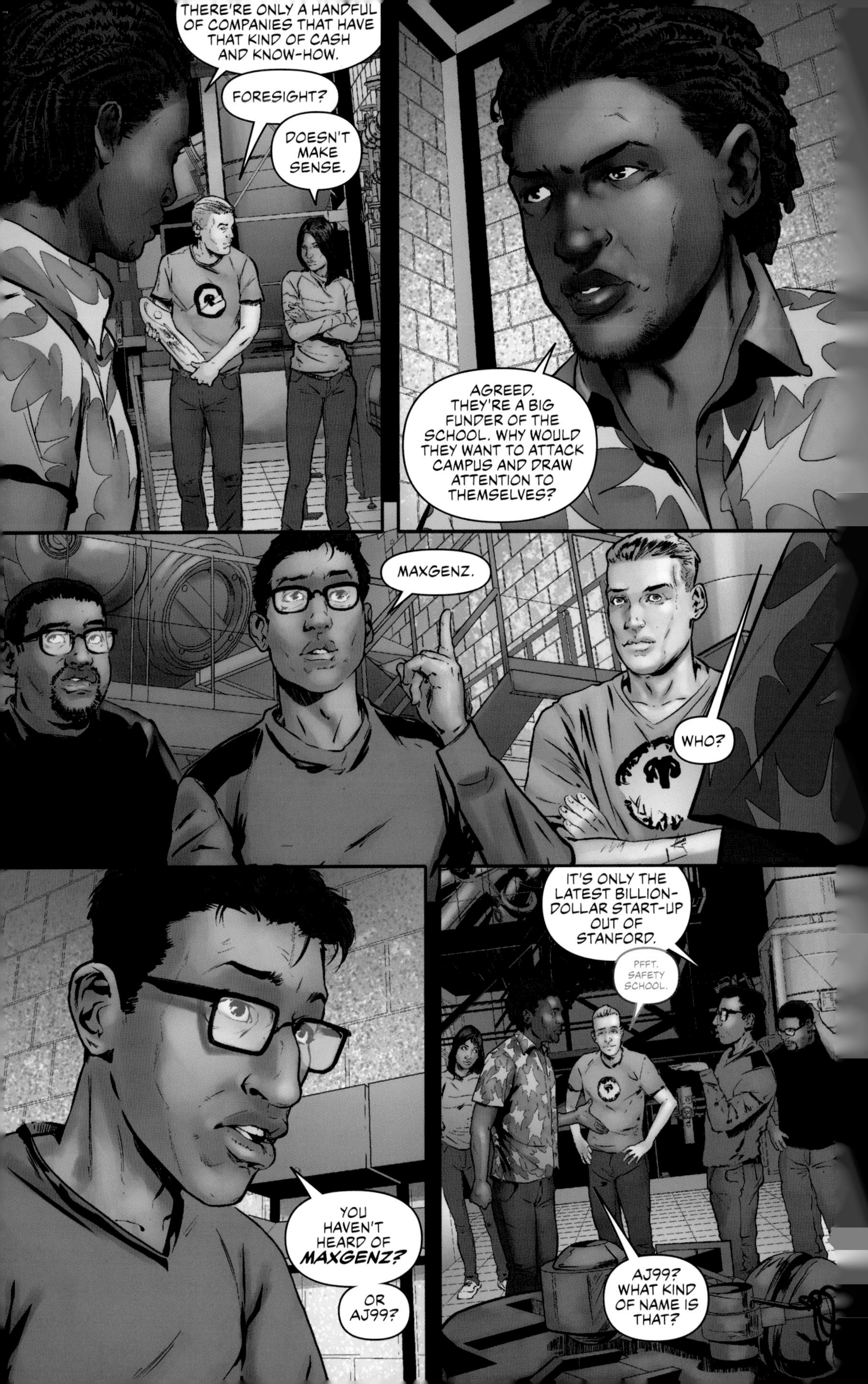
THERE'RE ONLY A HANDFUL OF COMPANIES THAT HAVE THAT KIND OF CASH AND KNOW-HOW.
FORESIGHT?
DOESN'T MAKE SENSE.
AGREED. THEY'RE A BIG FUNDER OF THE SCHOOL. WHY WOULD THEY WANT TO ATTACK CAMPUS AND DRAW ATTENTION TO THEMSELVES?
MAXGENZ.
WHO?
YOU HAVEN'T HEARD OF *MAXGENZ?*
OR AJ99?
IT'S ONLY THE LATEST BILLION-DOLLAR START-UP OUT OF STANFORD.
PFFT. SAFETY SCHOOL.
AJ99? WHAT KIND OF NAME IS THAT?

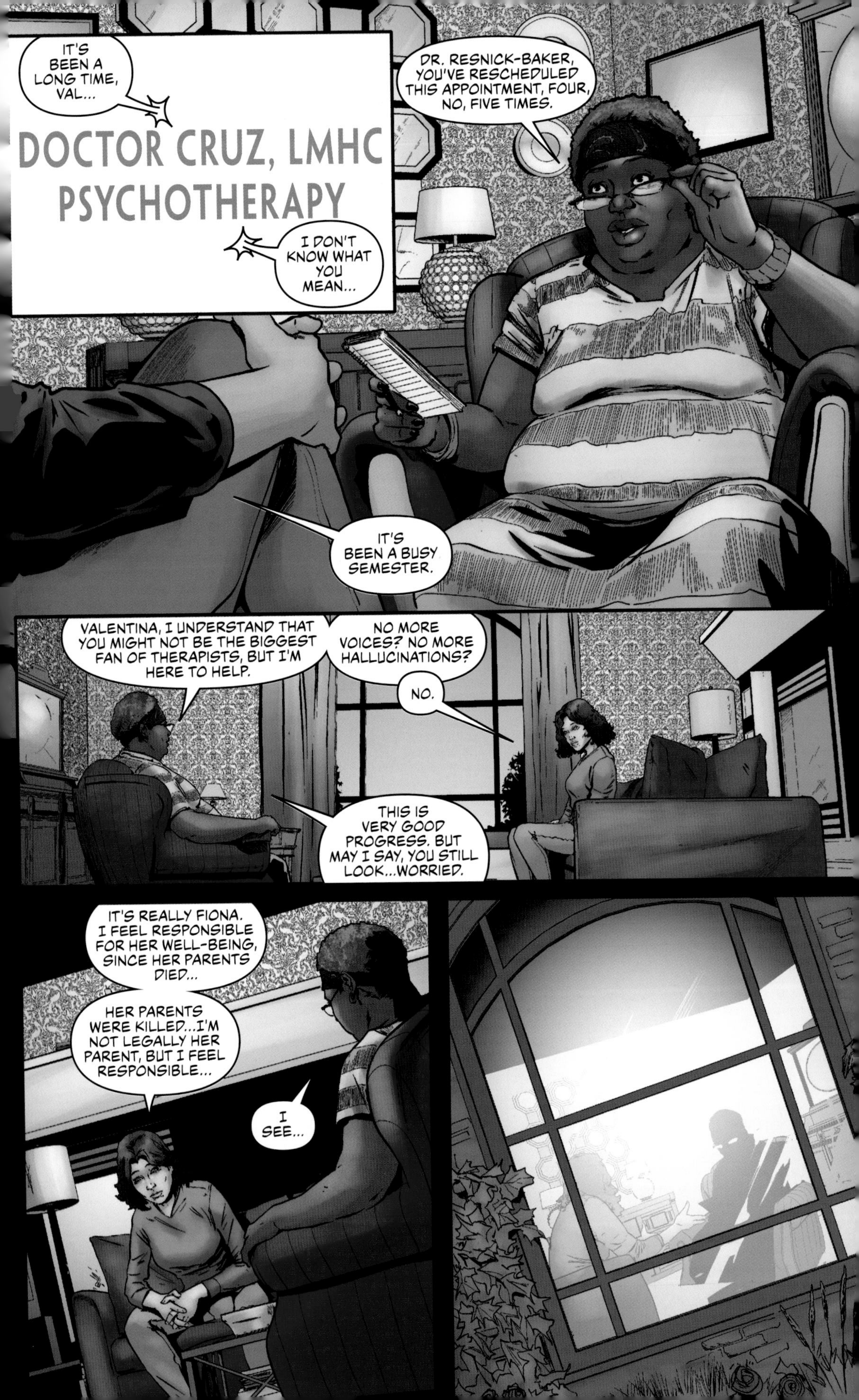

IT'S BEEN A LONG TIME, VAL...
DOCTOR CRUZ, LMHC
PSYCHOTHERAPY
I DON'T KNOW WHAT YOU MEAN...
DR. RESNICK-BAKER, YOU'VE RESCHEDULED THIS APPOINTMENT, FOUR, NO, FIVE TIMES.
IT'S BEEN A BUSY SEMESTER.
VALENTINA, I UNDERSTAND THAT YOU MIGHT NOT BE THE BIGGEST FAN OF THERAPISTS, BUT I'M HERE TO HELP.
NO MORE VOICES? NO MORE HALLUCINATIONS?
NO.
THIS IS VERY GOOD PROGRESS. BUT MAY I SAY, YOU STILL LOOK...WORRIED.
IT'S REALLY FIONA. I FEEL RESPONSIBLE FOR HER WELL-BEING, SINCE HER PARENTS DIED...
HER PARENTS WERE KILLED...I'M NOT LEGALLY HER PARENT, BUT I FEEL RESPONSIBLE...
I SEE...

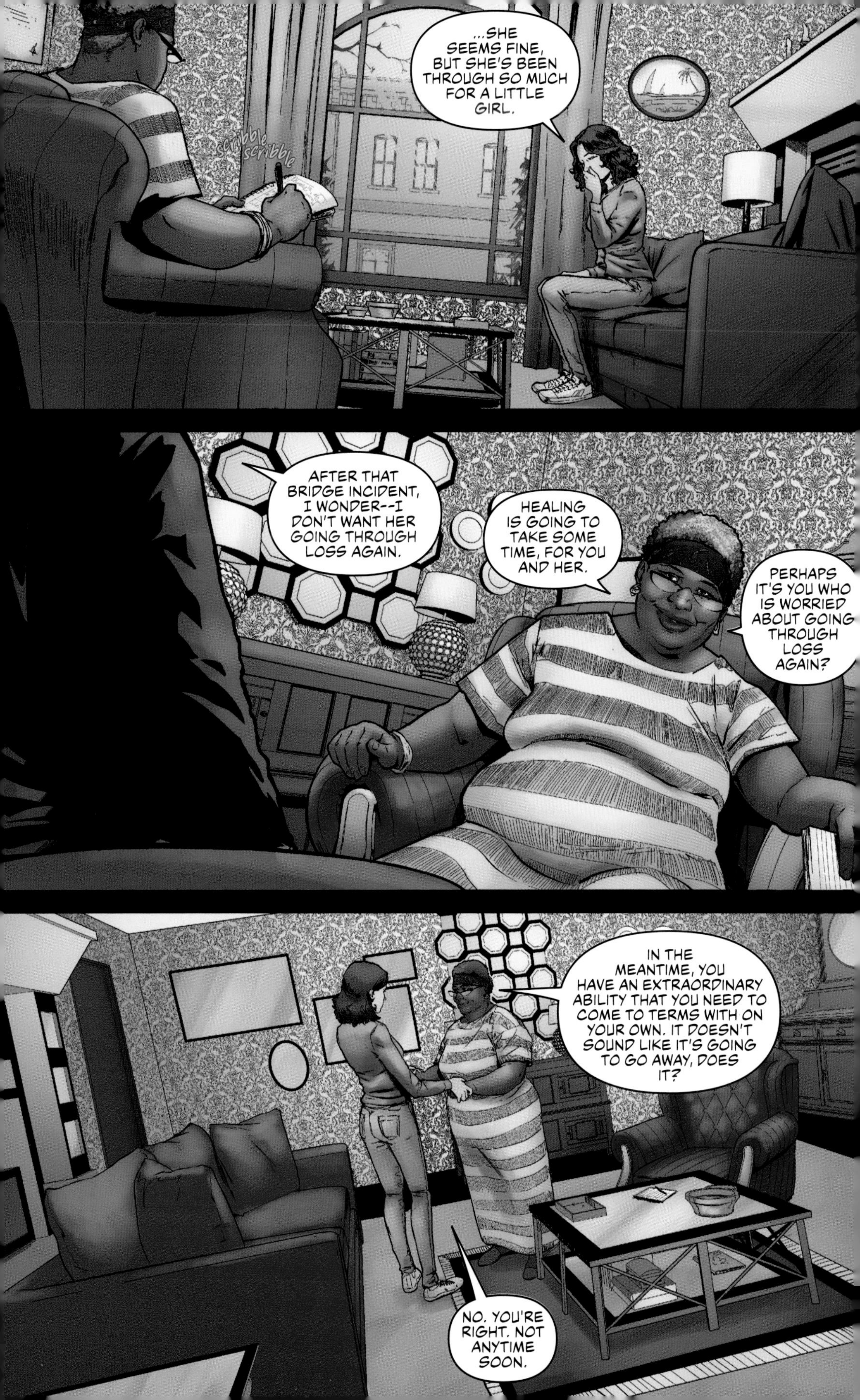
...SHE SEEMS FINE, BUT SHE'S BEEN THROUGH SO MUCH FOR A LITTLE GIRL.
scribble scribble
AFTER THAT BRIDGE INCIDENT, I WONDER--I DON'T WANT HER GOING THROUGH LOSS AGAIN.
HEALING IS GOING TO TAKE SOME TIME, FOR YOU AND HER.
PERHAPS IT'S YOU WHO IS WORRIED ABOUT GOING THROUGH LOSS AGAIN?
IN THE MEANTIME, YOU HAVE AN EXTRAORDINARY ABILITY THAT YOU NEED TO COME TO TERMS WITH ON YOUR OWN. IT DOESN'T SOUND LIKE IT'S GOING TO GO AWAY, DOES IT?
NO. YOU'RE RIGHT. NOT ANYTIME SOON.

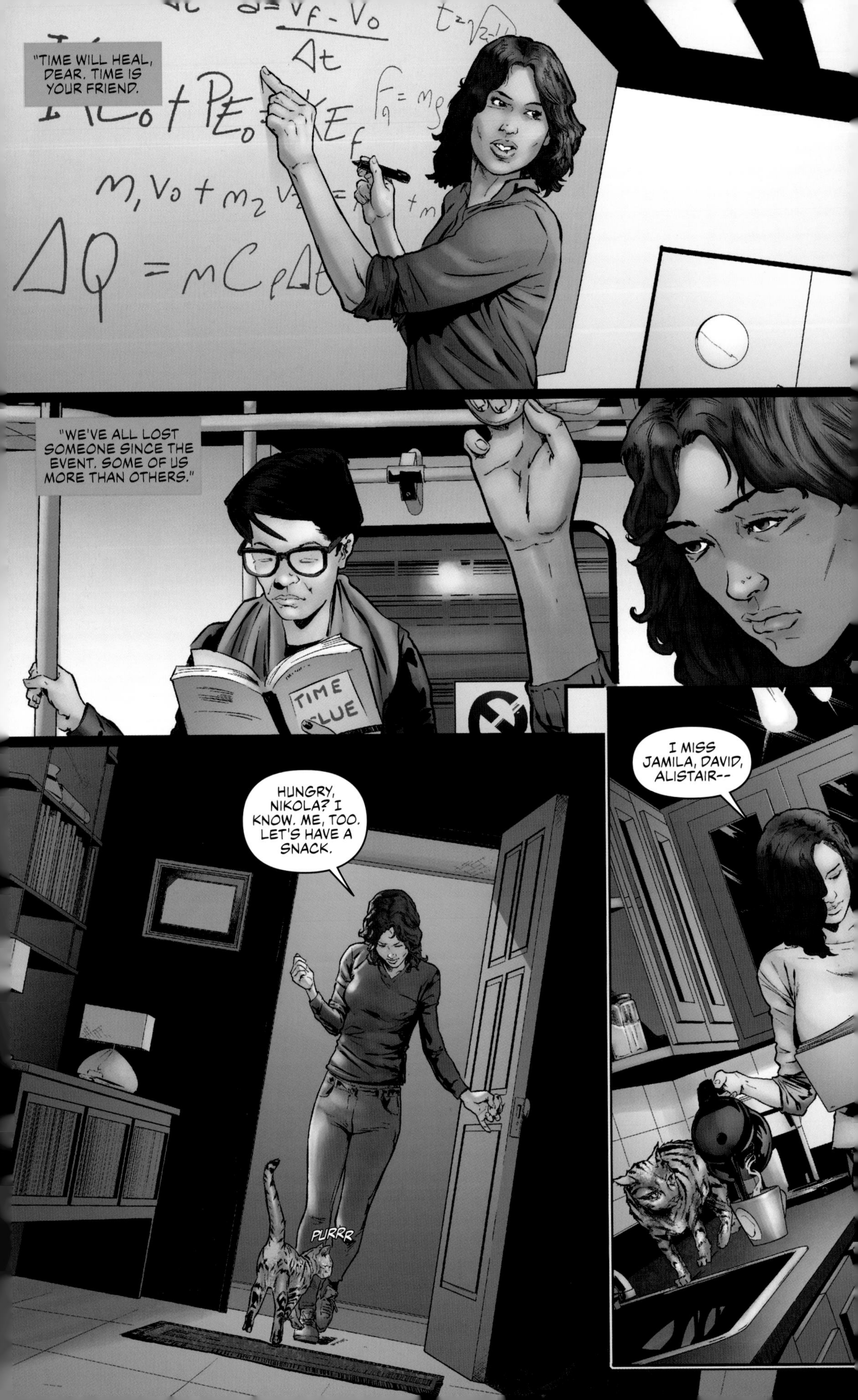
"TIME WILL HEAL, DEAR. TIME IS YOUR FRIEND.
"WE'VE ALL LOST SOMEONE SINCE THE EVENT. SOME OF US MORE THAN OTHERS."
HUNGRY, NIKOLA? I KNOW. ME, TOO. LET'S HAVE A SNACK.
PURRR
I MISS JAMILA, DAVID, ALISTAIR--

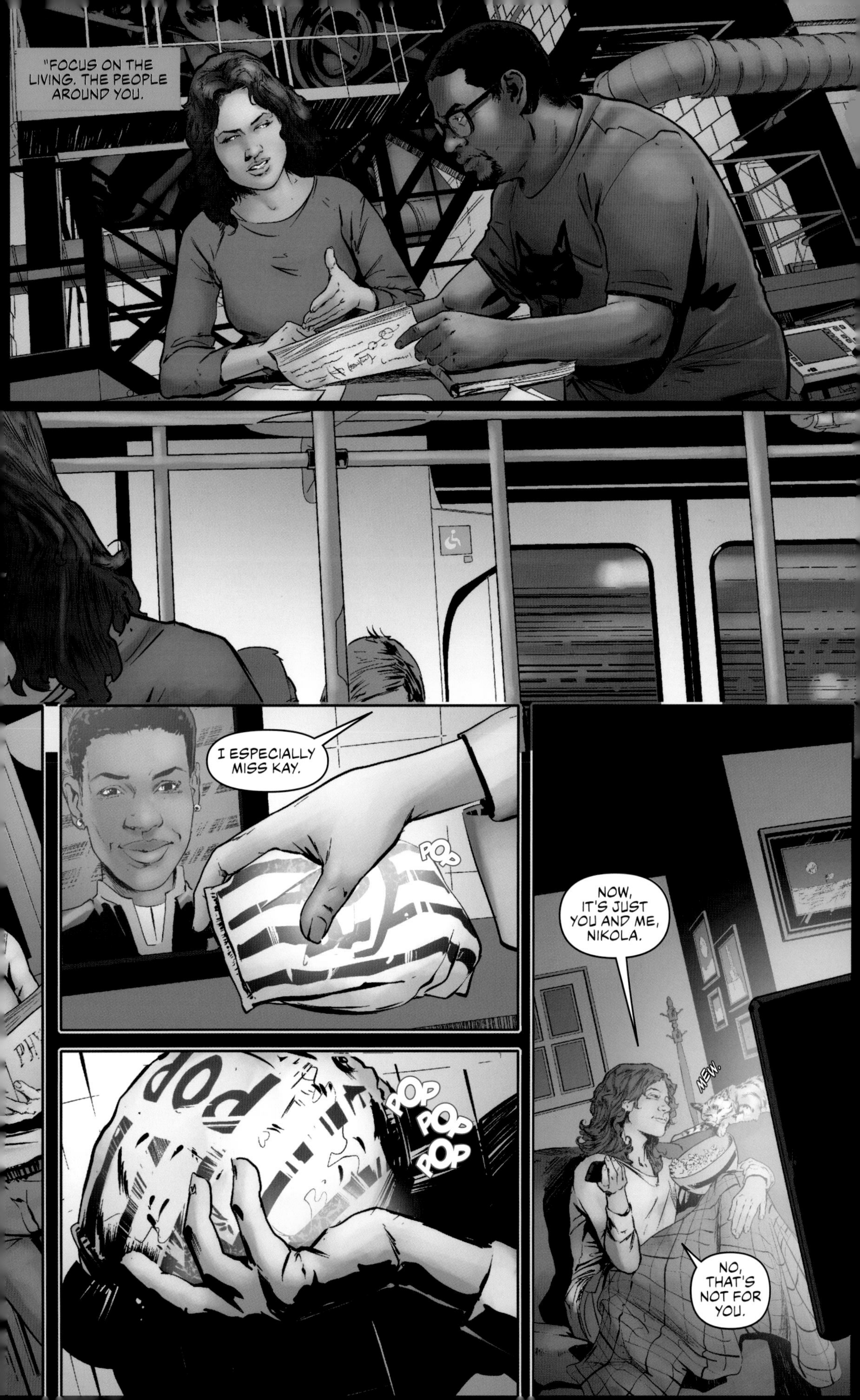
"FOCUS ON THE LIVING. THE PEOPLE AROUND YOU.
I ESPECIALLY MISS KAY.
POP
POP
POP
POP
POP
NOW, IT'S JUST YOU AND ME, NIKOLA.
MEW.
NO, THAT'S NOT FOR YOU.

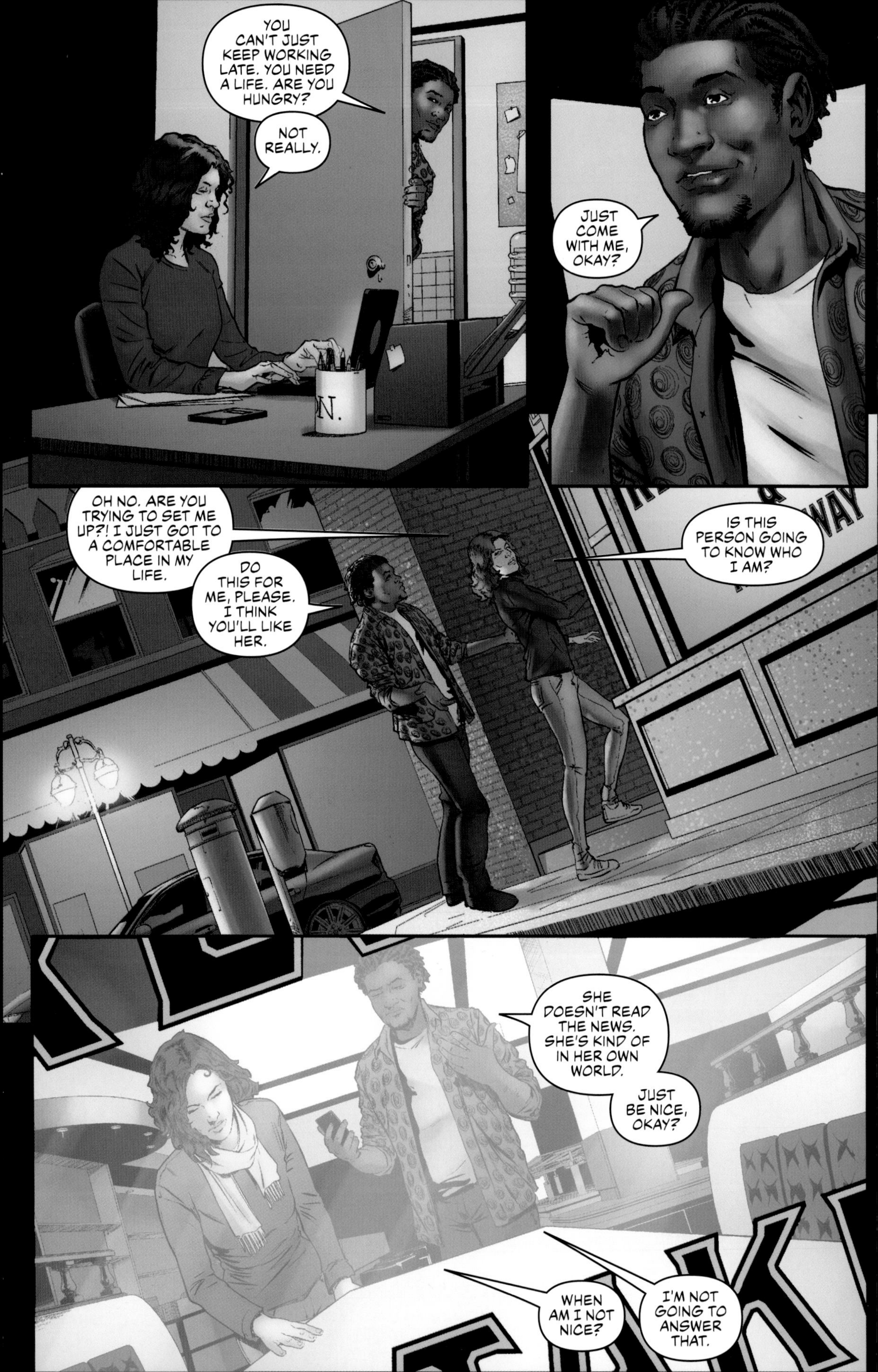
YOU CAN'T JUST KEEP WORKING LATE. YOU NEED A LIFE. ARE YOU HUNGRY?
NOT REALLY.
JUST COME WITH ME, OKAY?
OH NO. ARE YOU TRYING TO SET ME UP?! I JUST GOT TO A COMFORTABLE PLACE IN MY LIFE.
DO THIS FOR ME, PLEASE. I THINK YOU'LL LIKE HER.
IS THIS PERSON GOING TO KNOW WHO I AM?
SHE DOESN'T READ THE NEWS. SHE'S KIND OF IN HER OWN WORLD.
JUST BE NICE, OKAY?
WHEN AM I NOT NICE?
I'M NOT GOING TO ANSWER THAT.

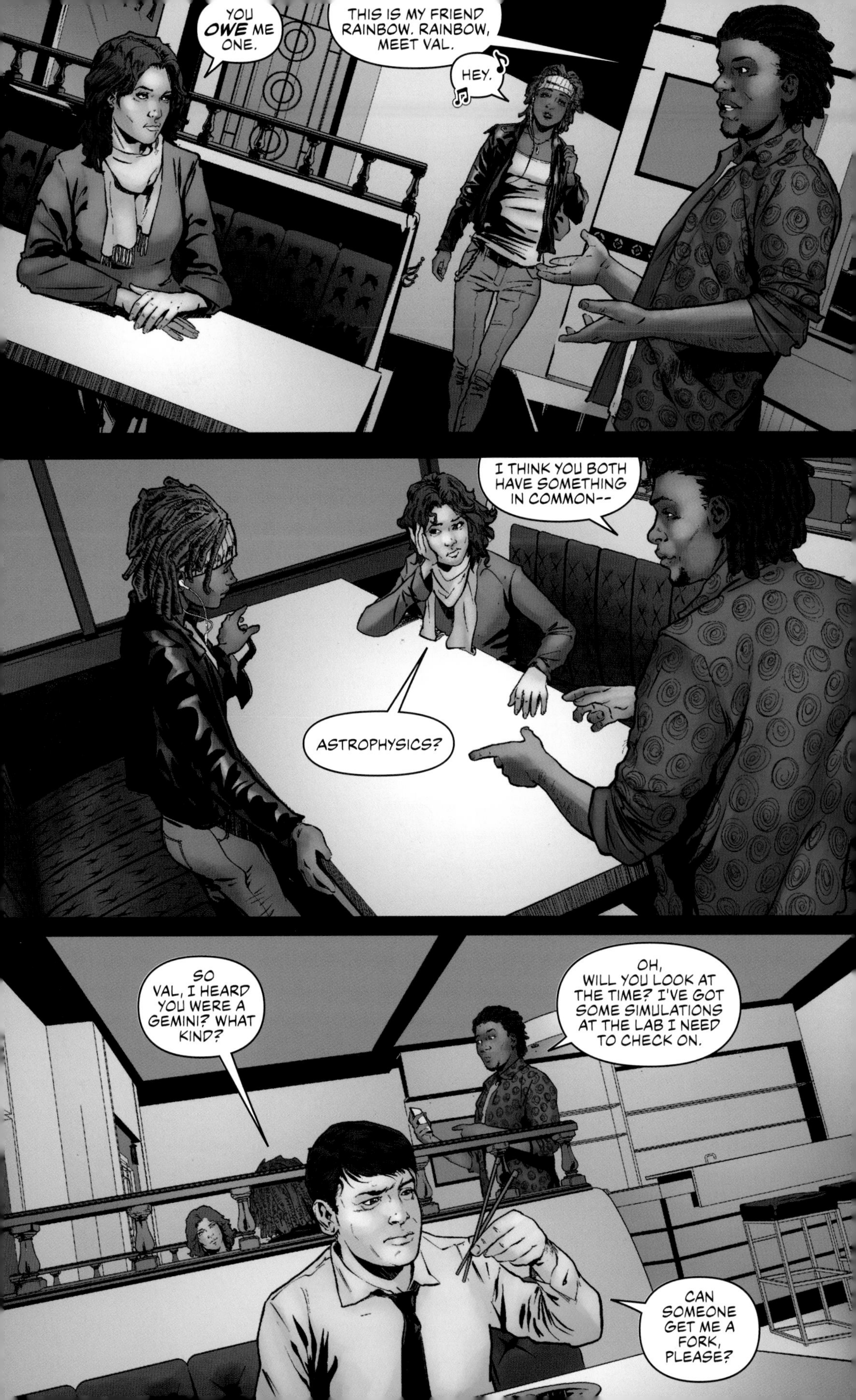
YOU OWE ME ONE.
THIS IS MY FRIEND RAINBOW. RAINBOW, MEET VAL.
HEY.
I THINK YOU BOTH HAVE SOMETHING IN COMMON--
ASTROPHYSICS?
SO VAL, I HEARD YOU WERE A GEMINI? WHAT KIND?
OH, WILL YOU LOOK AT THE TIME? I'VE GOT SOME SIMULATIONS AT THE LAB I NEED TO CHECK ON.
CAN SOMEONE GET ME A FORK, PLEASE?

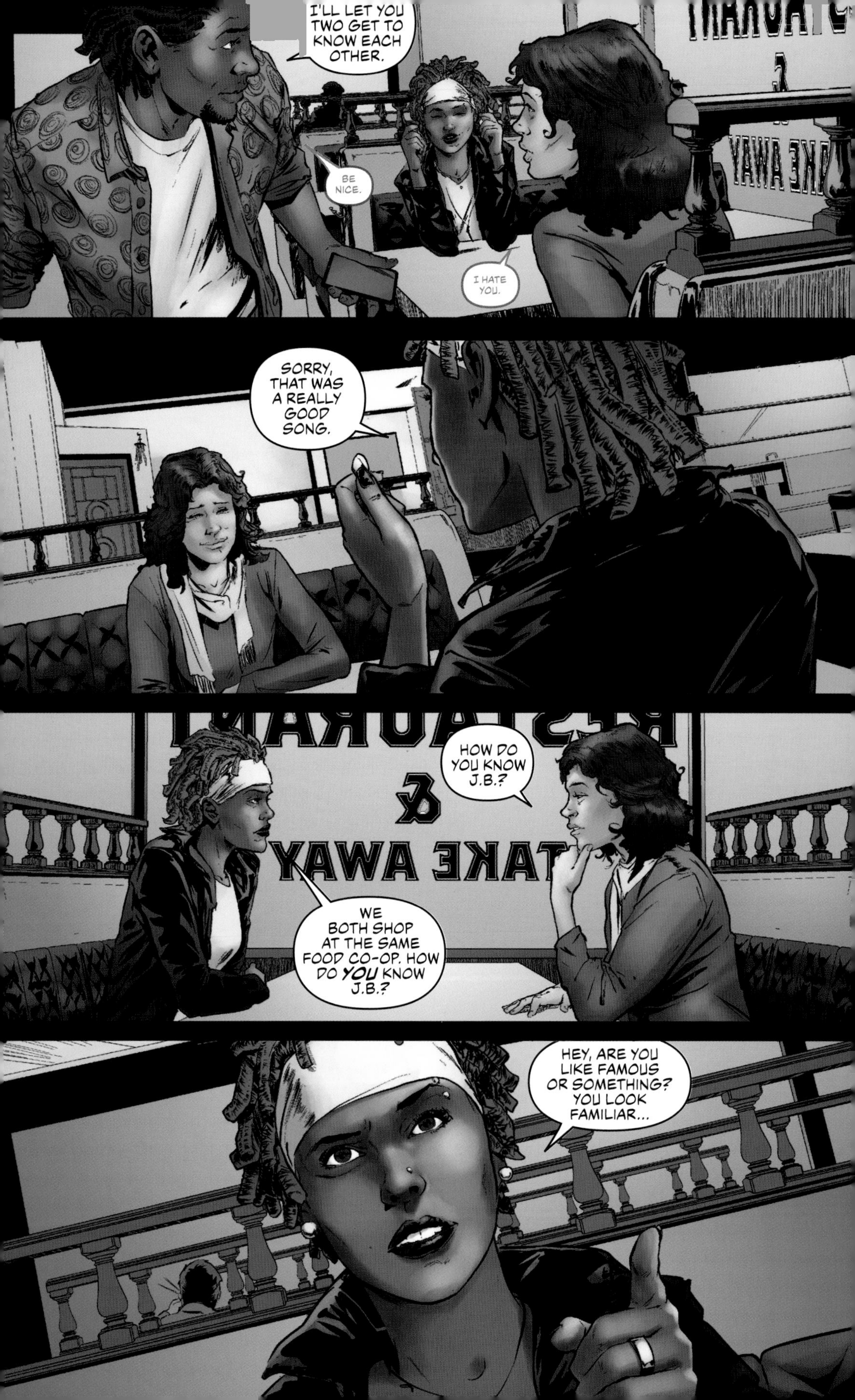
I'LL LET YOU TWO GET TO KNOW EACH OTHER.
BE NICE.
I HATE YOU.
SORRY, THAT WAS A REALLY GOOD SONG.
HOW DO YOU KNOW J.B.?
WE BOTH SHOP AT THE SAME FOOD CO-OP. HOW DO *YOU* KNOW J.B.?
HEY, ARE YOU LIKE FAMOUS OR SOMETHING? YOU LOOK FAMILIAR...

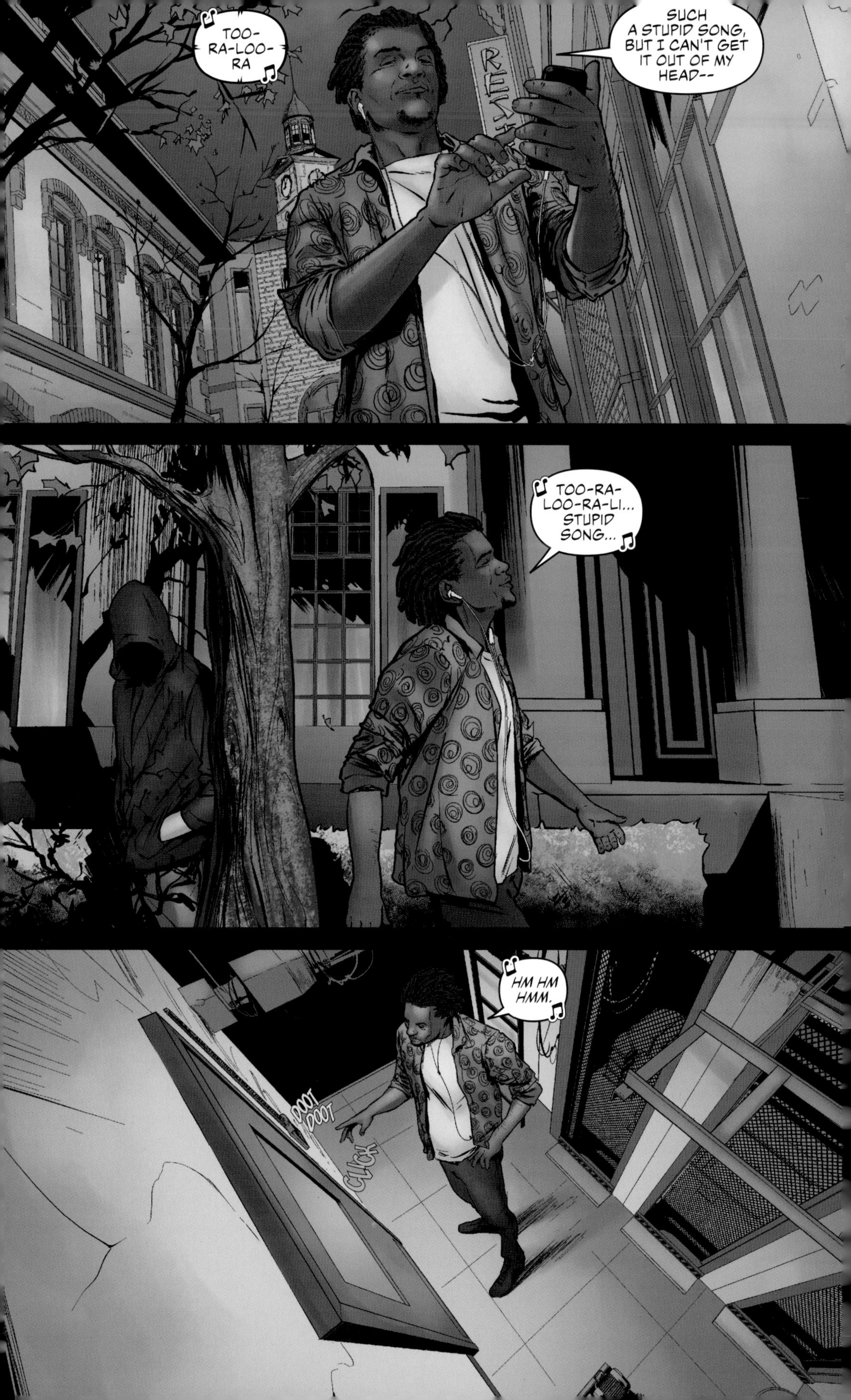
TOO-RA-LOO-RA
SUCH A STUPID SONG, BUT I CAN'T GET IT OUT OF MY HEAD--
TOO-RA-LOO-RA-LI... STUPID SONG...
HM HM HMM.
DOOT DOOT
CLICK

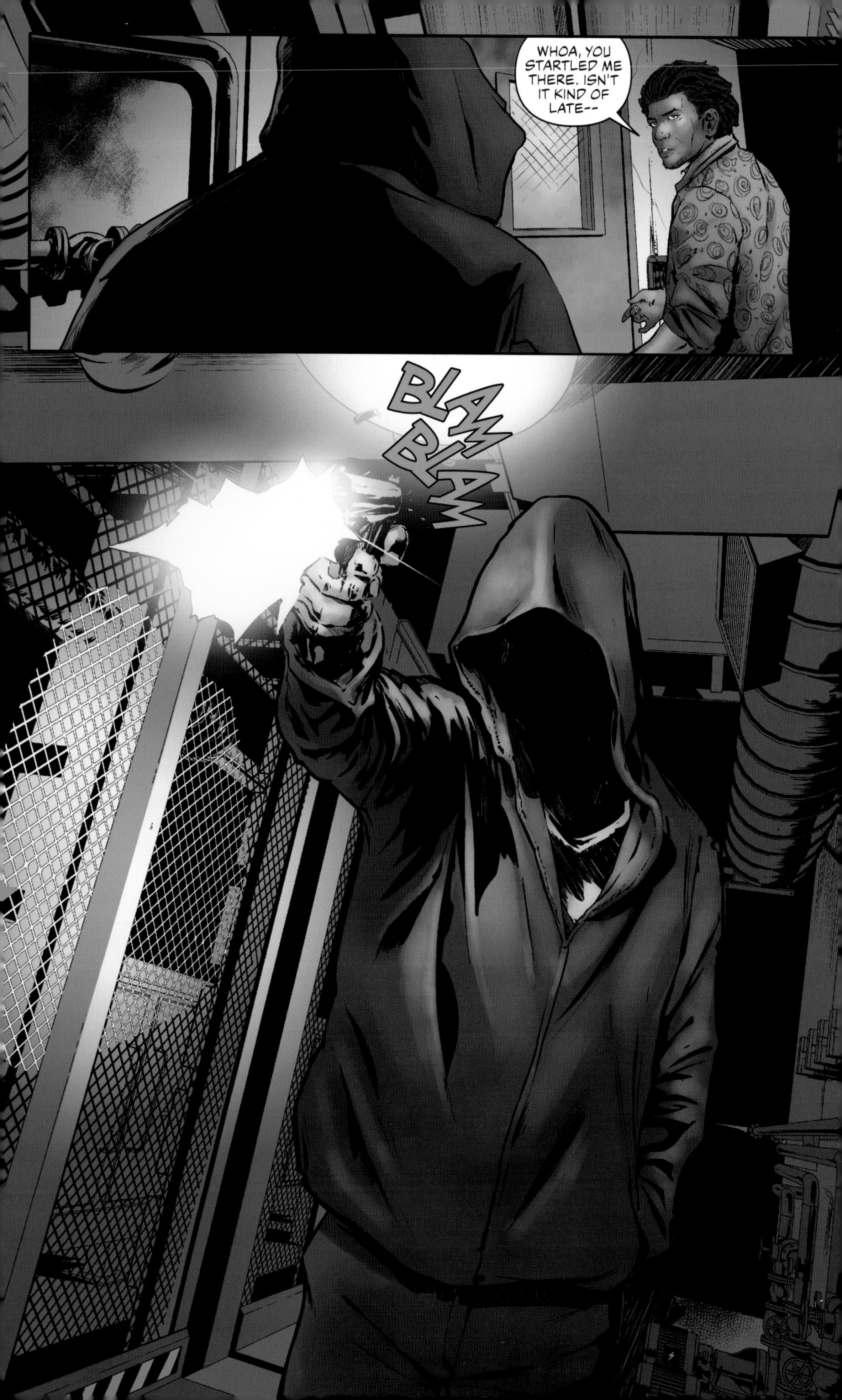
WHOA, YOU STARTLED ME THERE. ISN'T IT KIND OF LATE--
BLAM BLAM

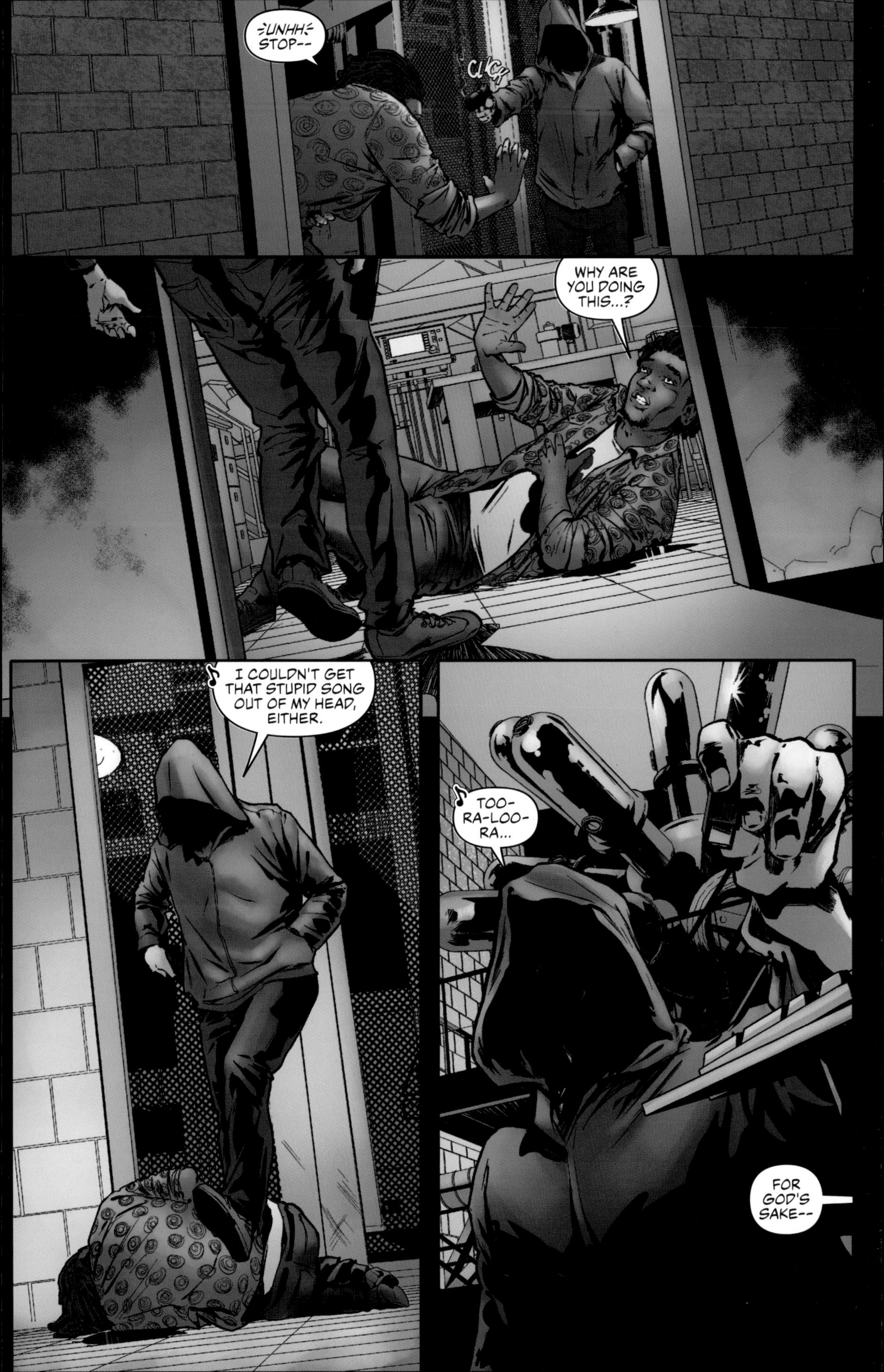
UNHH STOP--
CLICK
WHY ARE YOU DOING THIS...?
I COULDN'T GET THAT STUPID SONG OUT OF MY HEAD, EITHER.
TOO-RA-LOO-RA...
FOR GOD'S SAKE--

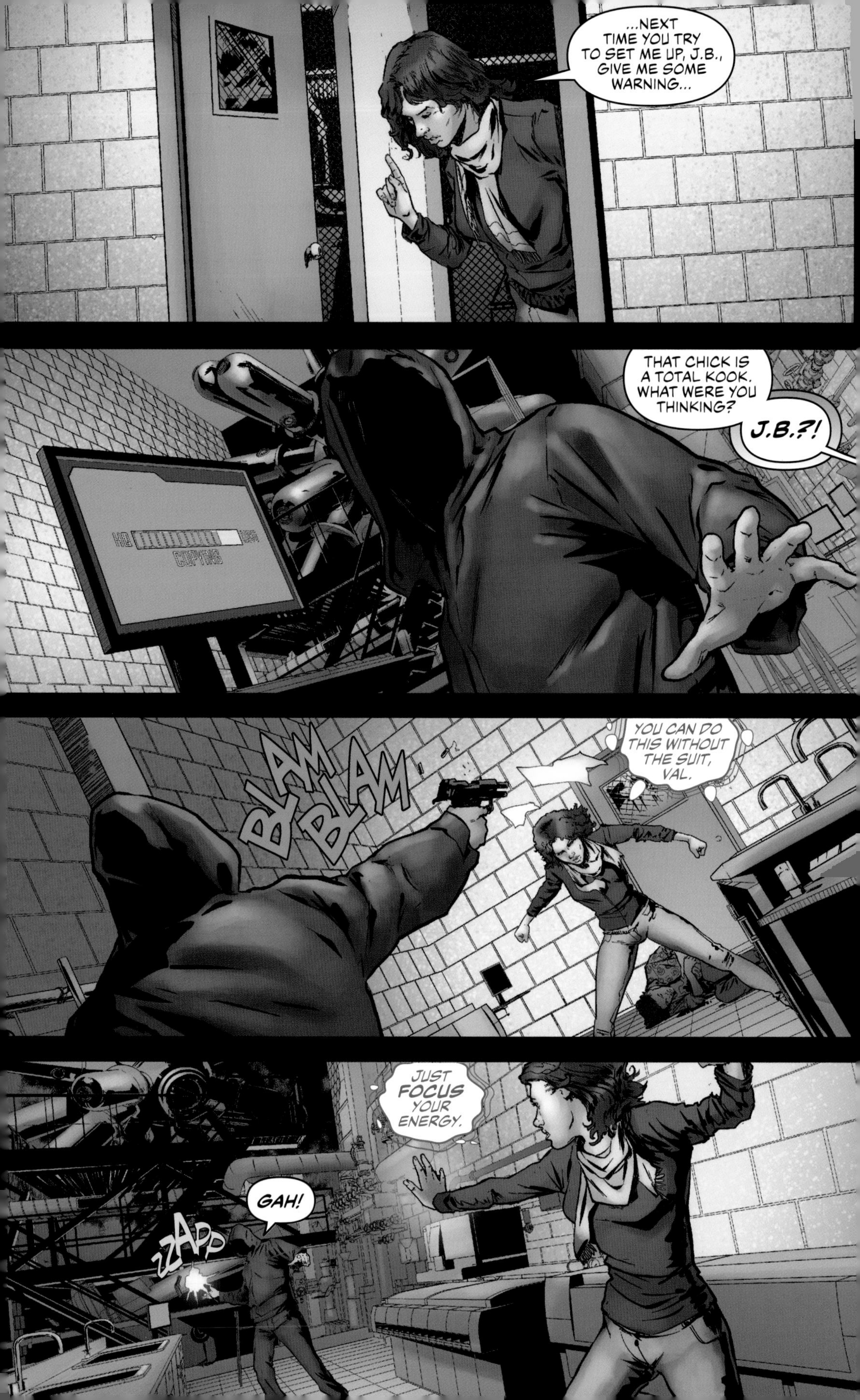
...NEXT TIME YOU TRY TO SET ME UP, J.B., GIVE ME SOME WARNING...
THAT CHICK IS A TOTAL KOOK. WHAT WERE YOU THINKING?
J.B.?!
COPYING
BLAM BLAM
YOU CAN DO THIS WITHOUT THE SUIT, VAL.
JUST FOCUS YOUR ENERGY.
GAH!
ZZAPP

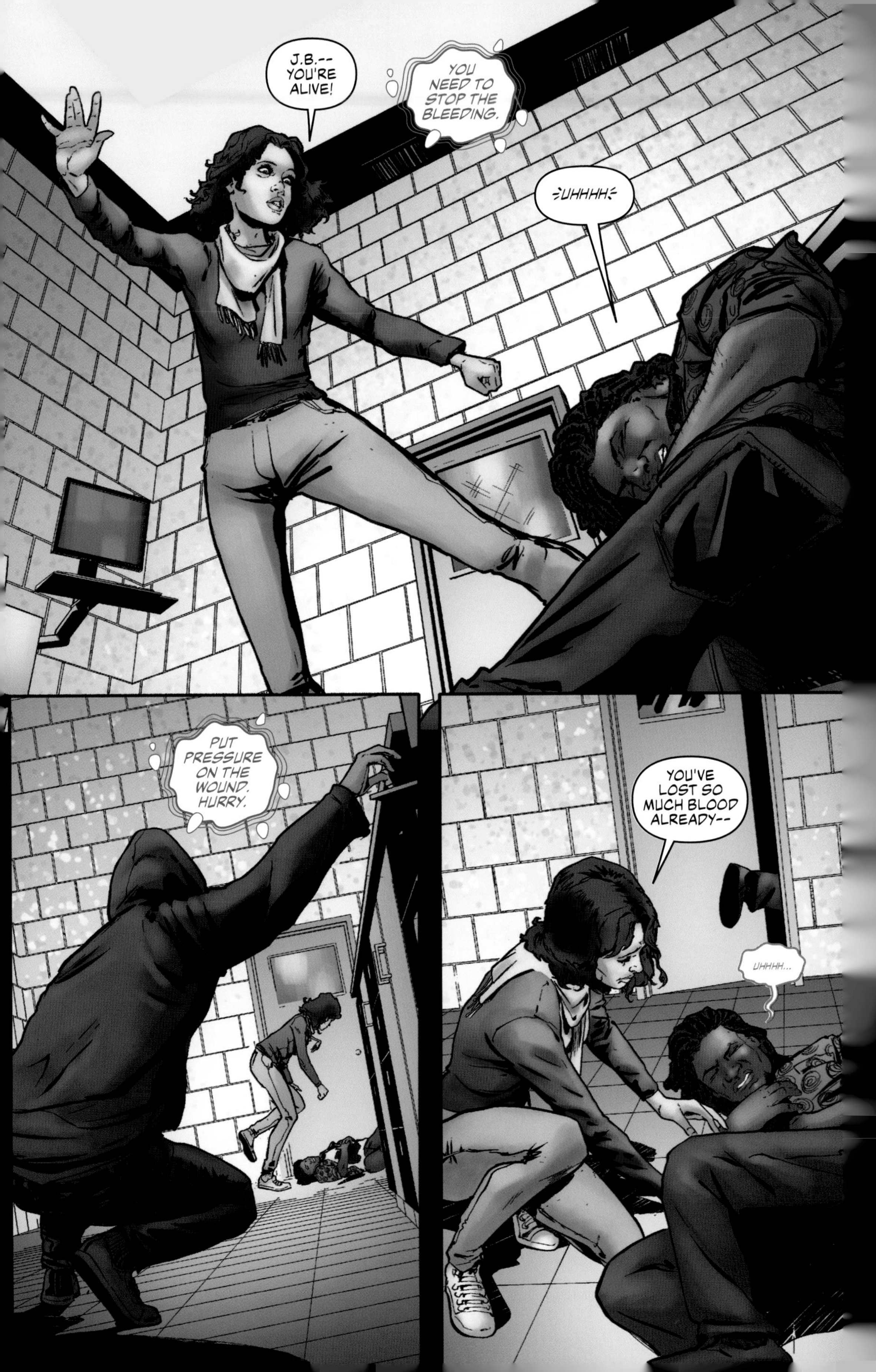
J.B.-- YOU'RE ALIVE!
YOU NEED TO STOP THE BLEEDING.
UHHHH.
PUT PRESSURE ON THE WOUND. HURRY.
YOU'VE LOST SO MUCH BLOOD ALREADY--
UHHHH...

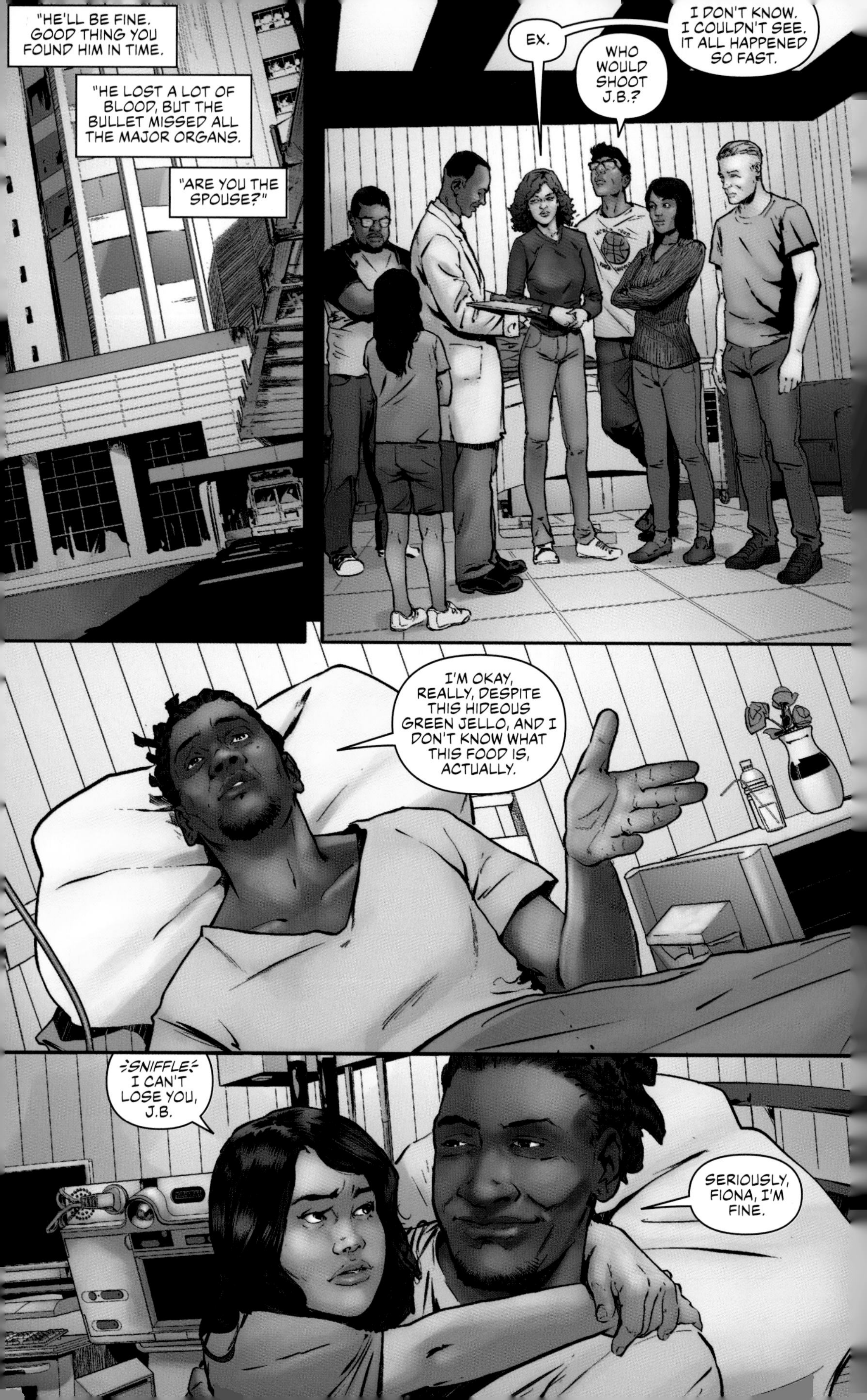
"HE'LL BE FINE. GOOD THING YOU FOUND HIM IN TIME.
"HE LOST A LOT OF BLOOD, BUT THE BULLET MISSED ALL THE MAJOR ORGANS.
"ARE YOU THE SPOUSE?"
EX.
WHO WOULD SHOOT J.B.?
I DON'T KNOW. I COULDN'T SEE. IT ALL HAPPENED SO FAST.
I'M OKAY, REALLY, DESPITE THIS HIDEOUS GREEN JELLO, AND I DON'T KNOW WHAT THIS FOOD IS, ACTUALLY.
SNIFFLE I CAN'T LOSE YOU, J.B.
SERIOUSLY, FIONA, I'M FINE.

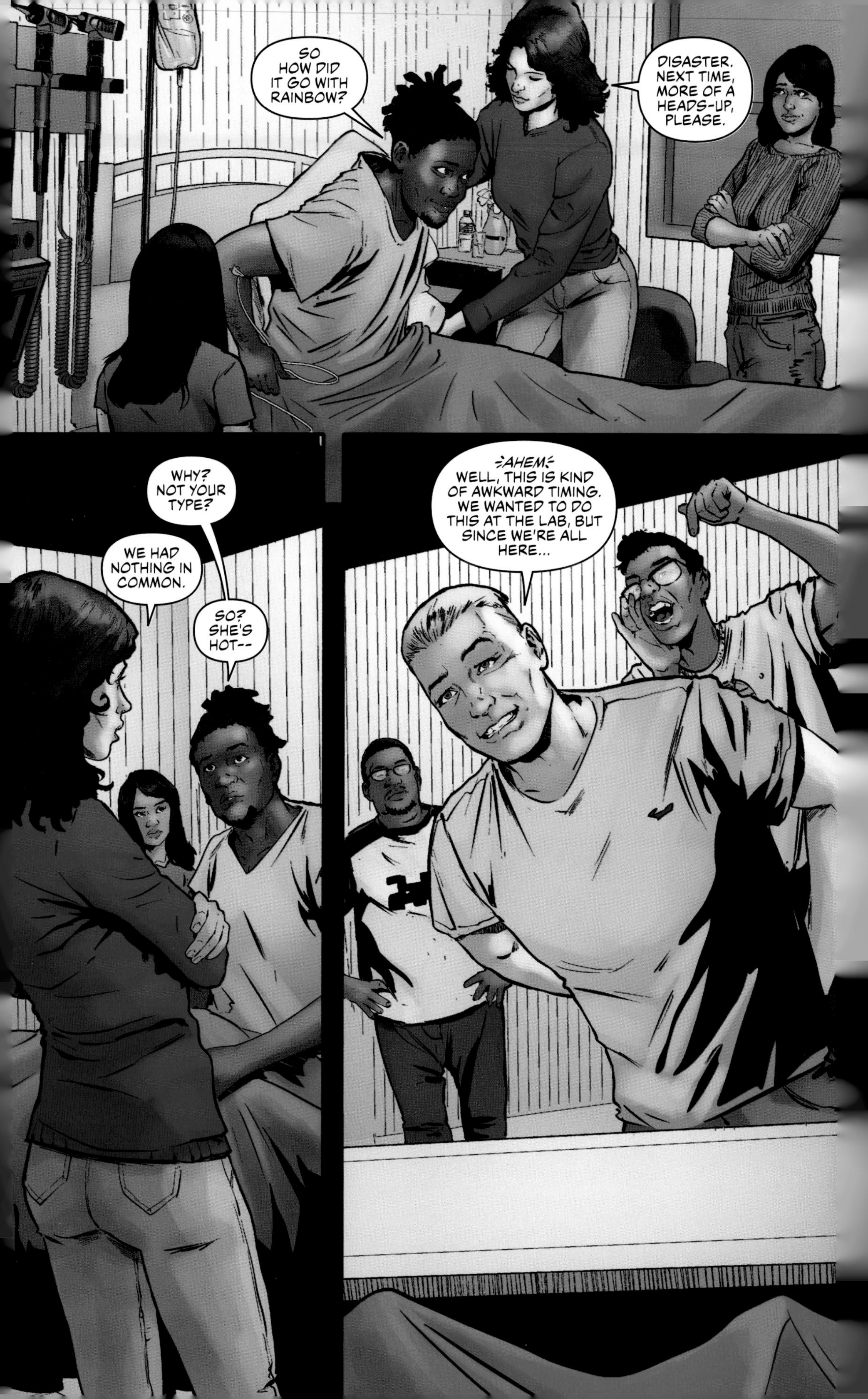
SO HOW DID IT GO WITH RAINBOW?
DISASTER. NEXT TIME, MORE OF A HEADS-UP, PLEASE.
WHY? NOT YOUR TYPE?
WE HAD NOTHING IN COMMON.
SO? SHE'S HOT--
AHEM
WELL, THIS IS KIND OF AWKWARD TIMING. WE WANTED TO DO THIS AT THE LAB, BUT SINCE WE'RE ALL HERE...

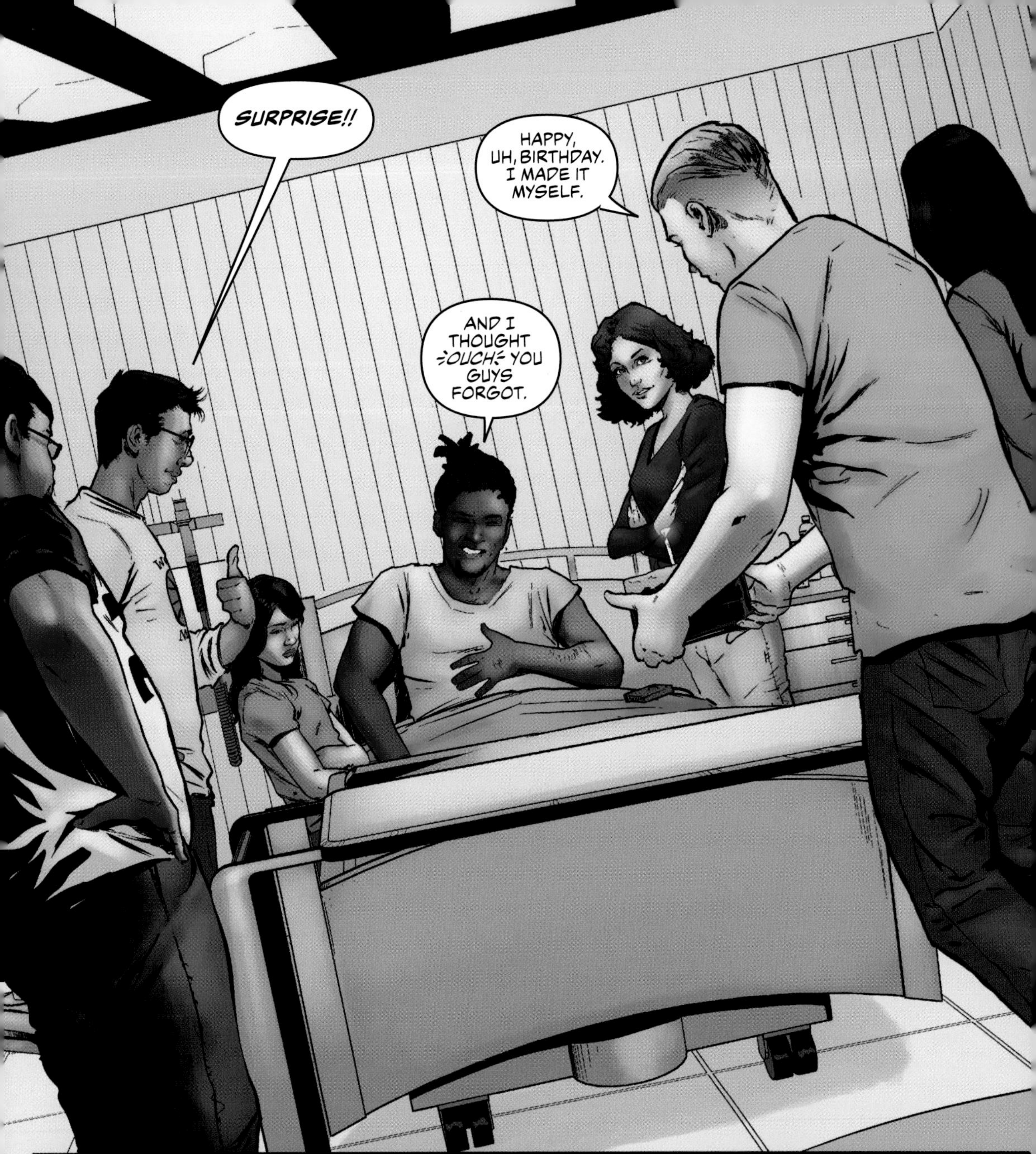
SURPRISE!!
HAPPY, UH, BIRTHDAY. I MADE IT MYSELF.
AND I THOUGHT -OUCH- YOU GUYS FORGOT.
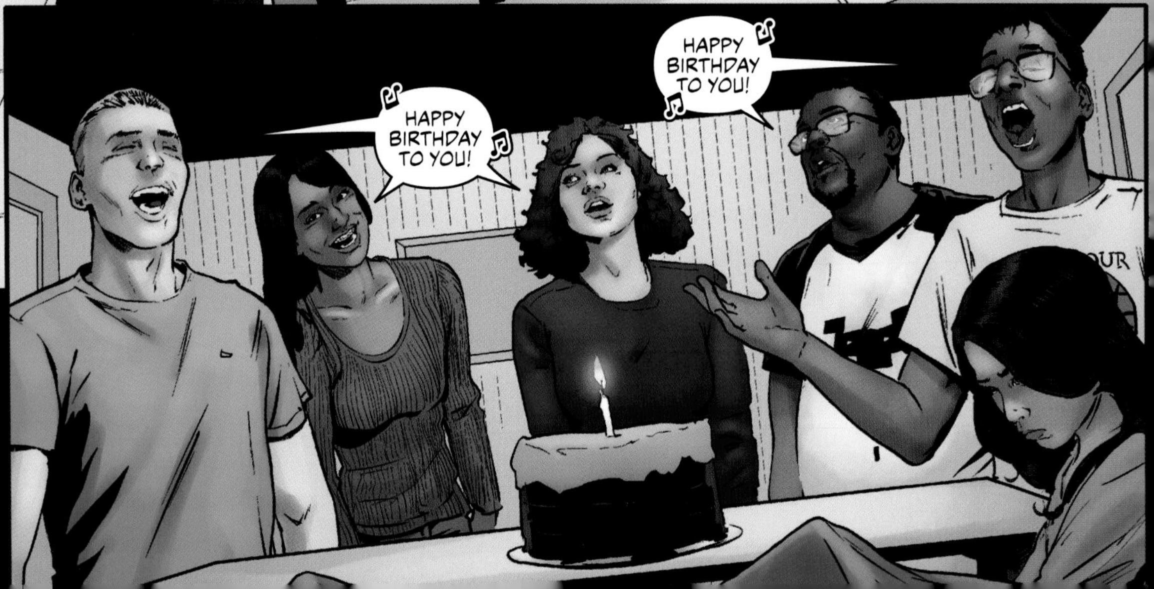
HAPPY BIRTHDAY TO YOU!
HAPPY BIRTHDAY TO YOU!

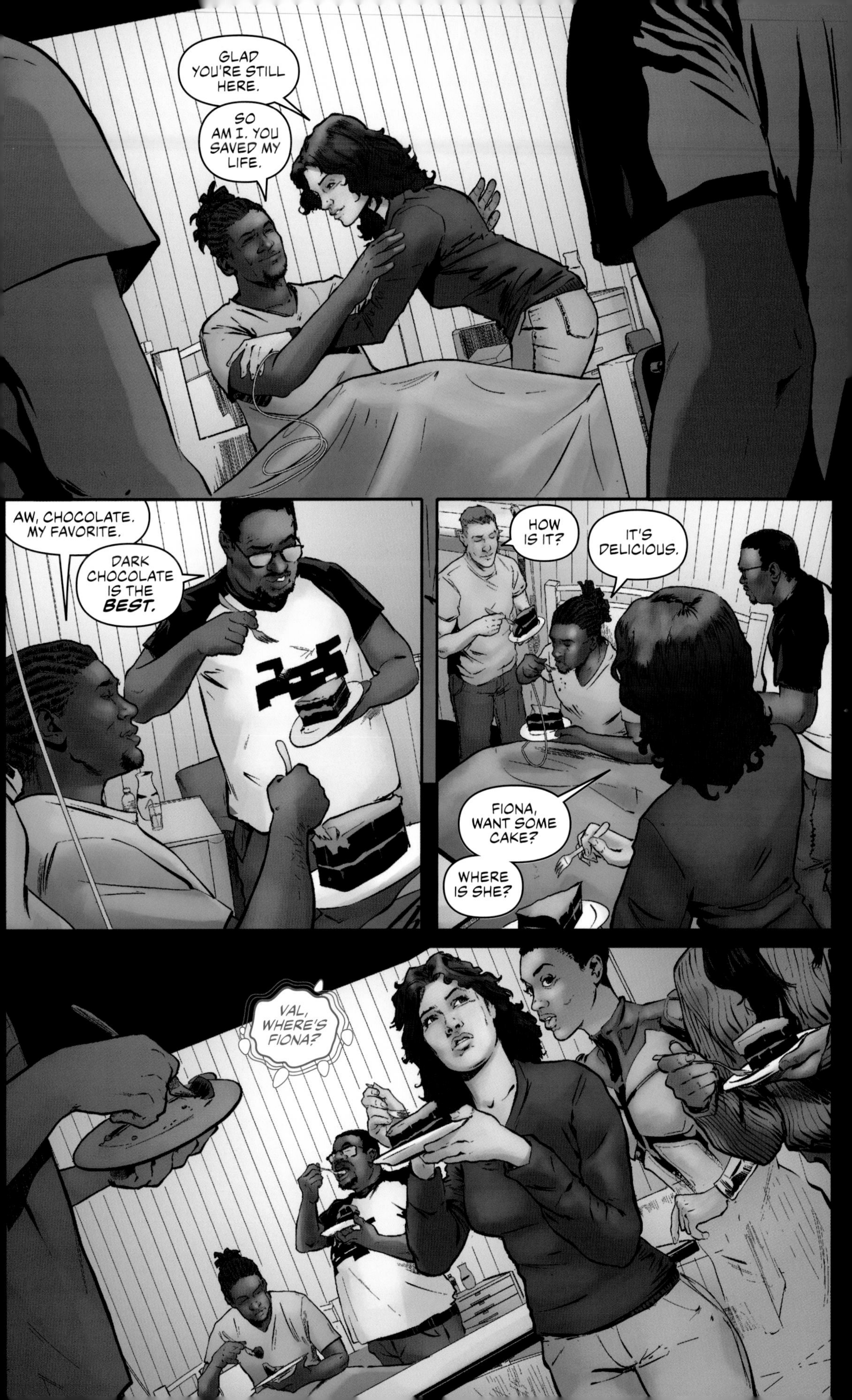
GLAD YOU'RE STILL HERE.
SO AM I. YOU SAVED MY LIFE.
AW, CHOCOLATE. MY FAVORITE.
DARK CHOCOLATE IS THE BEST.
HOW IS IT?
IT'S DELICIOUS.
FIONA, WANT SOME CAKE?
WHERE IS SHE?
VAL, WHERE'S FIONA?

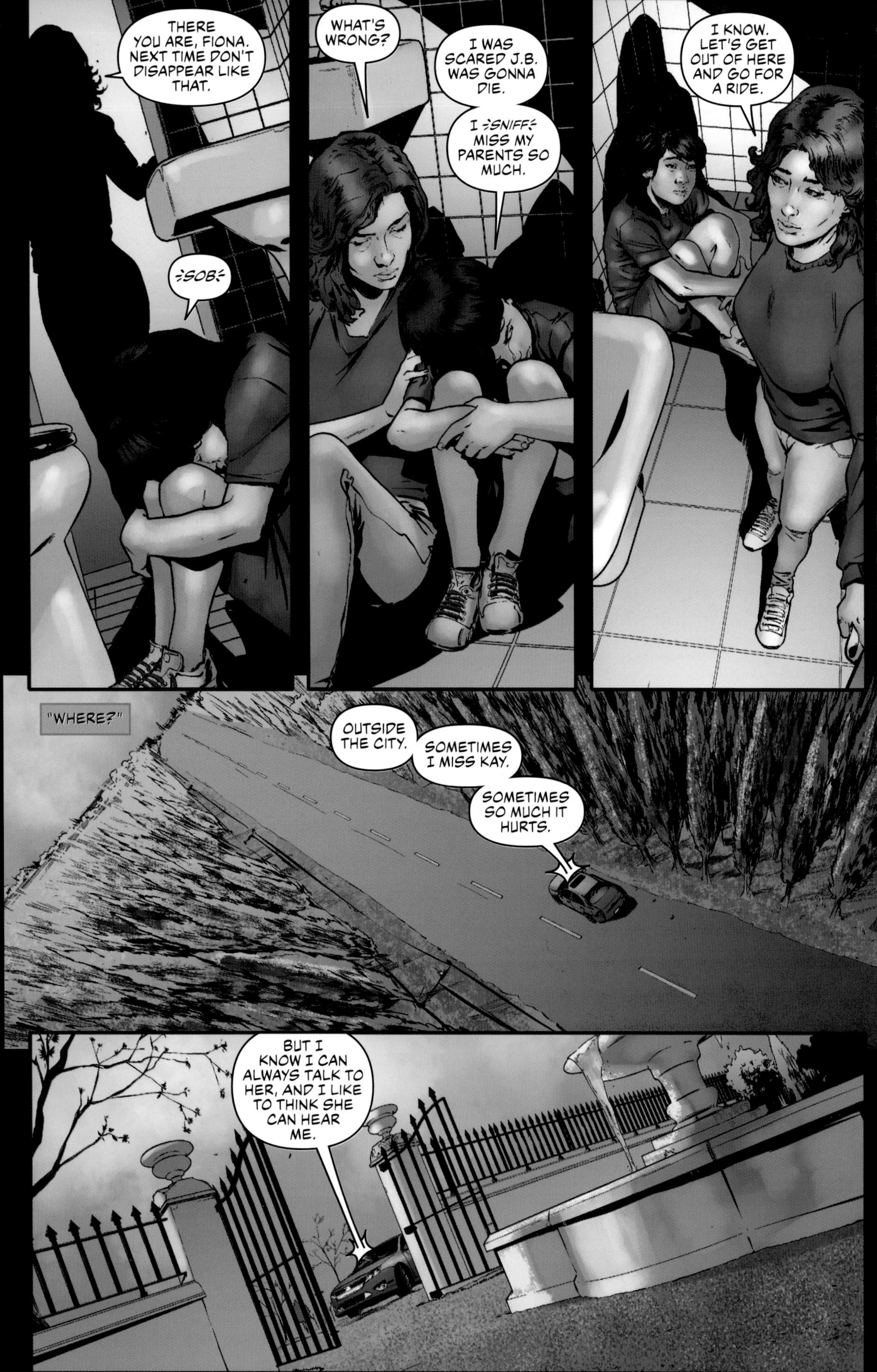
THERE YOU ARE, FIONA. NEXT TIME DON'T DISAPPEAR LIKE THAT.
-SOB-
WHAT'S WRONG?
I WAS SCARED J.B. WAS GONNA DIE.
I -SNIFF- MISS MY PARENTS SO MUCH.
I KNOW. LET'S GET OUT OF HERE AND GO FOR A RIDE.
"WHERE?"
OUTSIDE THE CITY.
SOMETIMES I MISS KAY.
SOMETIMES SO MUCH IT HURTS.
BUT I KNOW I CAN ALWAYS TALK TO HER, AND I LIKE TO THINK SHE CAN HEAR ME.

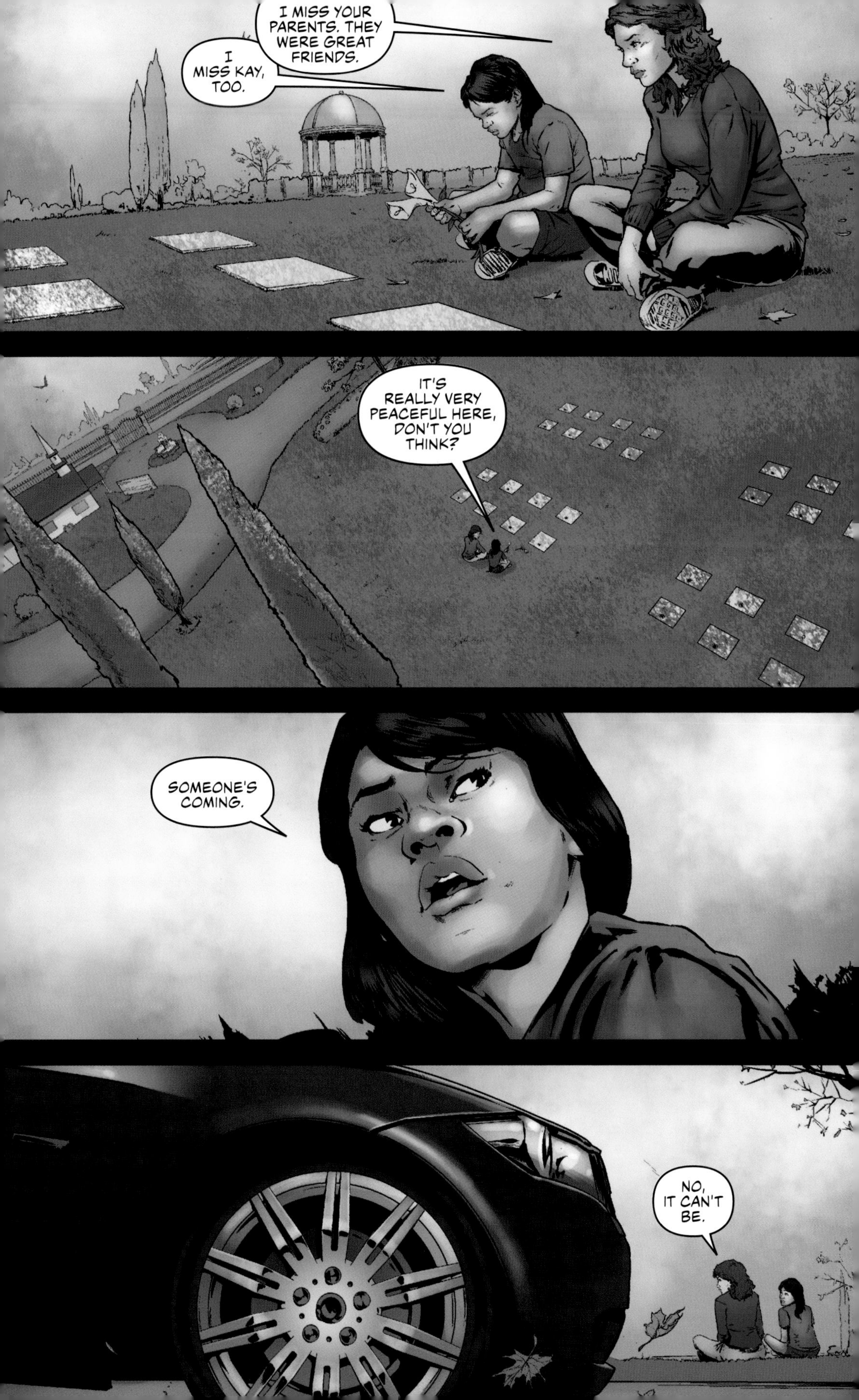
I MISS YOUR PARENTS. THEY WERE GREAT FRIENDS.
I MISS KAY, TOO.
IT'S REALLY VERY PEACEFUL HERE, DON'T YOU THINK?
SOMEONE'S COMING.
NO, IT CAN'T BE.

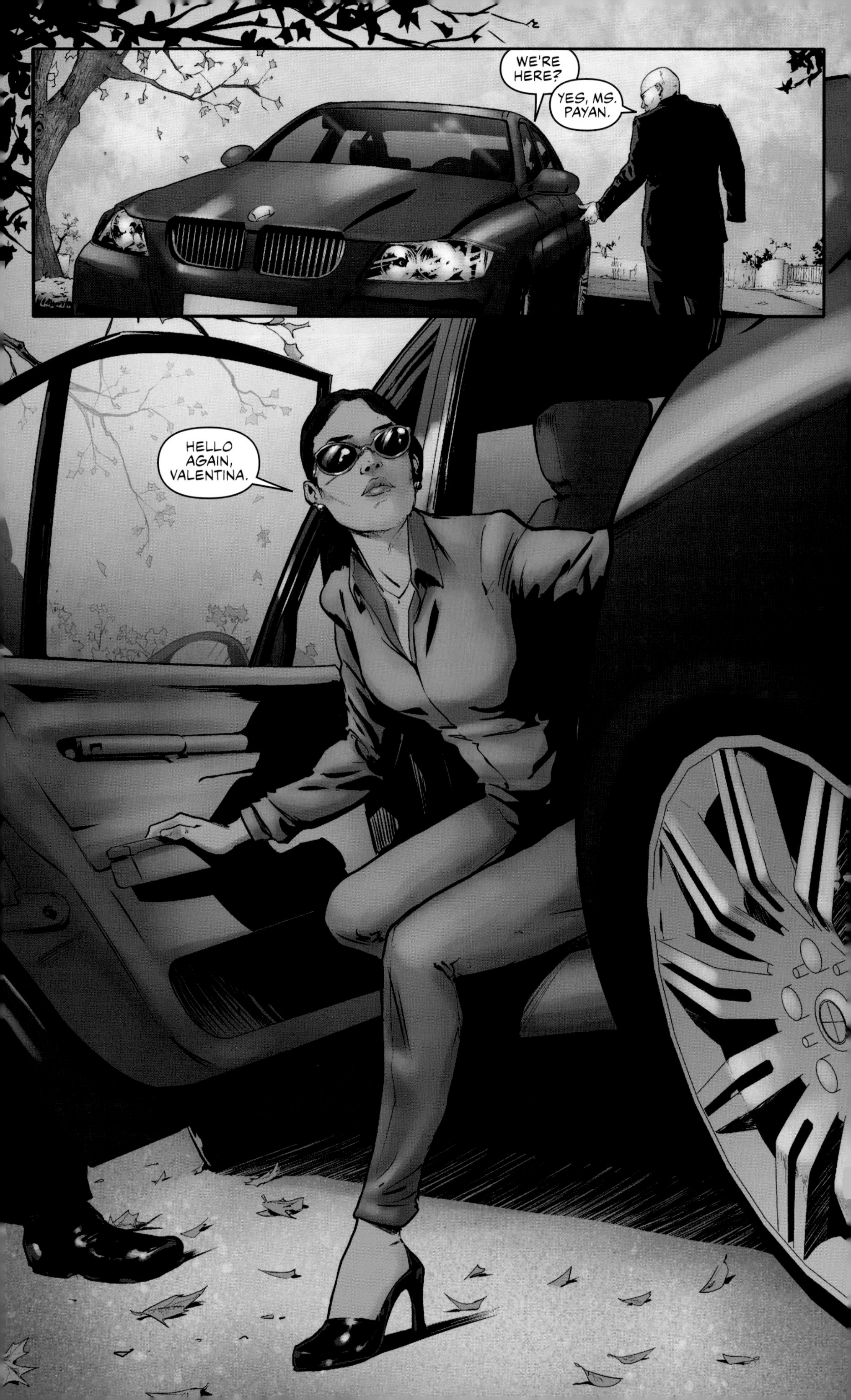

WE'RE HERE?
YES, MS. PAYAN.
HELLO AGAIN, VALENTINA.

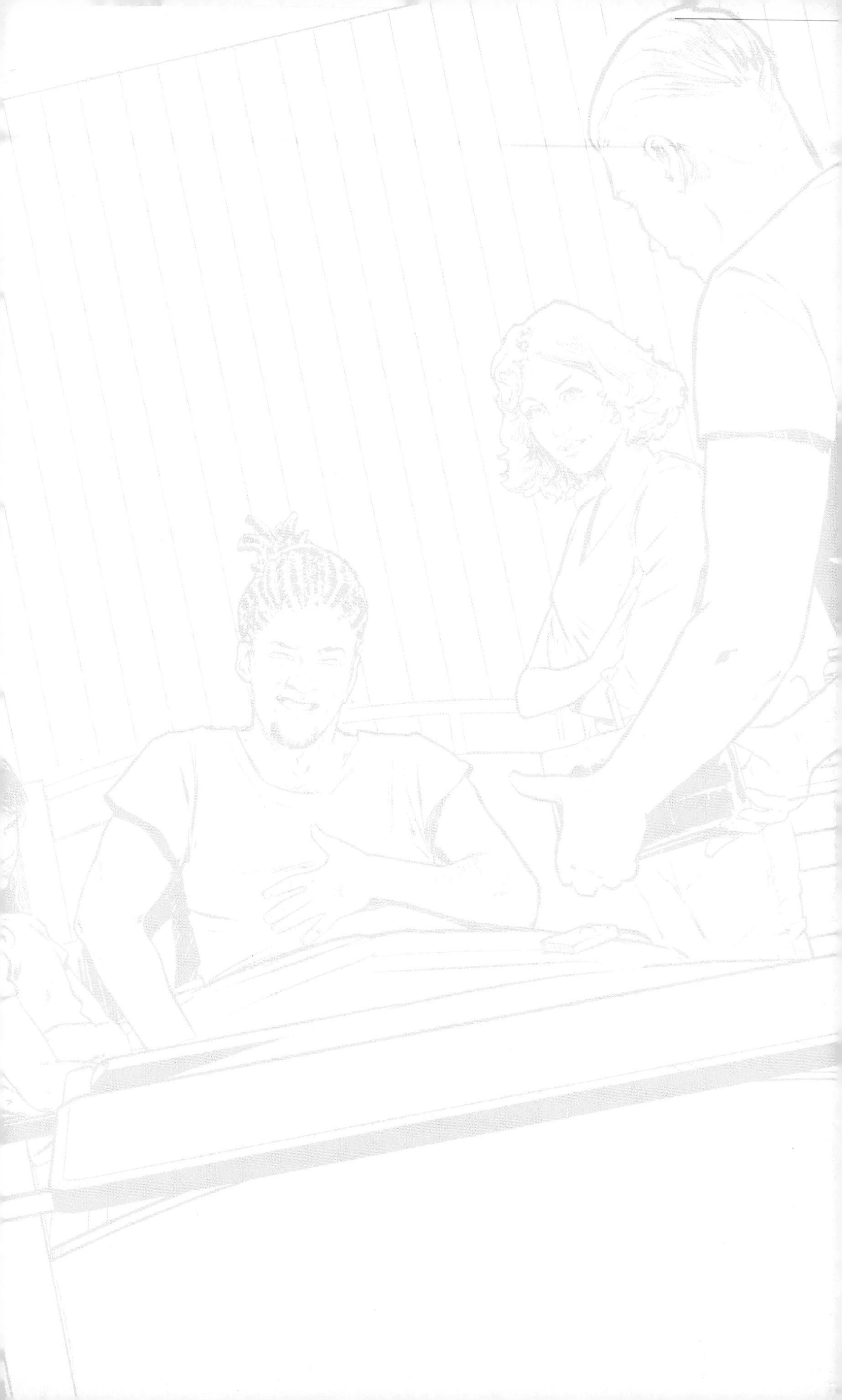

CHAPTER THREE

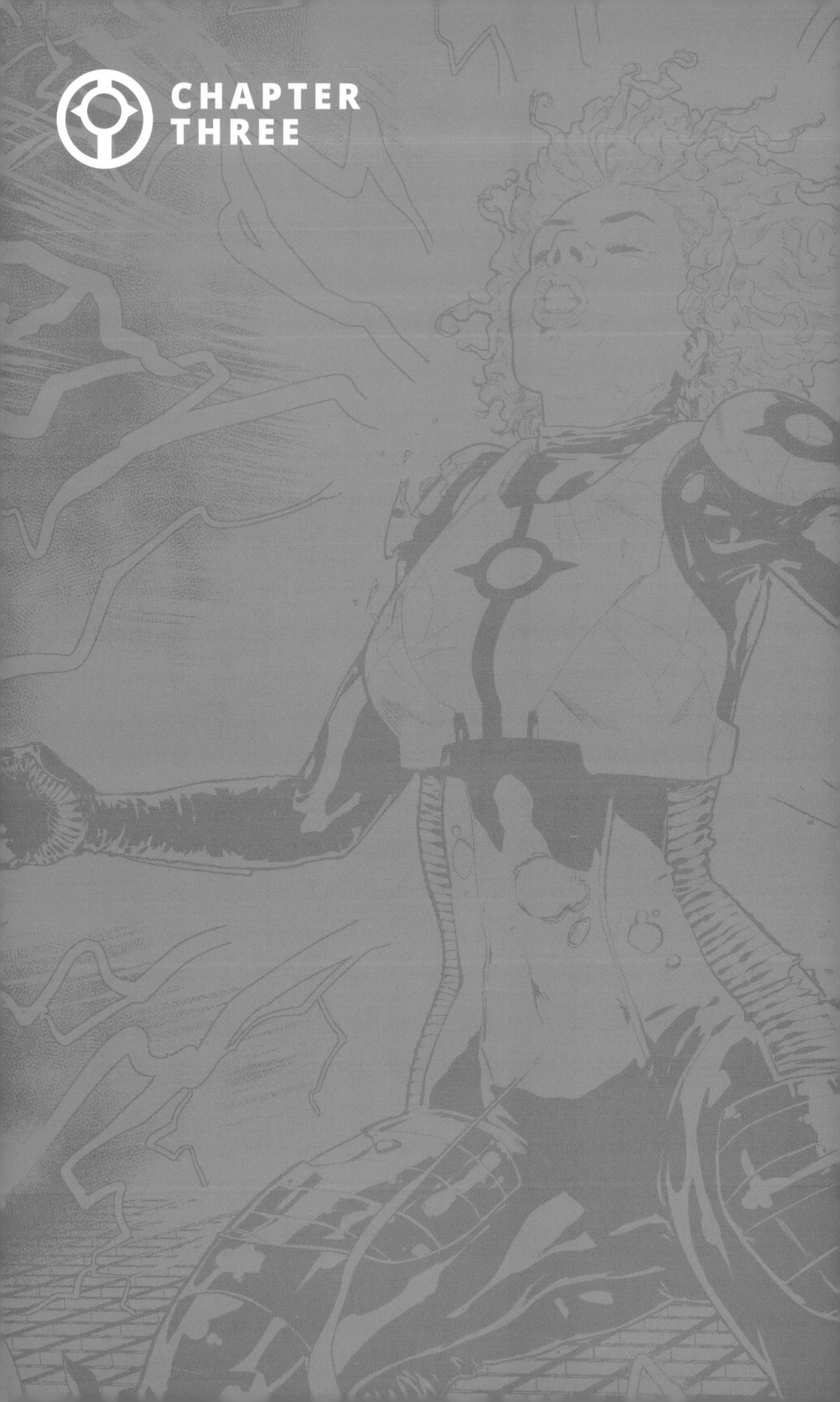

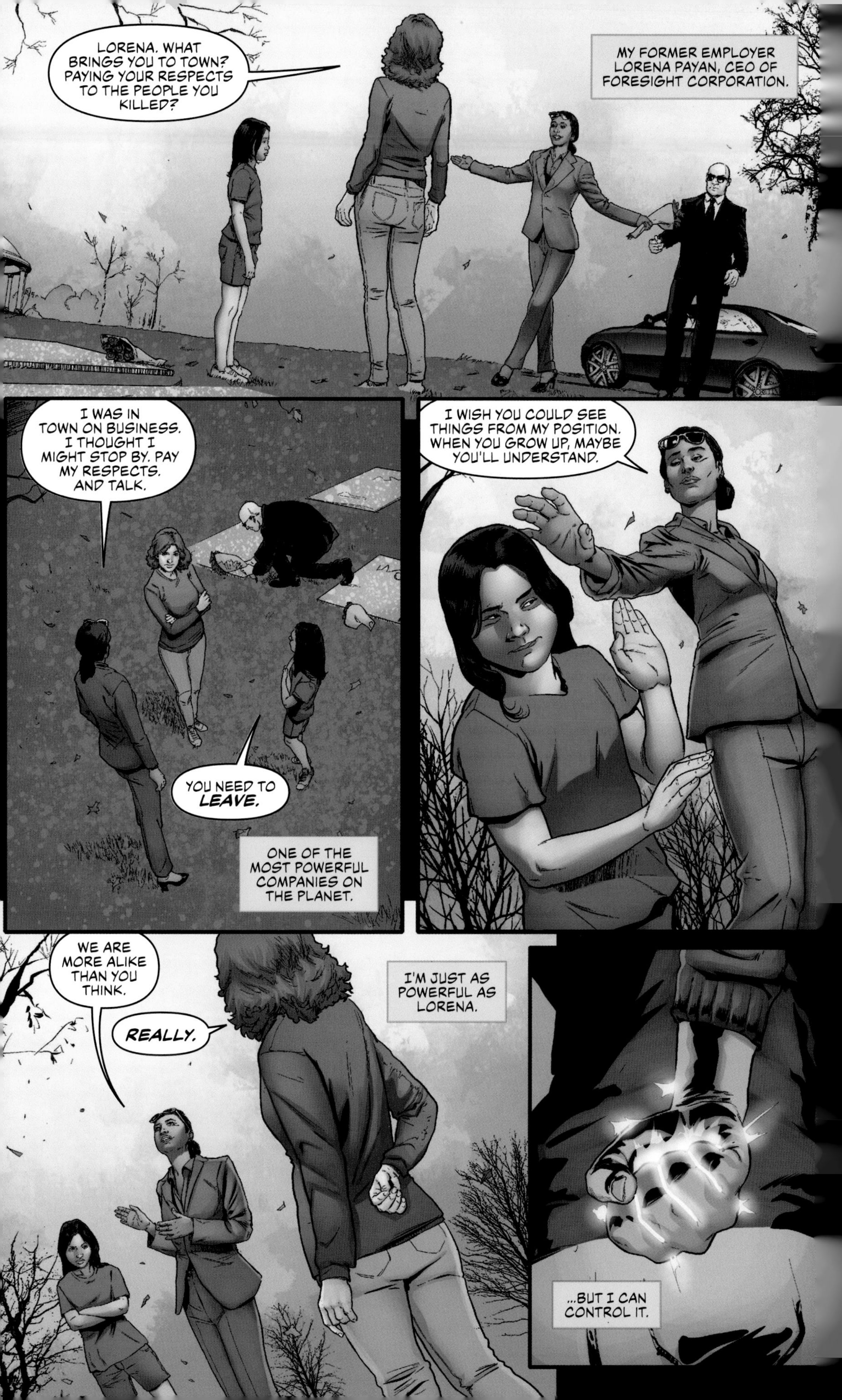
LORENA. WHAT BRINGS YOU TO TOWN? PAYING YOUR RESPECTS TO THE PEOPLE YOU KILLED?
MY FORMER EMPLOYER LORENA PAYAN, CEO OF FORESIGHT CORPORATION.
I WAS IN TOWN ON BUSINESS. I THOUGHT I MIGHT STOP BY. PAY MY RESPECTS. AND TALK.
YOU NEED TO LEAVE.
ONE OF THE MOST POWERFUL COMPANIES ON THE PLANET.
I WISH YOU COULD SEE THINGS FROM MY POSITION. WHEN YOU GROW UP, MAYBE YOU'LL UNDERSTAND.
WE ARE MORE ALIKE THAN YOU THINK.
REALLY.
I'M JUST AS POWERFUL AS LORENA.
...BUT I CAN CONTROL IT.

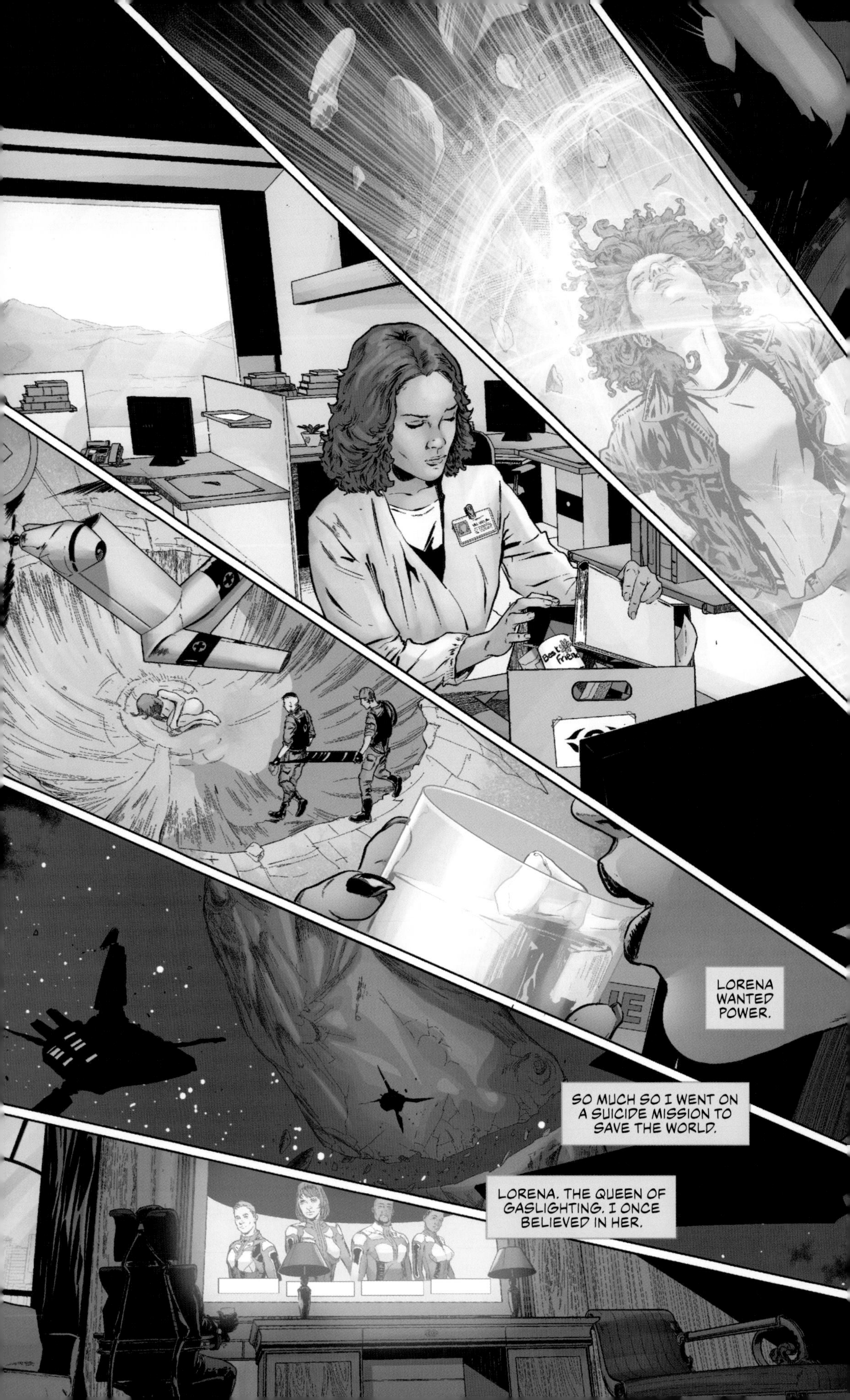

LORENA WANTED POWER.
SO MUCH SO I WENT ON A SUICIDE MISSION TO SAVE THE WORLD.
LORENA. THE QUEEN OF GASLIGHTING. I ONCE BELIEVED IN HER.

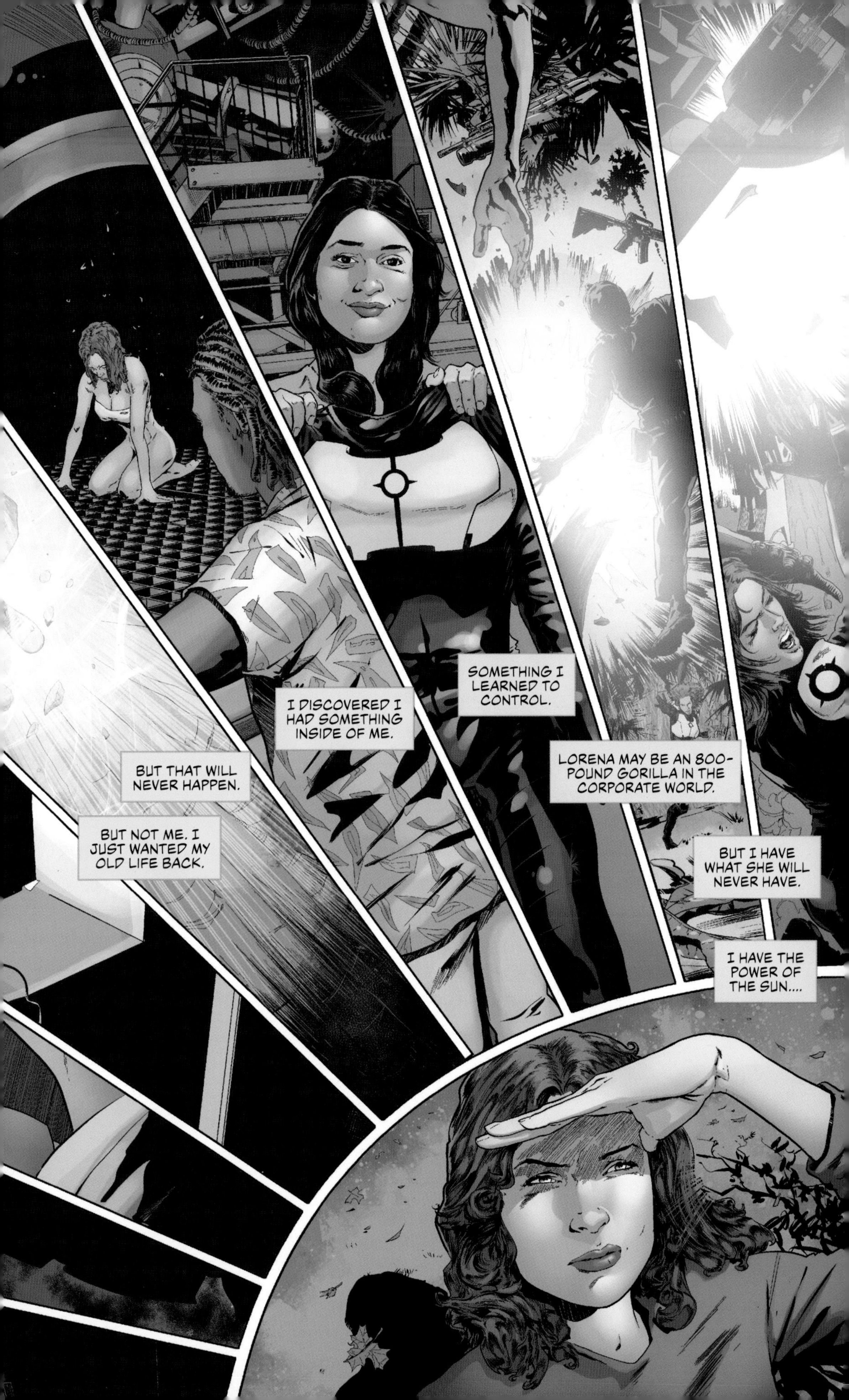
BUT NOT ME. I JUST WANTED MY OLD LIFE BACK.
BUT THAT WILL NEVER HAPPEN.
I DISCOVERED I HAD SOMETHING INSIDE OF ME.
SOMETHING I LEARNED TO CONTROL.
LORENA MAY BE AN 800-POUND GORILLA IN THE CORPORATE WORLD.
BUT I HAVE WHAT SHE WILL NEVER HAVE.
I HAVE THE POWER OF THE SUN....

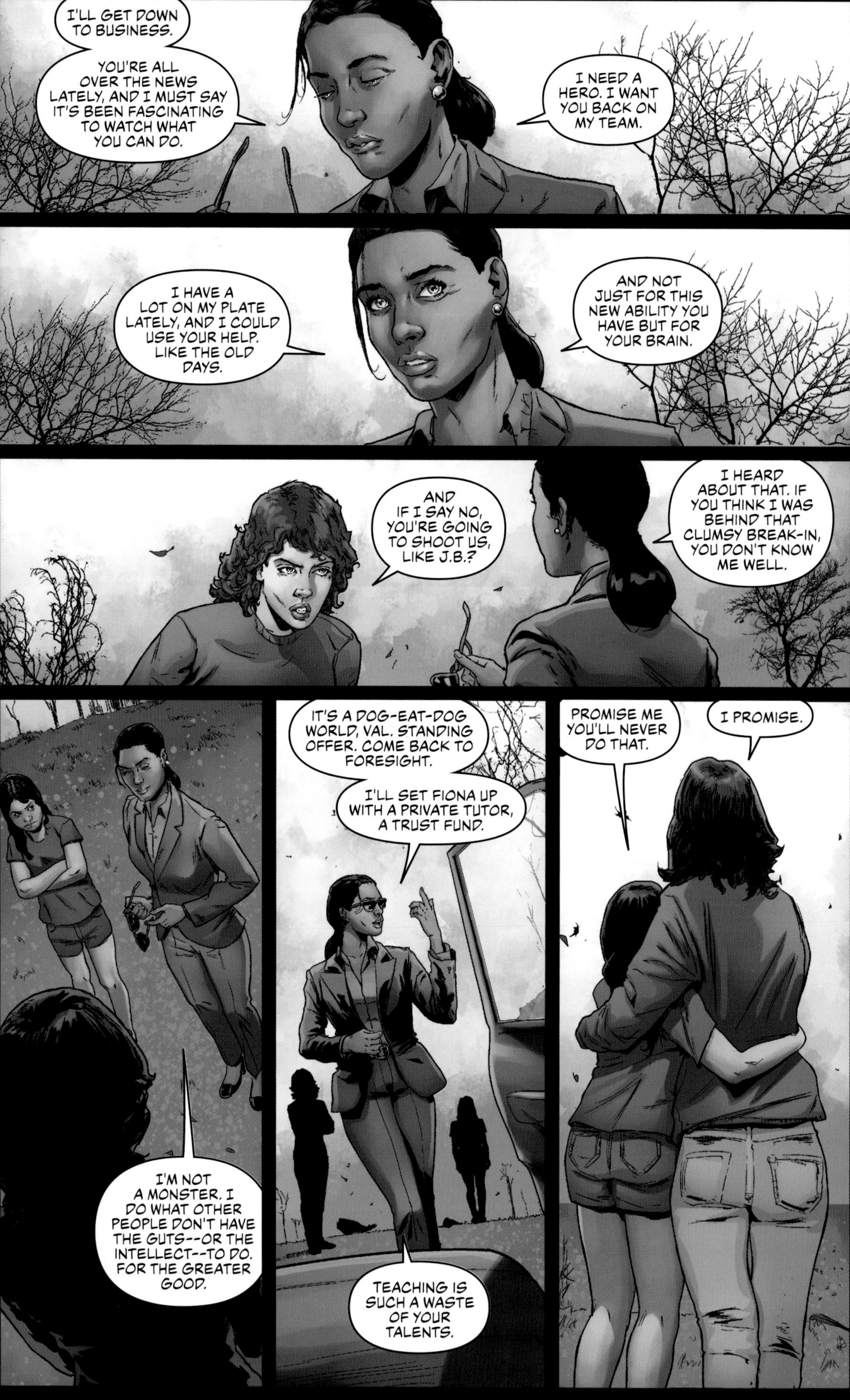

I'LL GET DOWN TO BUSINESS.
YOU'RE ALL OVER THE NEWS LATELY, AND I MUST SAY IT'S BEEN FASCINATING TO WATCH WHAT YOU CAN DO.
I NEED A HERO. I WANT YOU BACK ON MY TEAM.
I HAVE A LOT ON MY PLATE LATELY, AND I COULD USE YOUR HELP. LIKE THE OLD DAYS.
AND NOT JUST FOR THIS NEW ABILITY YOU HAVE BUT FOR YOUR BRAIN.
AND IF I SAY NO, YOU'RE GOING TO SHOOT US, LIKE J.B.?
I HEARD ABOUT THAT. IF YOU THINK I WAS BEHIND THAT CLUMSY BREAK-IN, YOU DON'T KNOW ME WELL.
I'M NOT A MONSTER. I DO WHAT OTHER PEOPLE DON'T HAVE THE GUTS--OR THE INTELLECT--TO DO. FOR THE GREATER GOOD.
IT'S A DOG-EAT-DOG WORLD, VAL. STANDING OFFER. COME BACK TO FORESIGHT.
I'LL SET FIONA UP WITH A PRIVATE TUTOR, A TRUST FUND.
TEACHING IS SUCH A WASTE OF YOUR TALENTS.
PROMISE ME YOU'LL NEVER DO THAT.
I PROMISE.

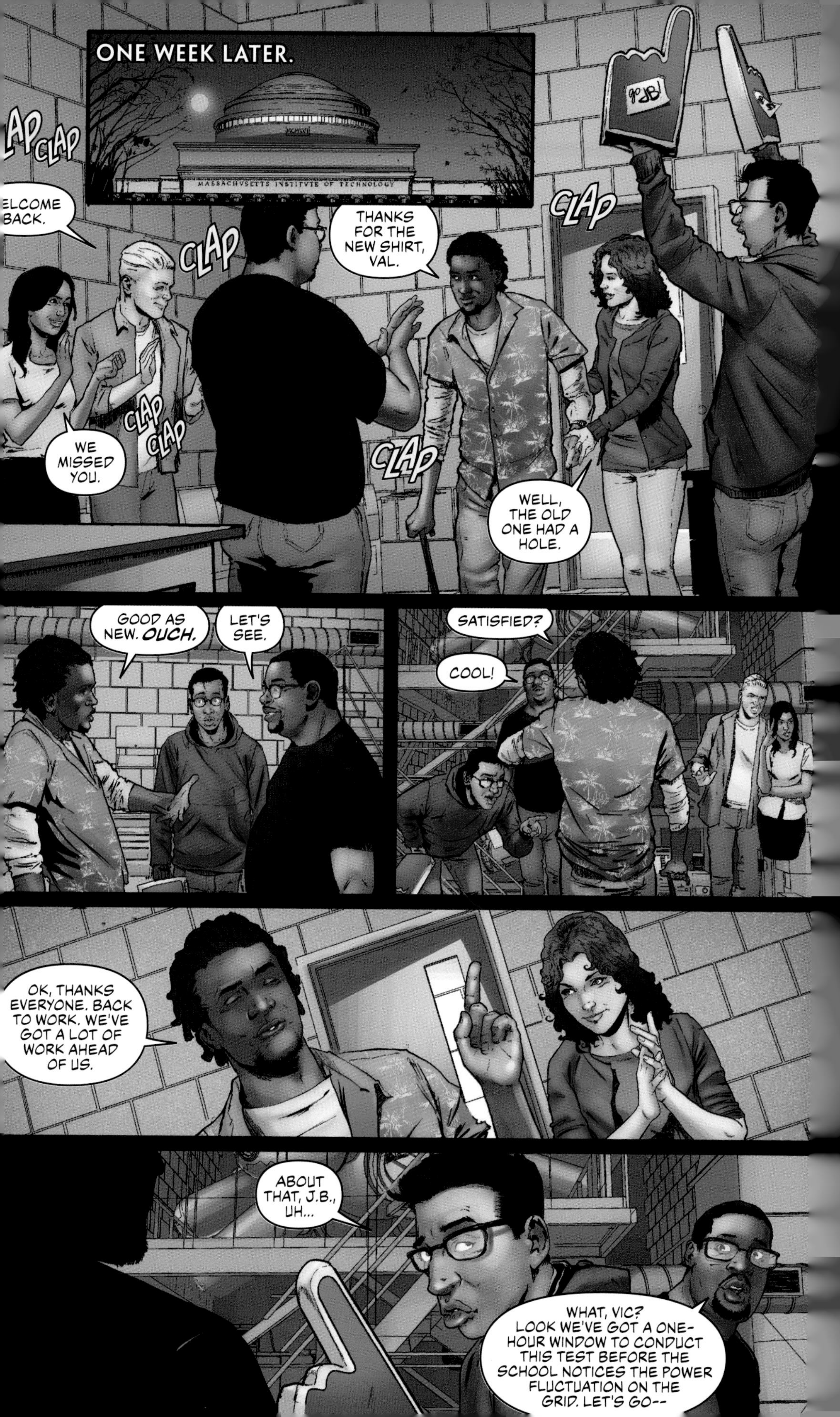
ONE WEEK LATER.
MASSACHVSETTS INSTITVTE OF TECHNOLOGY
CLAP CLAP
ELCOME BACK.
CLAP
THANKS FOR THE NEW SHIRT, VAL.
CLAP
WE MISSED YOU.
CLAP CLAP
CLAP
WELL, THE OLD ONE HAD A HOLE.
GOOD AS NEW. OUCH.
LET'S SEE.
SATISFIED?
COOL!
OK, THANKS EVERYONE. BACK TO WORK. WE'VE GOT A LOT OF WORK AHEAD OF US.
ABOUT THAT, J.B., UH...
WHAT, VIC? LOOK WE'VE GOT A ONE-HOUR WINDOW TO CONDUCT THIS TEST BEFORE THE SCHOOL NOTICES THE POWER FLUCTUATION ON THE GRID. LET'S GO--

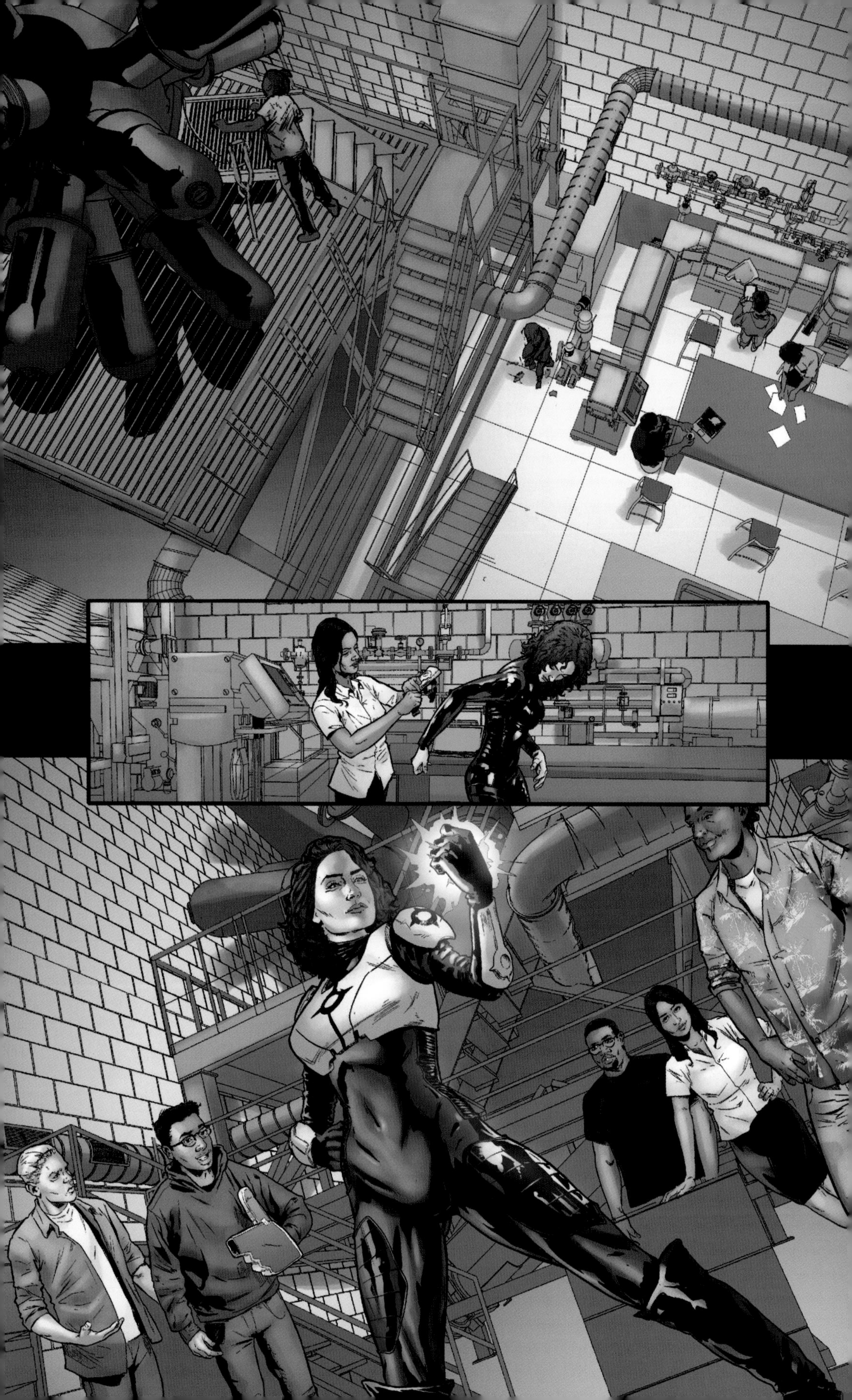

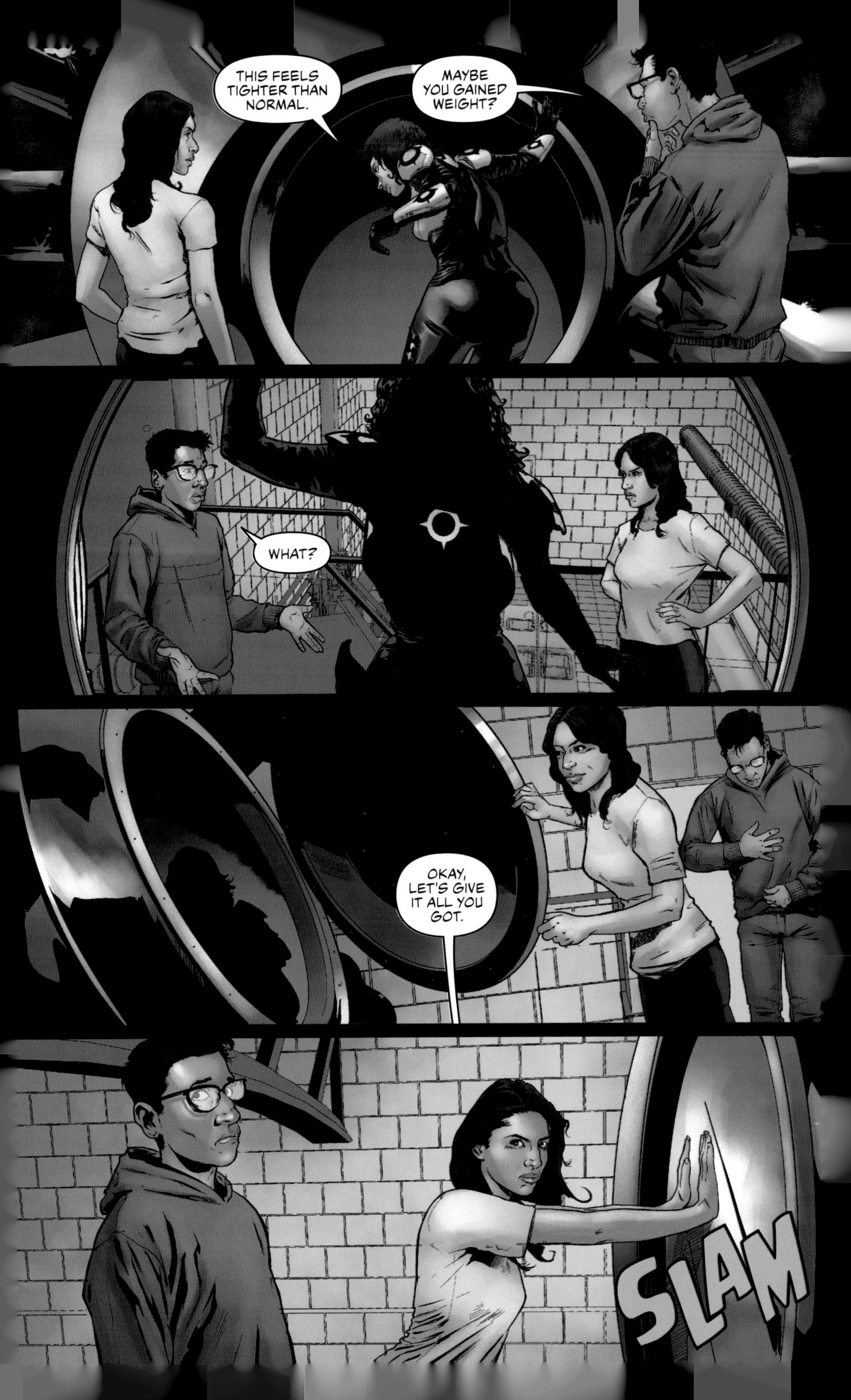
THIS FEELS TIGHTER THAN NORMAL.
MAYBE YOU GAINED WEIGHT?
WHAT?
OKAY, LET'S GIVE IT ALL YOU GOT.
SLAM

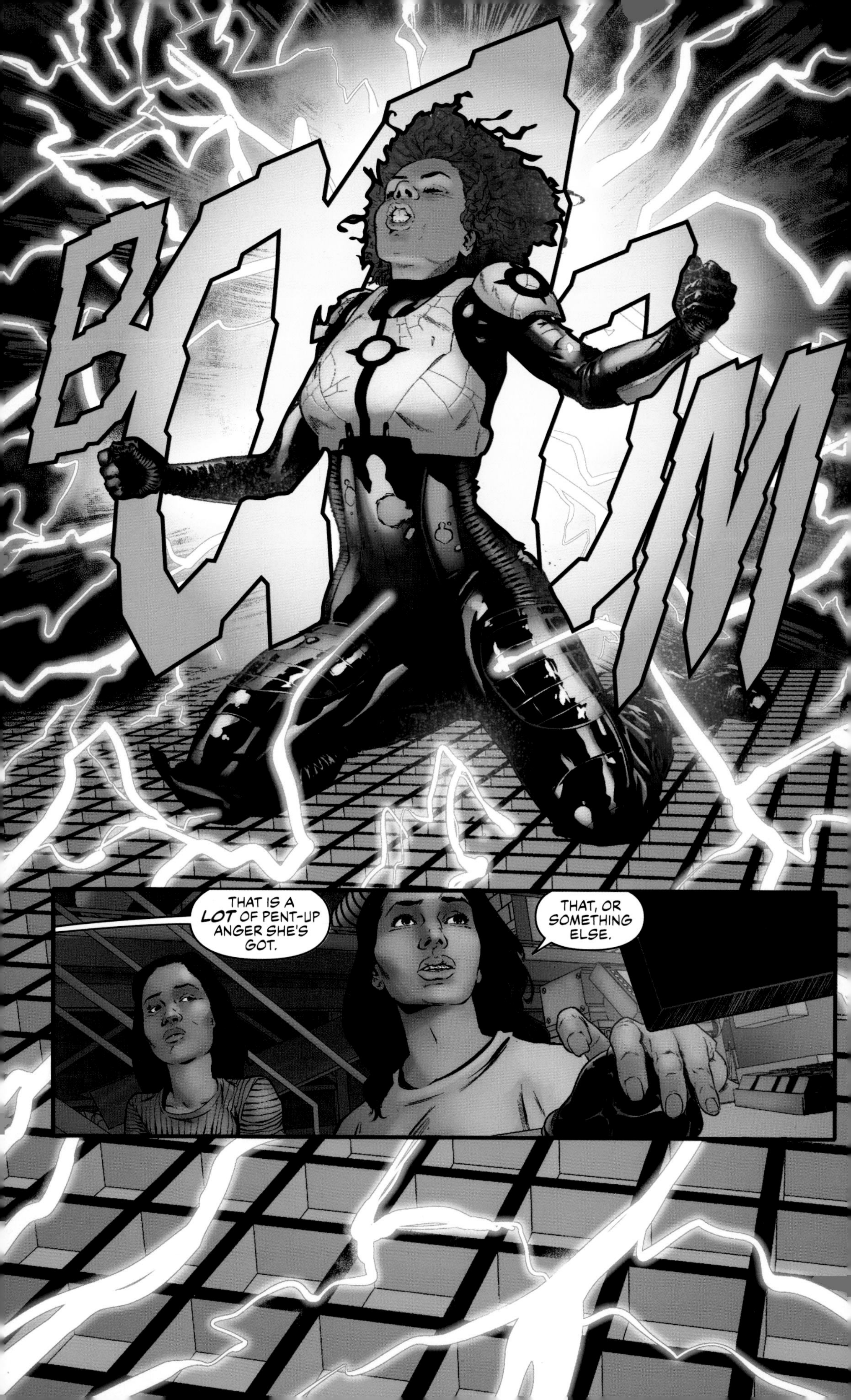
BOOM
THAT IS A LOT OF PENT-UP ANGER SHE'S GOT.
THAT, OR SOMETHING ELSE.

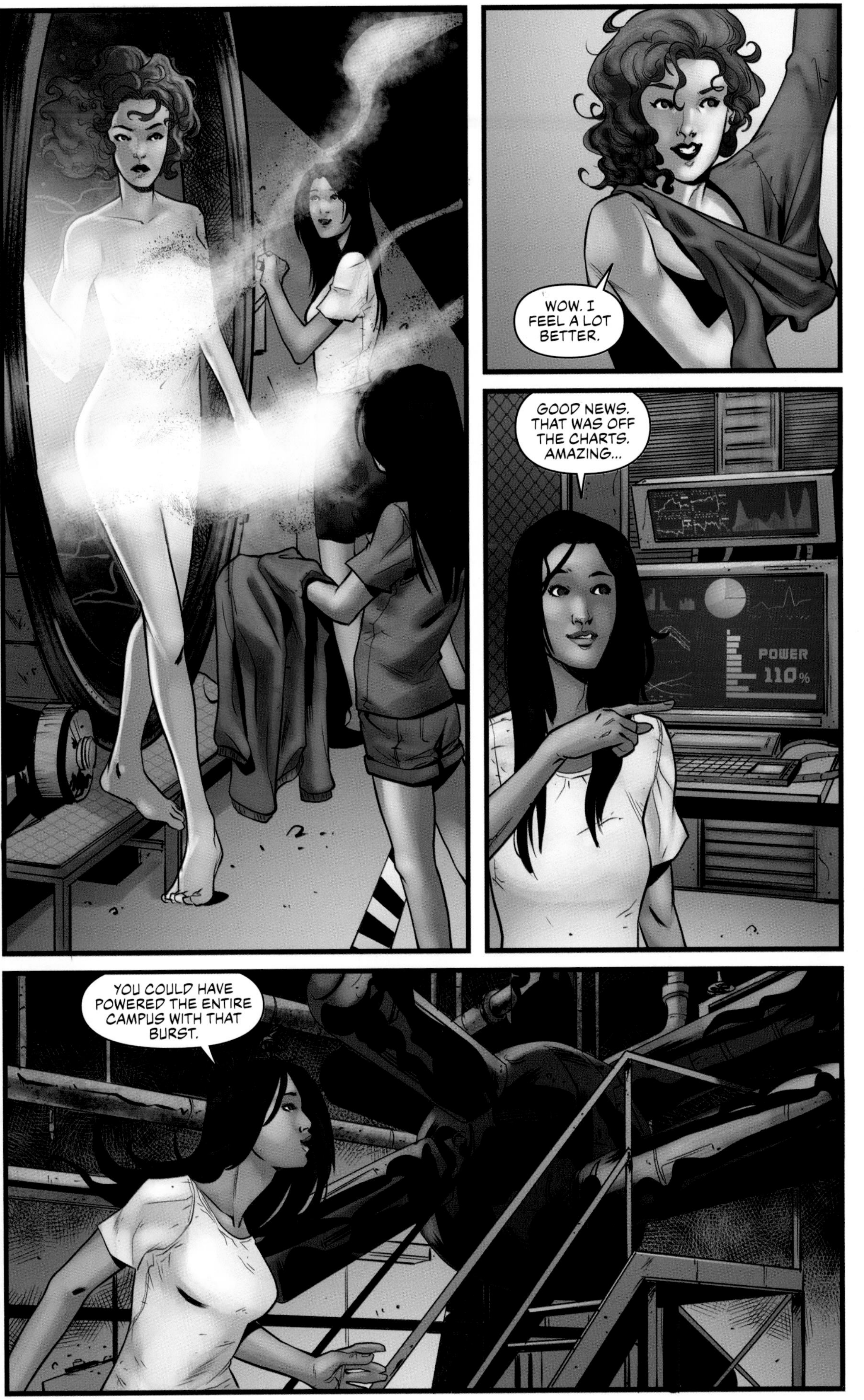
WOW. I FEEL A LOT BETTER.
GOOD NEWS. THAT WAS OFF THE CHARTS. AMAZING...
POWER 110%
YOU COULD HAVE POWERED THE ENTIRE CAMPUS WITH THAT BURST.

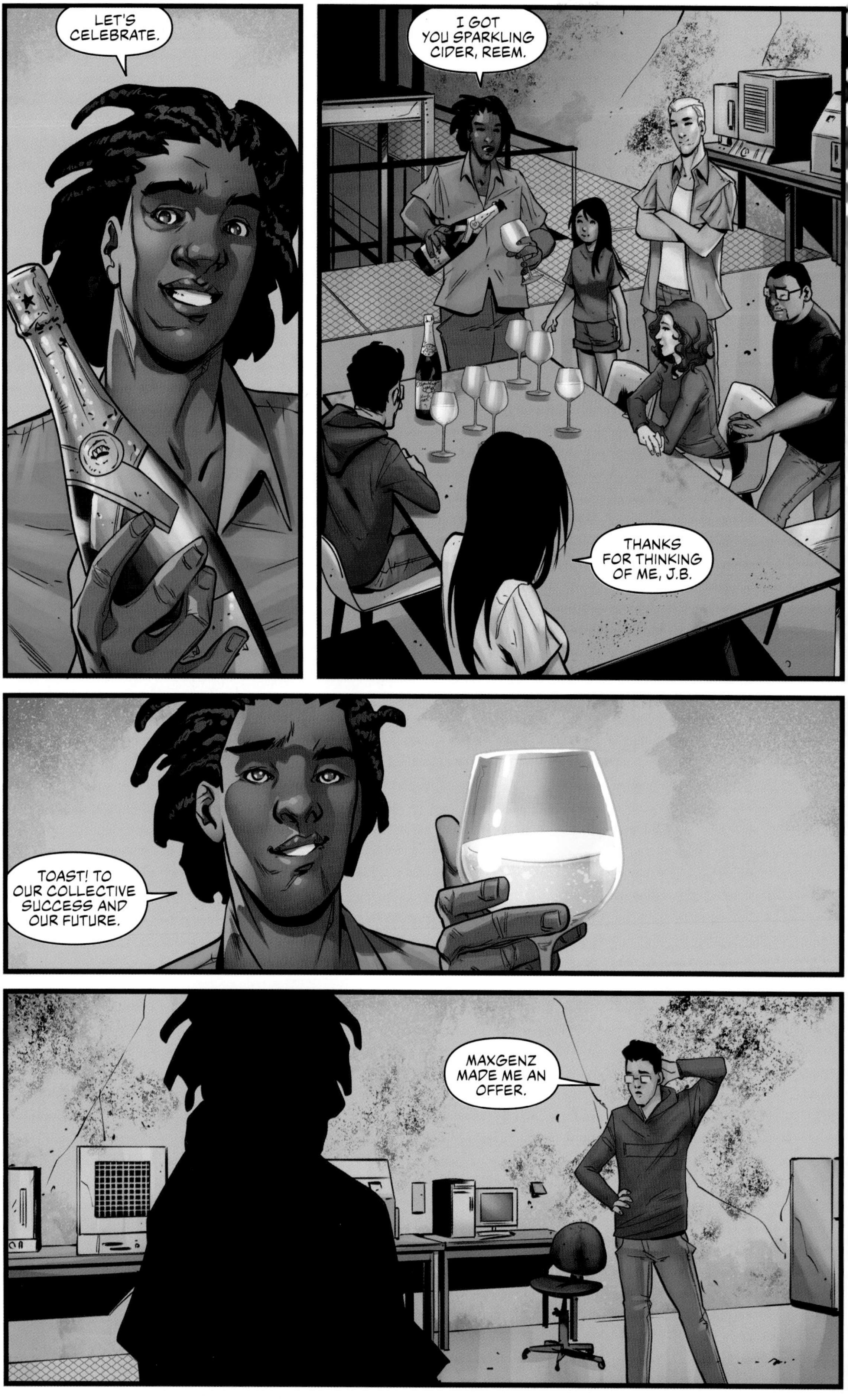
LET'S CELEBRATE.
I GOT YOU SPARKLING CIDER, REEM.
THANKS FOR THINKING OF ME, J.B.
TOAST! TO OUR COLLECTIVE SUCCESS AND OUR FUTURE.
MAXGENZ MADE ME AN OFFER.

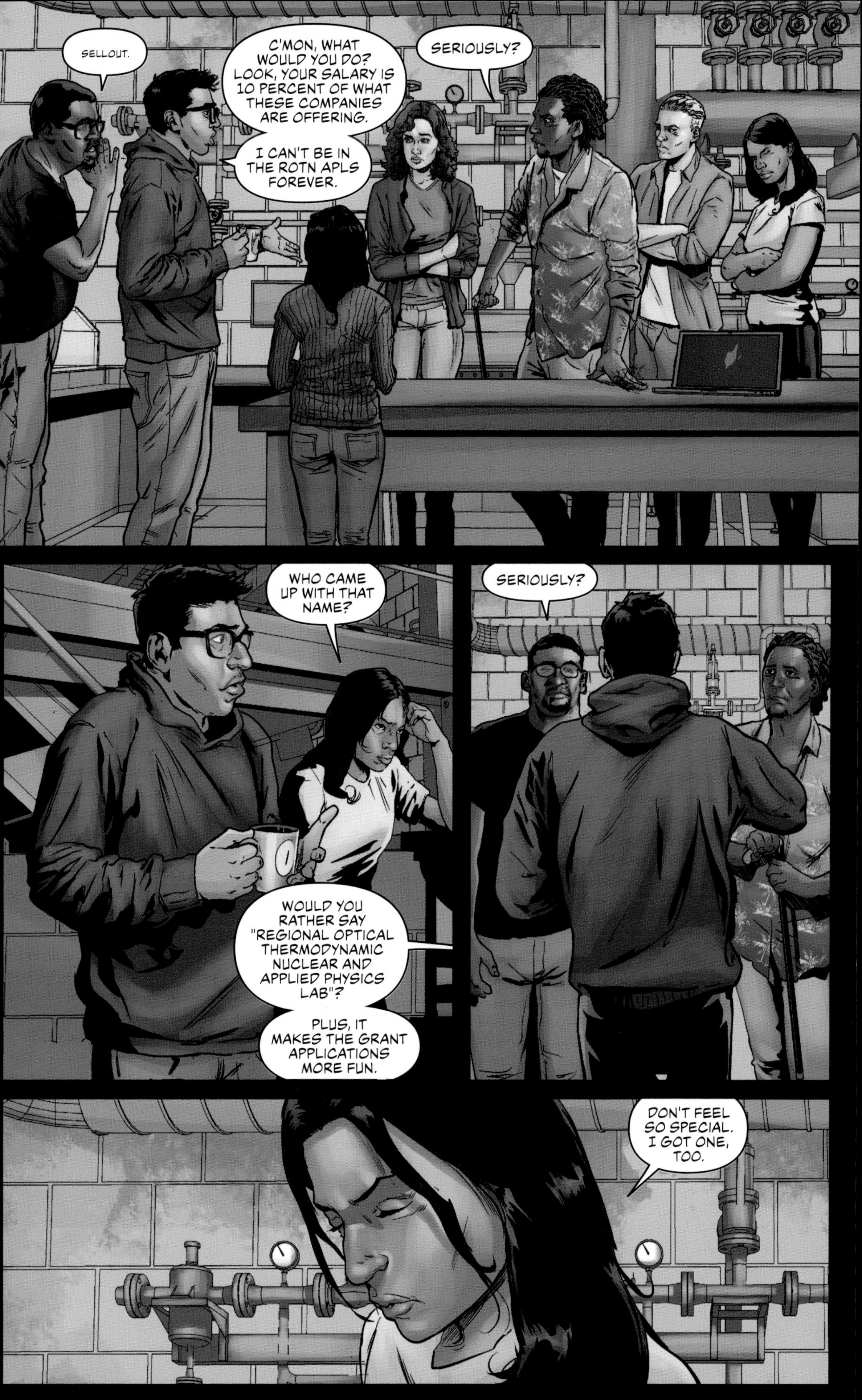
SELLOUT.
C'MON, WHAT WOULD YOU DO? LOOK, YOUR SALARY IS 10 PERCENT OF WHAT THESE COMPANIES ARE OFFERING.
I CAN'T BE IN THE ROTN APLS FOREVER.
SERIOUSLY?
WHO CAME UP WITH THAT NAME?
WOULD YOU RATHER SAY "REGIONAL OPTICAL THERMODYNAMIC NUCLEAR AND APPLIED PHYSICS LAB"?
PLUS, IT MAKES THE GRANT APPLICATIONS MORE FUN.
SERIOUSLY?
DON'T FEEL SO SPECIAL. I GOT ONE, TOO.

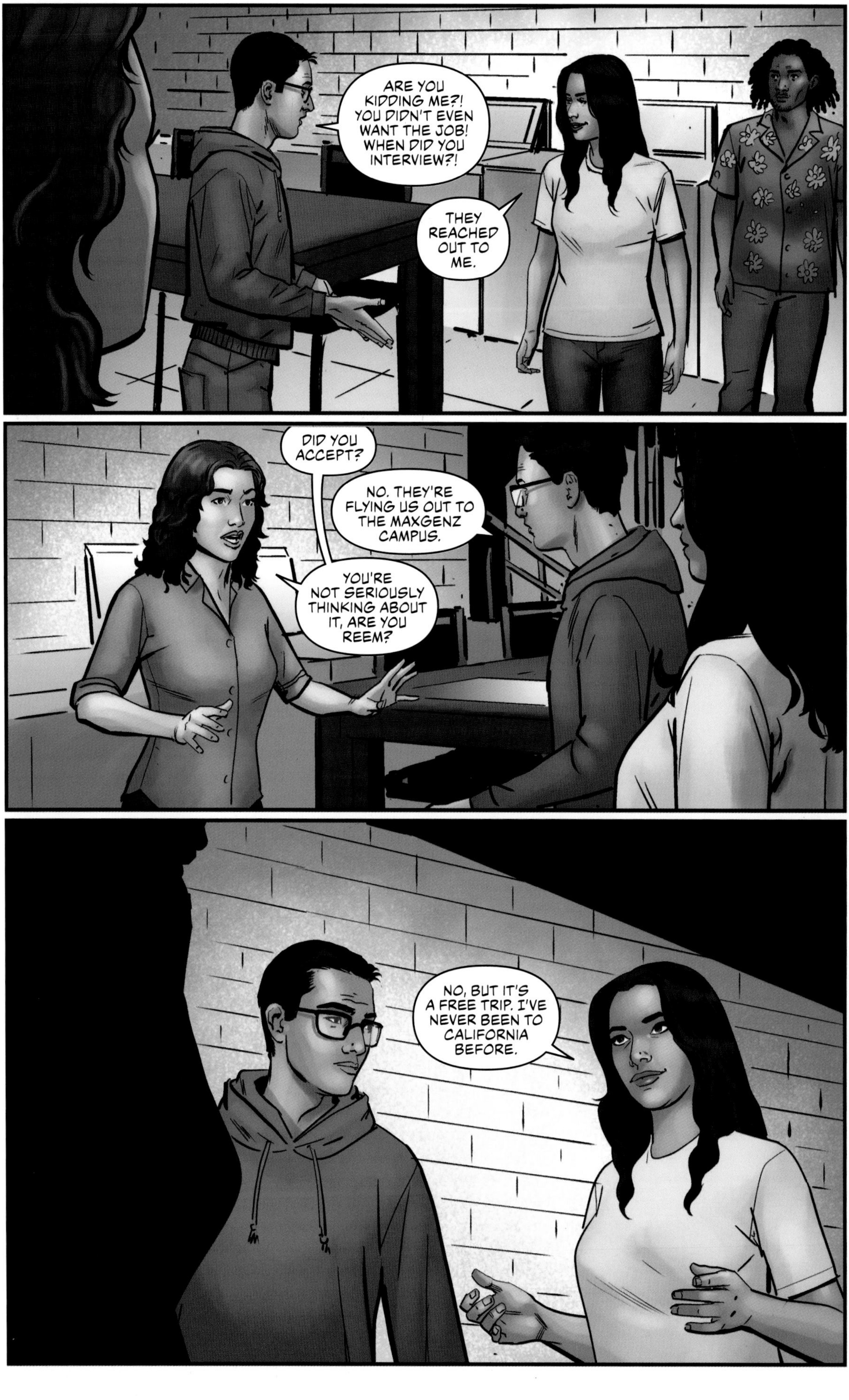

ARE YOU KIDDING ME?! YOU DIDN'T EVEN WANT THE JOB! WHEN DID YOU INTERVIEW?!
THEY REACHED OUT TO ME.
DID YOU ACCEPT?
NO. THEY'RE FLYING US OUT TO THE MAXGENZ CAMPUS.
YOU'RE NOT SERIOUSLY THINKING ABOUT IT, ARE YOU REEM?
NO, BUT IT'S A FREE TRIP. I'VE NEVER BEEN TO CALIFORNIA BEFORE.

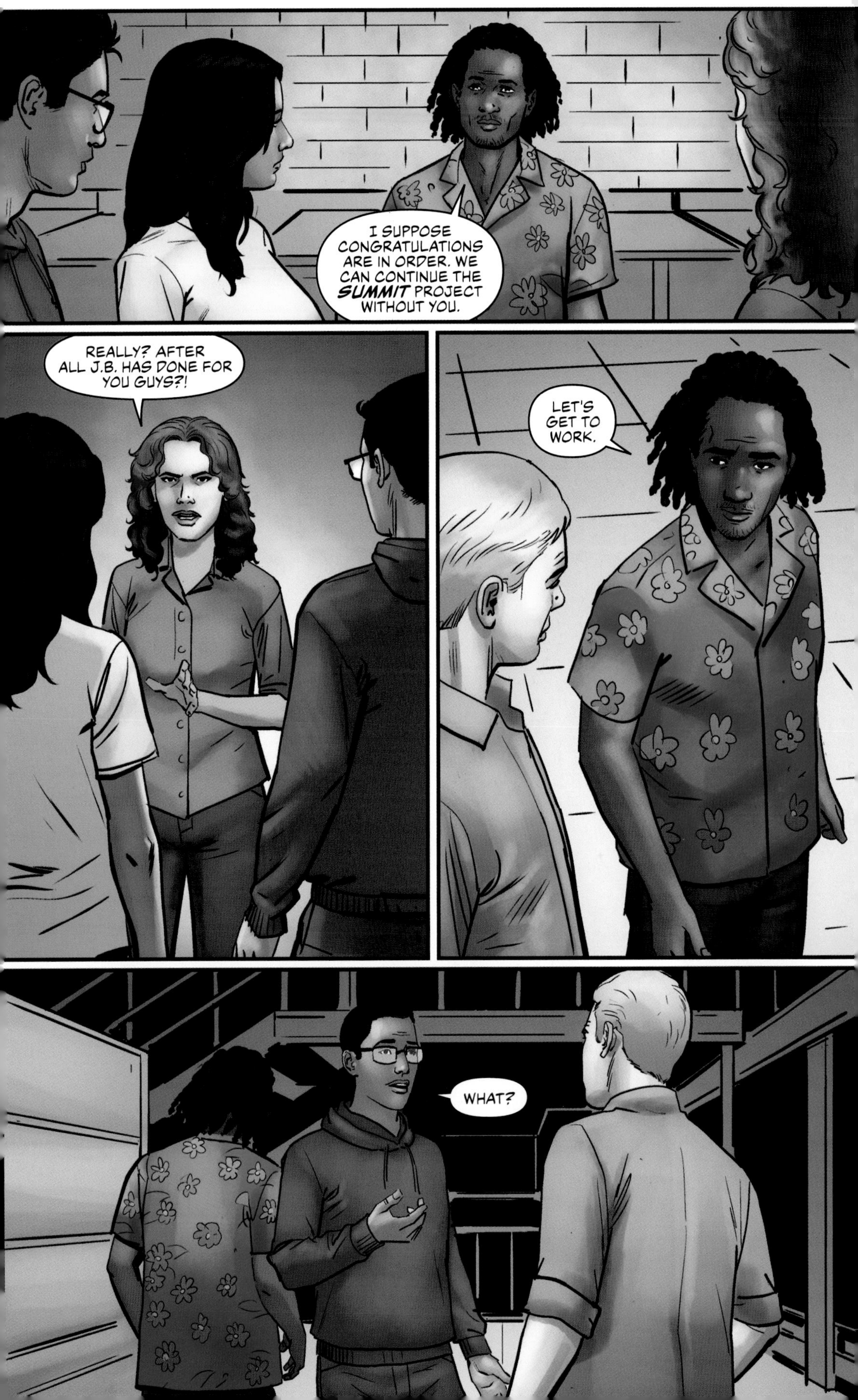
I SUPPOSE CONGRATULATIONS ARE IN ORDER. WE CAN CONTINUE THE *SUMMIT* PROJECT WITHOUT YOU.
REALLY? AFTER ALL J.B. HAS DONE FOR YOU GUYS?!
LET'S GET TO WORK.
WHAT?

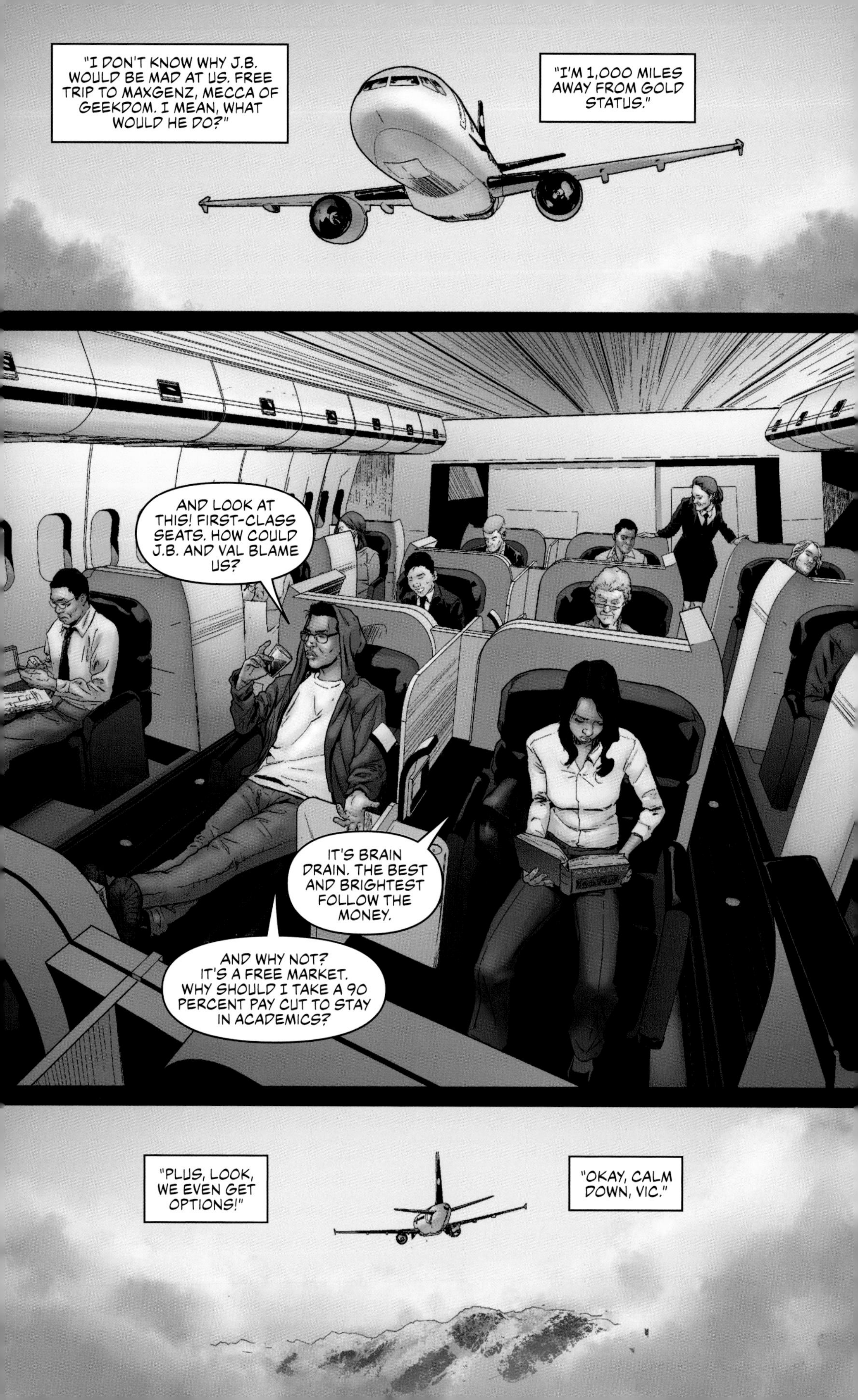
"I DON'T KNOW WHY J.B. WOULD BE MAD AT US. FREE TRIP TO MAXGENZ, MECCA OF GEEKDOM. I MEAN, WHAT WOULD HE DO?"
"I'M 1,000 MILES AWAY FROM GOLD STATUS."
AND LOOK AT THIS! FIRST-CLASS SEATS. HOW COULD J.B. AND VAL BLAME US?
IT'S BRAIN DRAIN. THE BEST AND BRIGHTEST FOLLOW THE MONEY.
AND WHY NOT? IT'S A FREE MARKET. WHY SHOULD I TAKE A 90 PERCENT PAY CUT TO STAY IN ACADEMICS?
"PLUS, LOOK, WE EVEN GET OPTIONS!"
"OKAY, CALM DOWN, VIC."

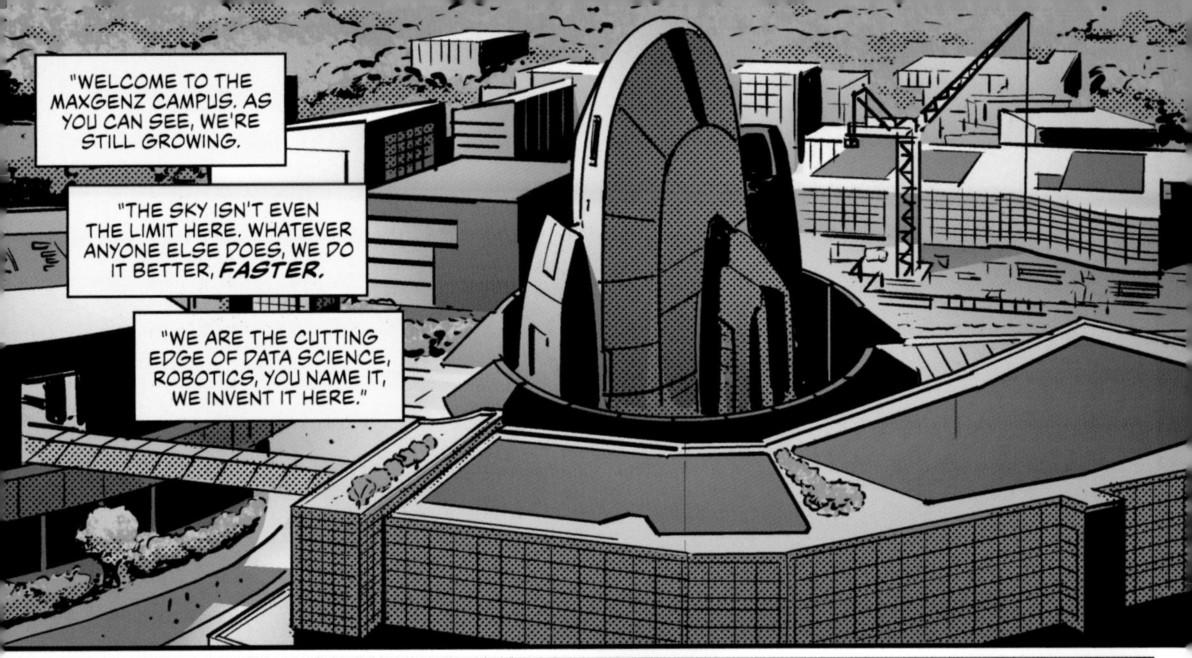
"WELCOME TO THE MAXGENZ CAMPUS. AS YOU CAN SEE, WE'RE STILL GROWING.
"THE SKY ISN'T EVEN THE LIMIT HERE. WHATEVER ANYONE ELSE DOES, WE DO IT BETTER, *FASTER.*
"WE ARE THE CUTTING EDGE OF DATA SCIENCE, ROBOTICS, YOU NAME IT, WE INVENT IT HERE."

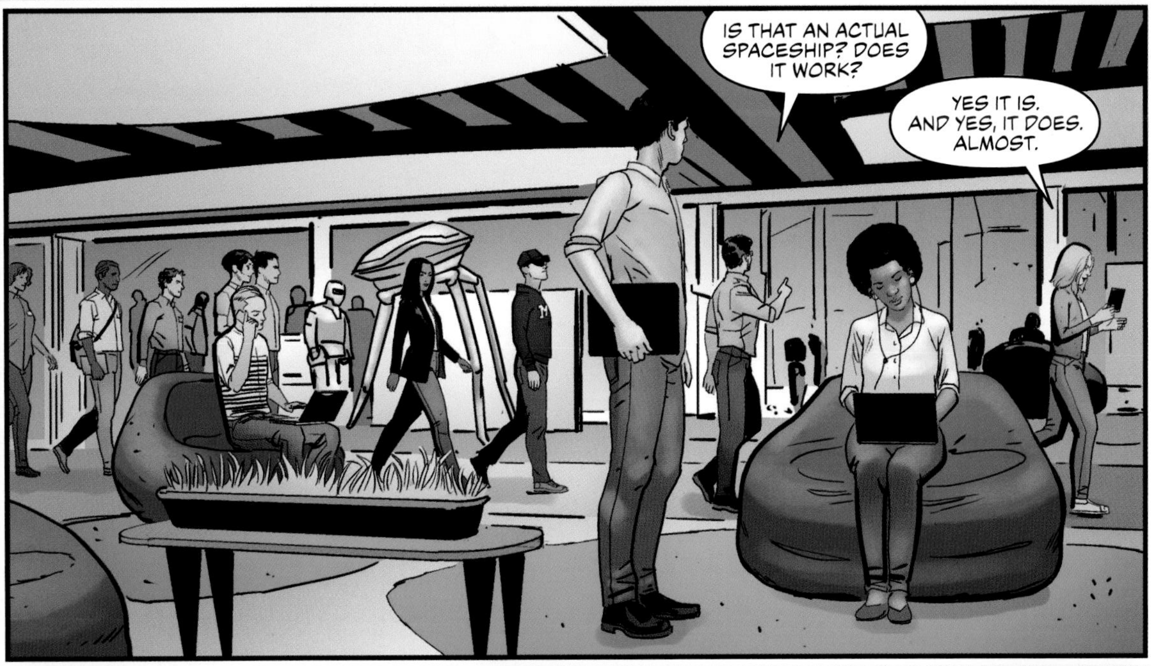
IS THAT AN ACTUAL SPACESHIP? DOES IT WORK?
YES IT IS. AND YES, IT DOES. ALMOST.

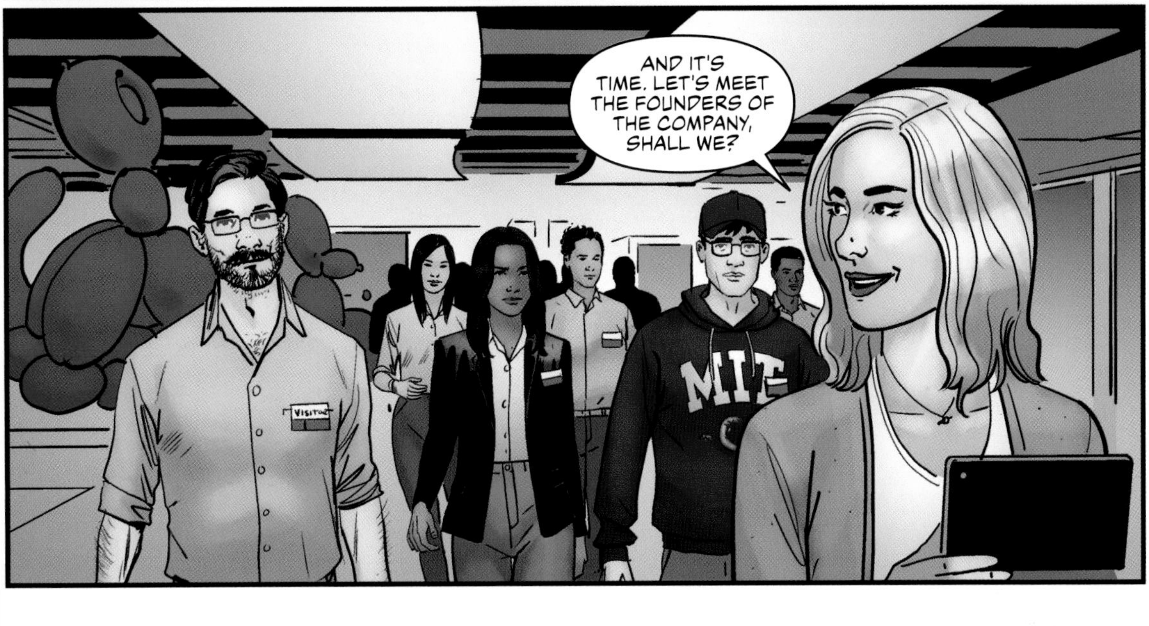
AND IT'S TIME. LET'S MEET THE FOUNDERS OF THE COMPANY, SHALL WE?
MIT

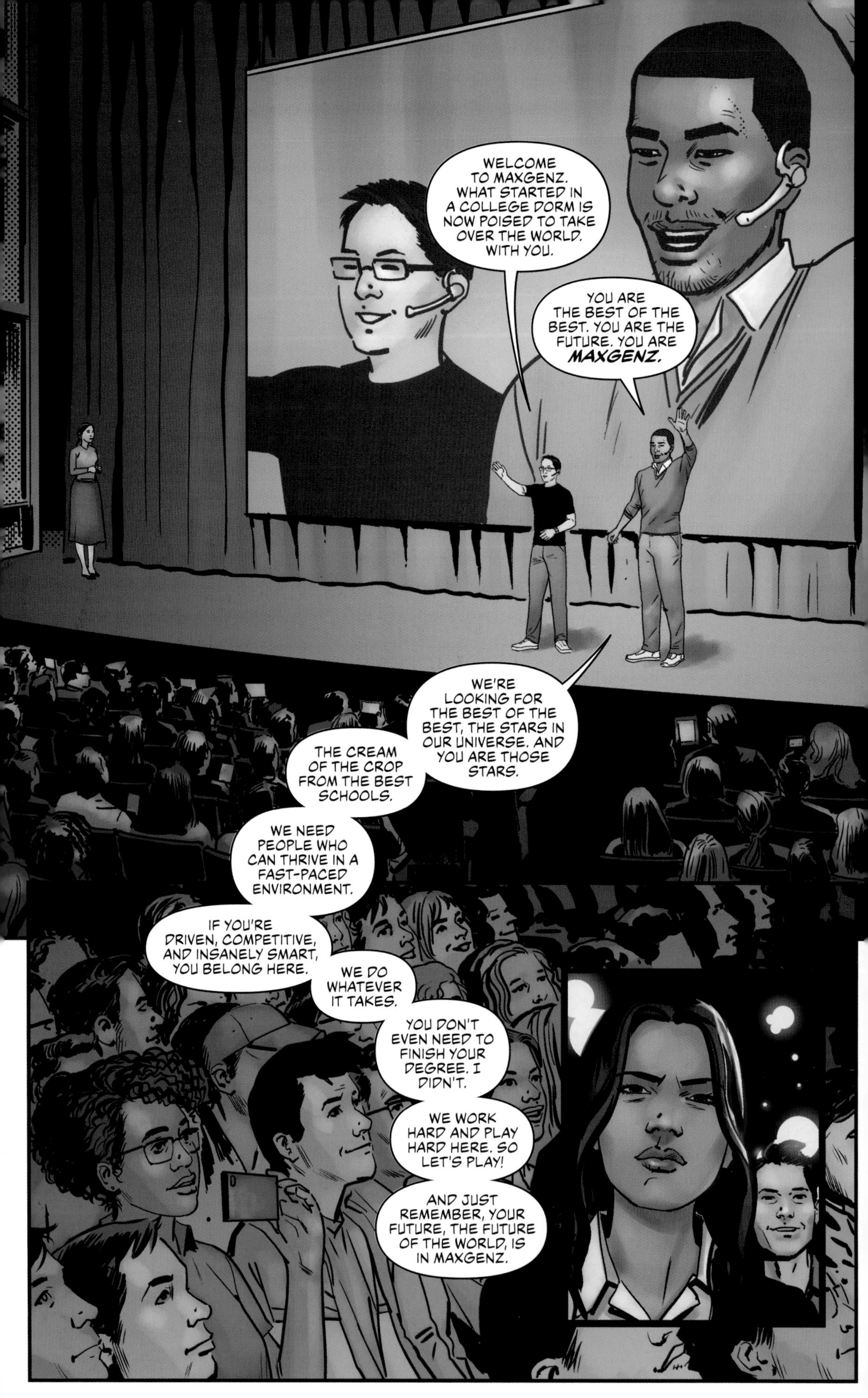
WELCOME TO MAXGENZ. WHAT STARTED IN A COLLEGE DORM IS NOW POISED TO TAKE OVER THE WORLD. WITH YOU.
YOU ARE THE BEST OF THE BEST. YOU ARE THE FUTURE. YOU ARE ***MAXGENZ.***
WE'RE LOOKING FOR THE BEST OF THE BEST, THE STARS IN OUR UNIVERSE. AND YOU ARE THOSE STARS.
THE CREAM OF THE CROP FROM THE BEST SCHOOLS.
WE NEED PEOPLE WHO CAN THRIVE IN A FAST-PACED ENVIRONMENT.
IF YOU'RE DRIVEN, COMPETITIVE, AND INSANELY SMART, YOU BELONG HERE.
WE DO WHATEVER IT TAKES.
YOU DON'T EVEN NEED TO FINISH YOUR DEGREE. I DIDN'T.
WE WORK HARD AND PLAY HARD HERE. SO LET'S PLAY!
AND JUST REMEMBER, YOUR FUTURE, THE FUTURE OF THE WORLD, IS IN MAXGENZ.

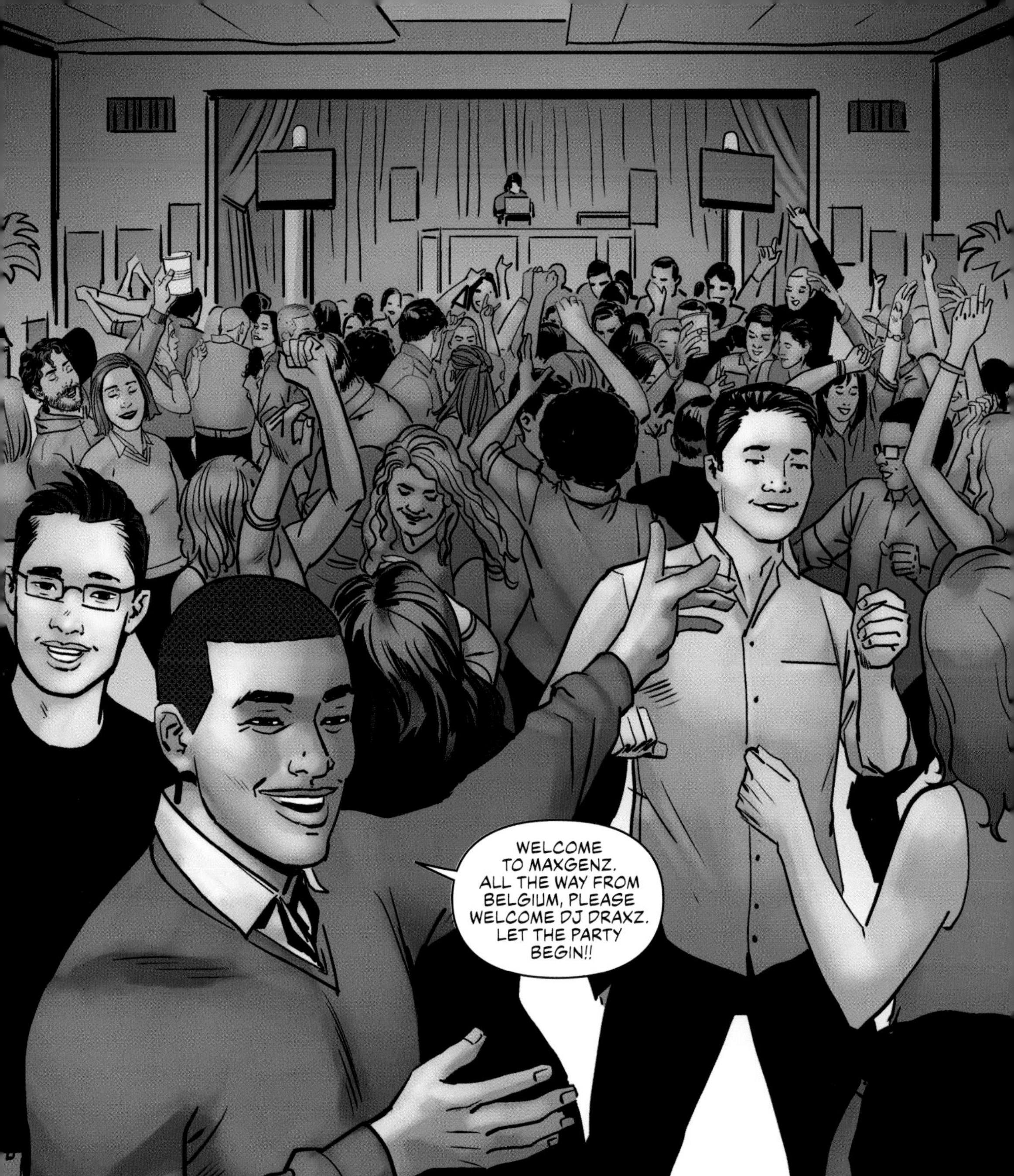
WELCOME TO MAXGENZ. ALL THE WAY FROM BELGIUM, PLEASE WELCOME DJ DRAXZ. LET THE PARTY BEGIN!!

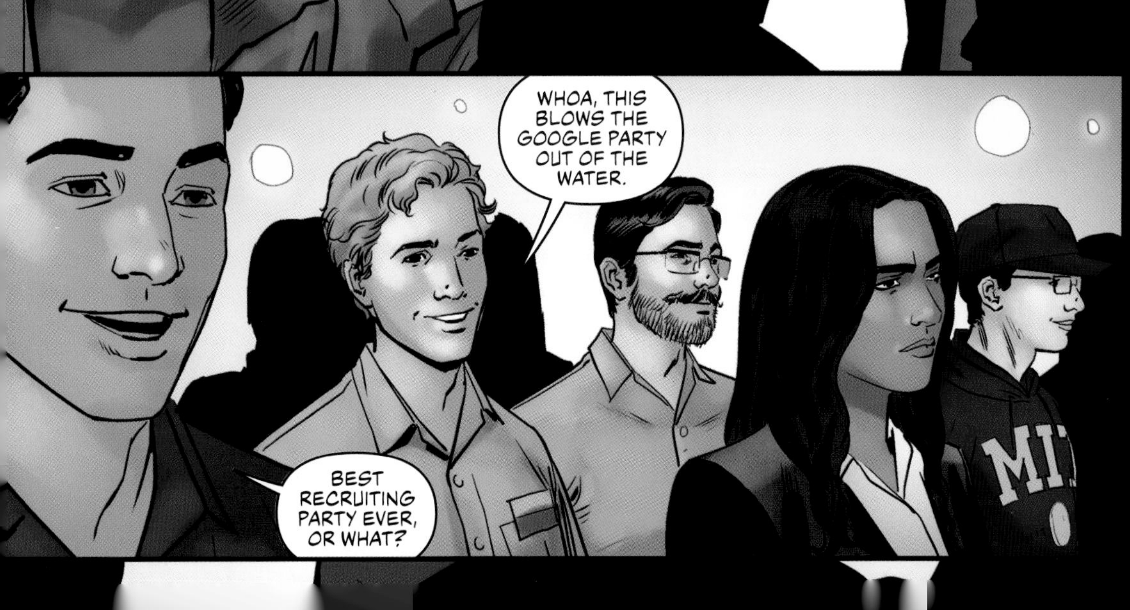
BEST RECRUITING PARTY EVER, OR WHAT?
WHOA, THIS BLOWS THE GOOGLE PARTY OUT OF THE WATER.
MIT

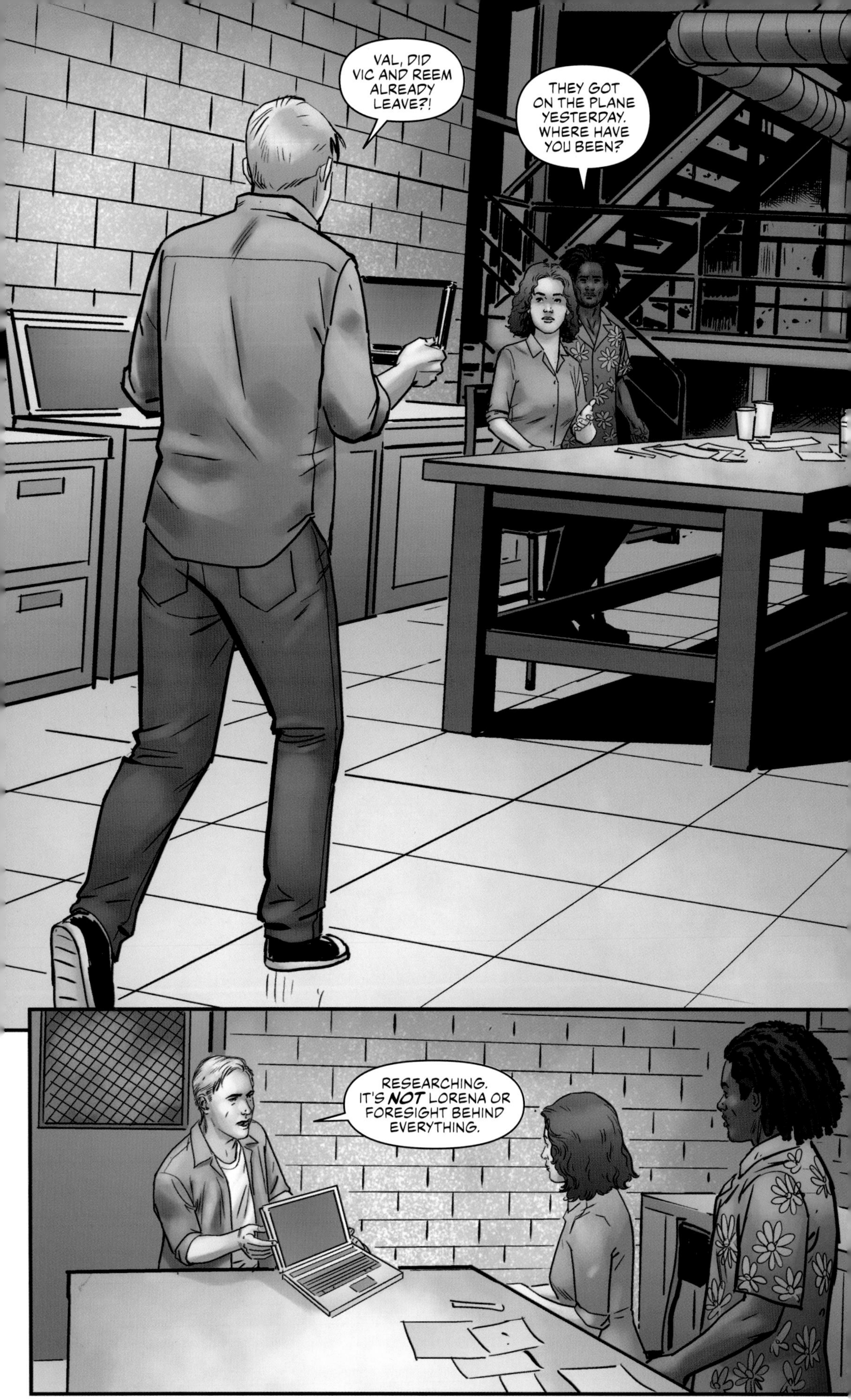
VAL, DID VIC AND REEM ALREADY LEAVE?!
THEY GOT ON THE PLANE YESTERDAY. WHERE HAVE YOU BEEN?
RESEARCHING. IT'S NOT LORENA OR FORESIGHT BEHIND EVERYTHING.

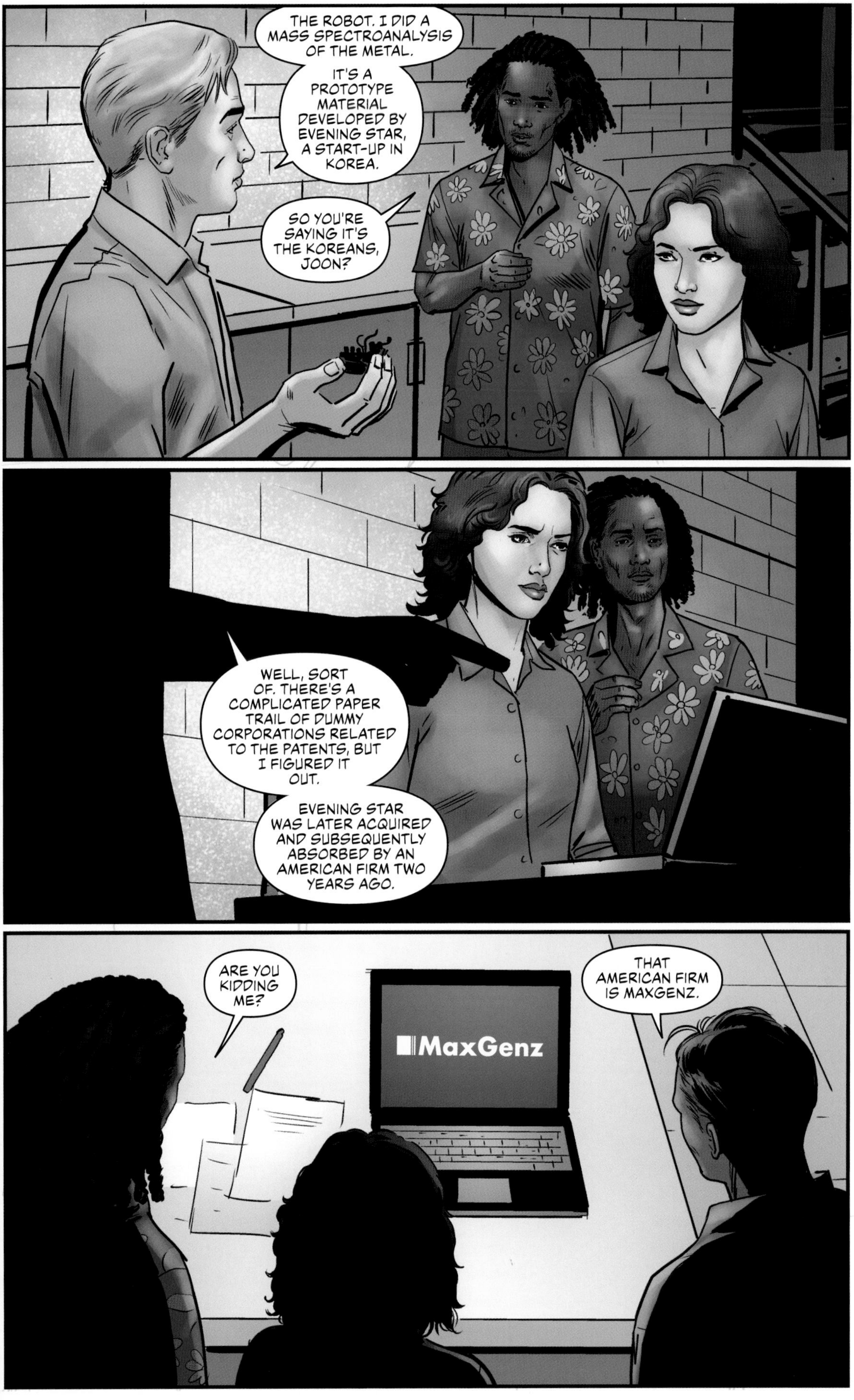
THE ROBOT. I DID A MASS SPECTROANALYSIS OF THE METAL.
IT'S A PROTOTYPE MATERIAL DEVELOPED BY EVENING STAR, A START-UP IN KOREA.
SO YOU'RE SAYING IT'S THE KOREANS, JOON?
WELL, SORT OF. THERE'S A COMPLICATED PAPER TRAIL OF DUMMY CORPORATIONS RELATED TO THE PATENTS, BUT I FIGURED IT OUT.
EVENING STAR WAS LATER ACQUIRED AND SUBSEQUENTLY ABSORBED BY AN AMERICAN FIRM TWO YEARS AGO.
ARE YOU KIDDING ME?
MaxGenz
THAT AMERICAN FIRM IS MAXGENZ.

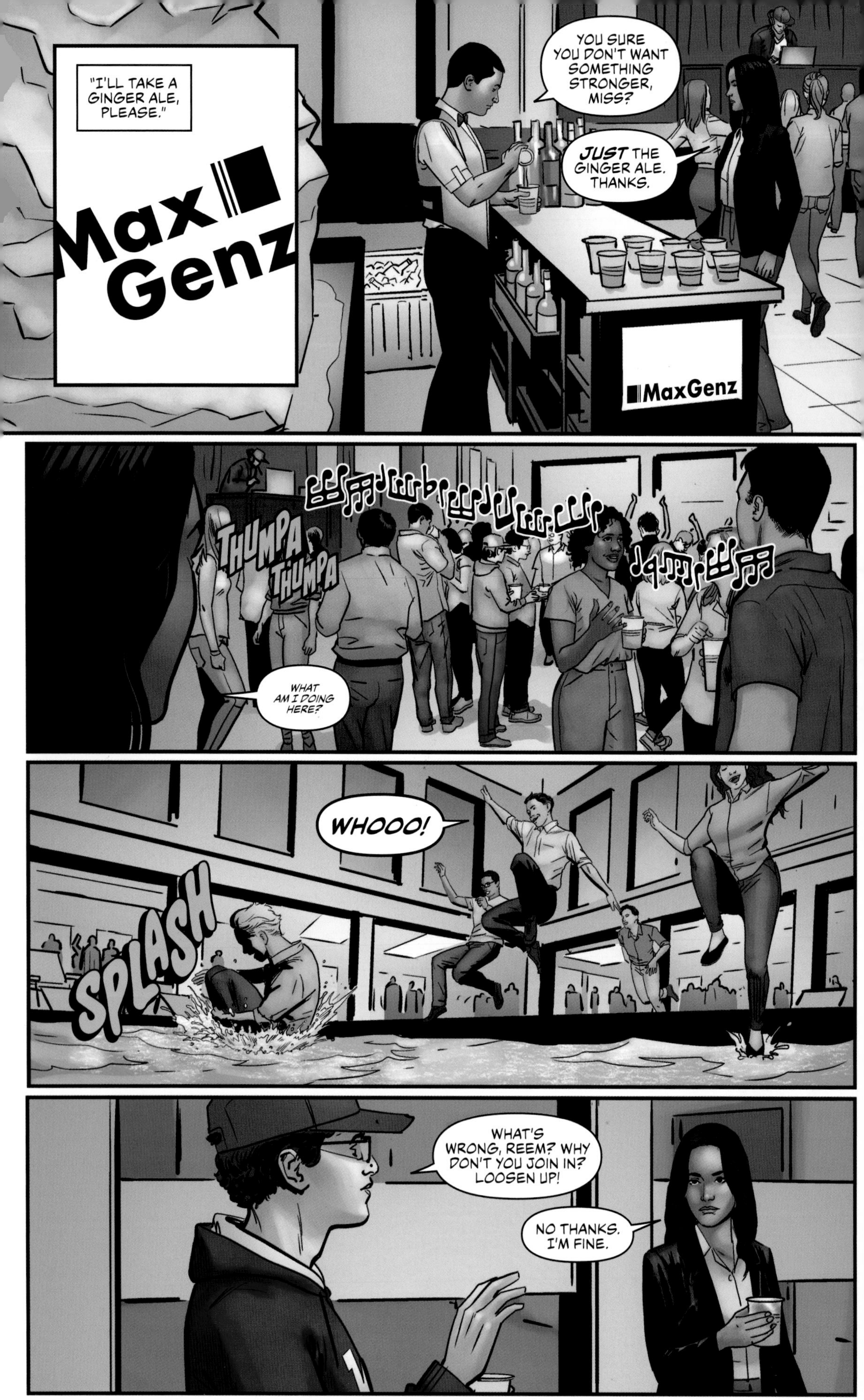
"I'LL TAKE A GINGER ALE, PLEASE."
Max Genz
YOU SURE YOU DON'T WANT SOMETHING STRONGER, MISS?
JUST THE GINGER ALE. THANKS.
MaxGenz
THUMPA THUMPA
WHAT AM I DOING HERE?
WHOOO!
SPLASH
WHAT'S WRONG, REEM? WHY DON'T YOU JOIN IN? LOOSEN UP!
NO THANKS. I'M FINE.

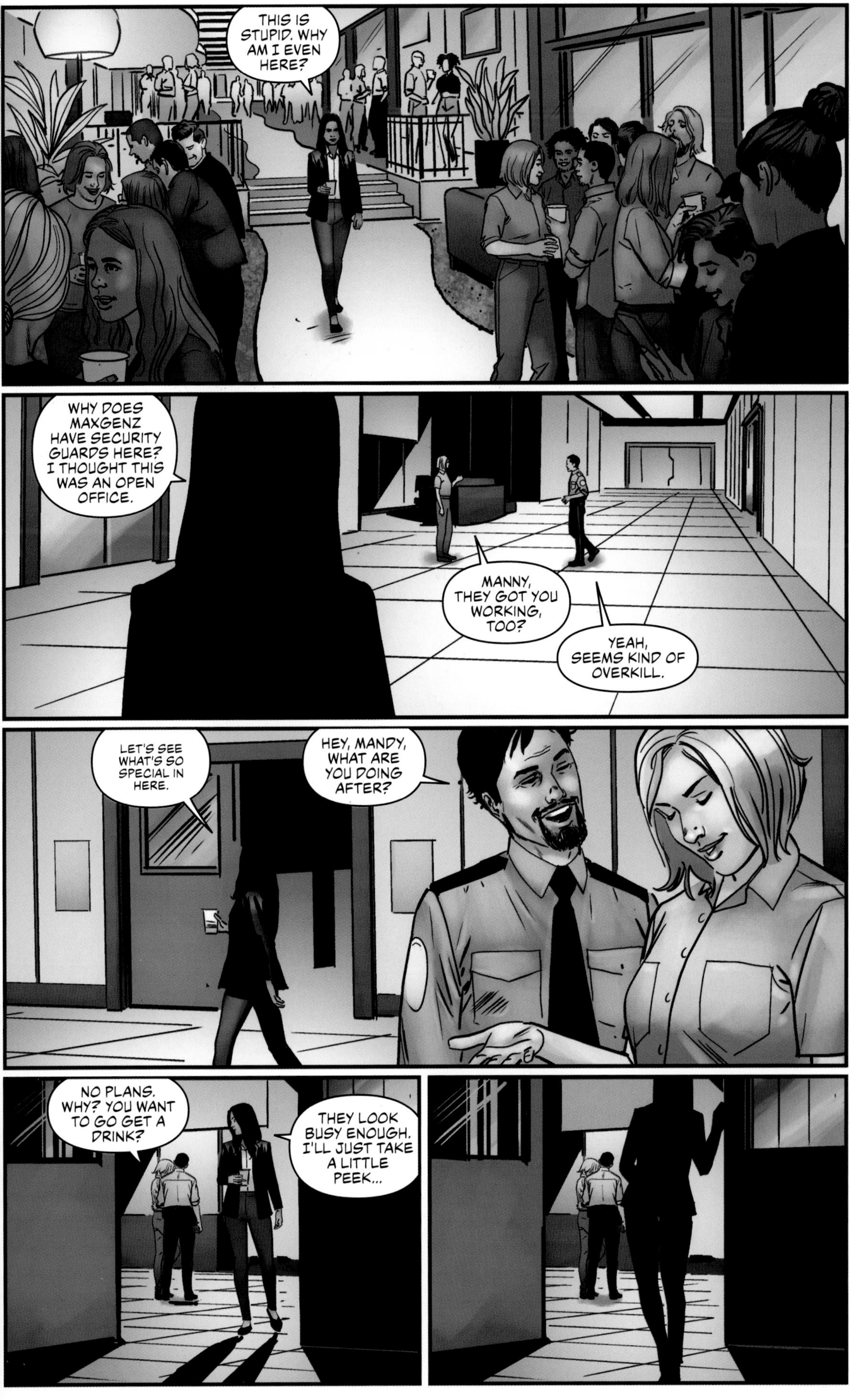
THIS IS STUPID. WHY AM I EVEN HERE?
WHY DOES MAXGENZ HAVE SECURITY GUARDS HERE? I THOUGHT THIS WAS AN OPEN OFFICE.
MANNY, THEY GOT YOU WORKING, TOO?
YEAH, SEEMS KIND OF OVERKILL.
LET'S SEE WHAT'S SO SPECIAL IN HERE.
HEY, MANDY, WHAT ARE YOU DOING AFTER?
NO PLANS. WHY? YOU WANT TO GO GET A DRINK?
THEY LOOK BUSY ENOUGH. I'LL JUST TAKE A LITTLE PEEK...

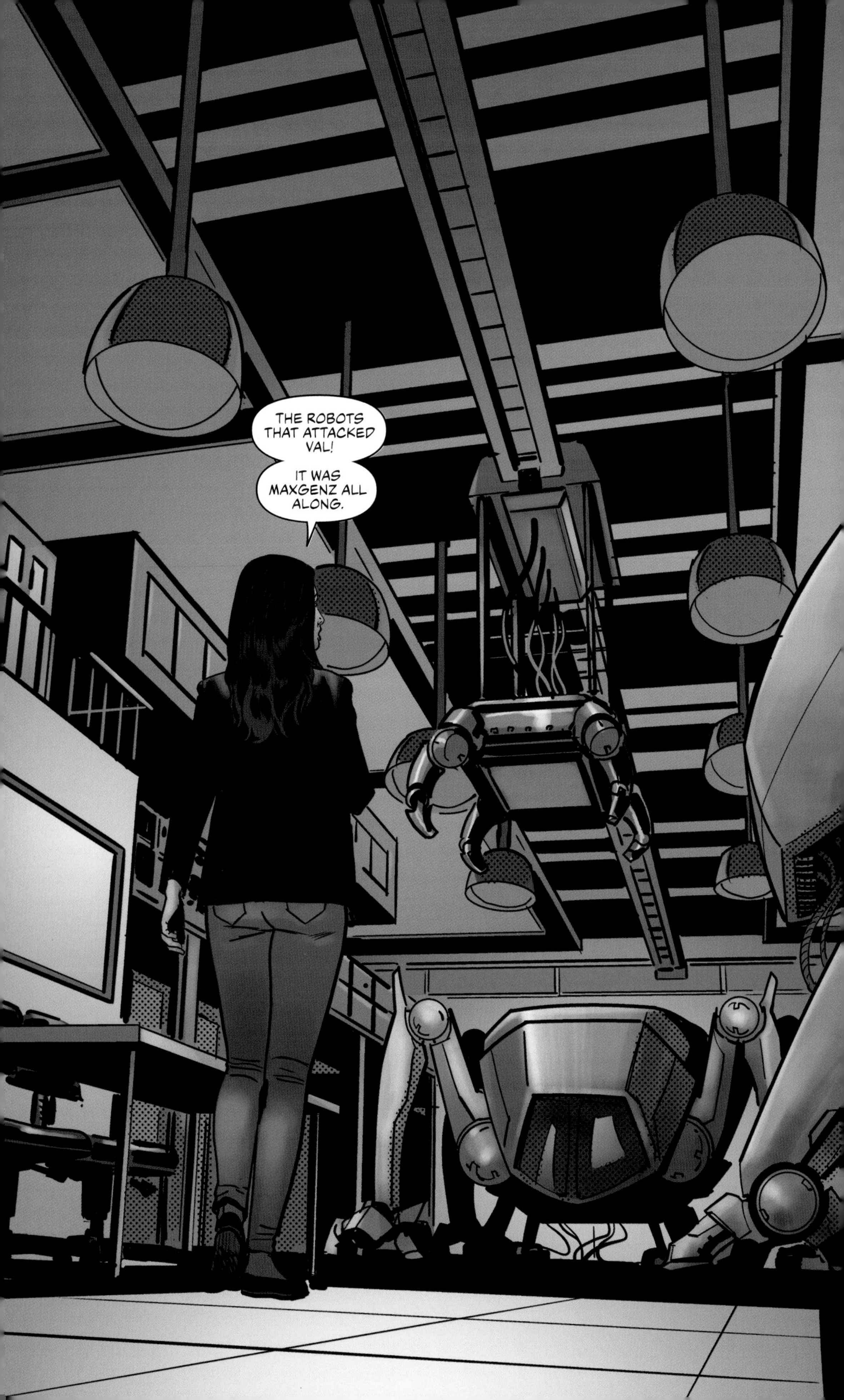
THE ROBOTS THAT ATTACKED VAL!
IT WAS MAXGENZ ALL ALONG.

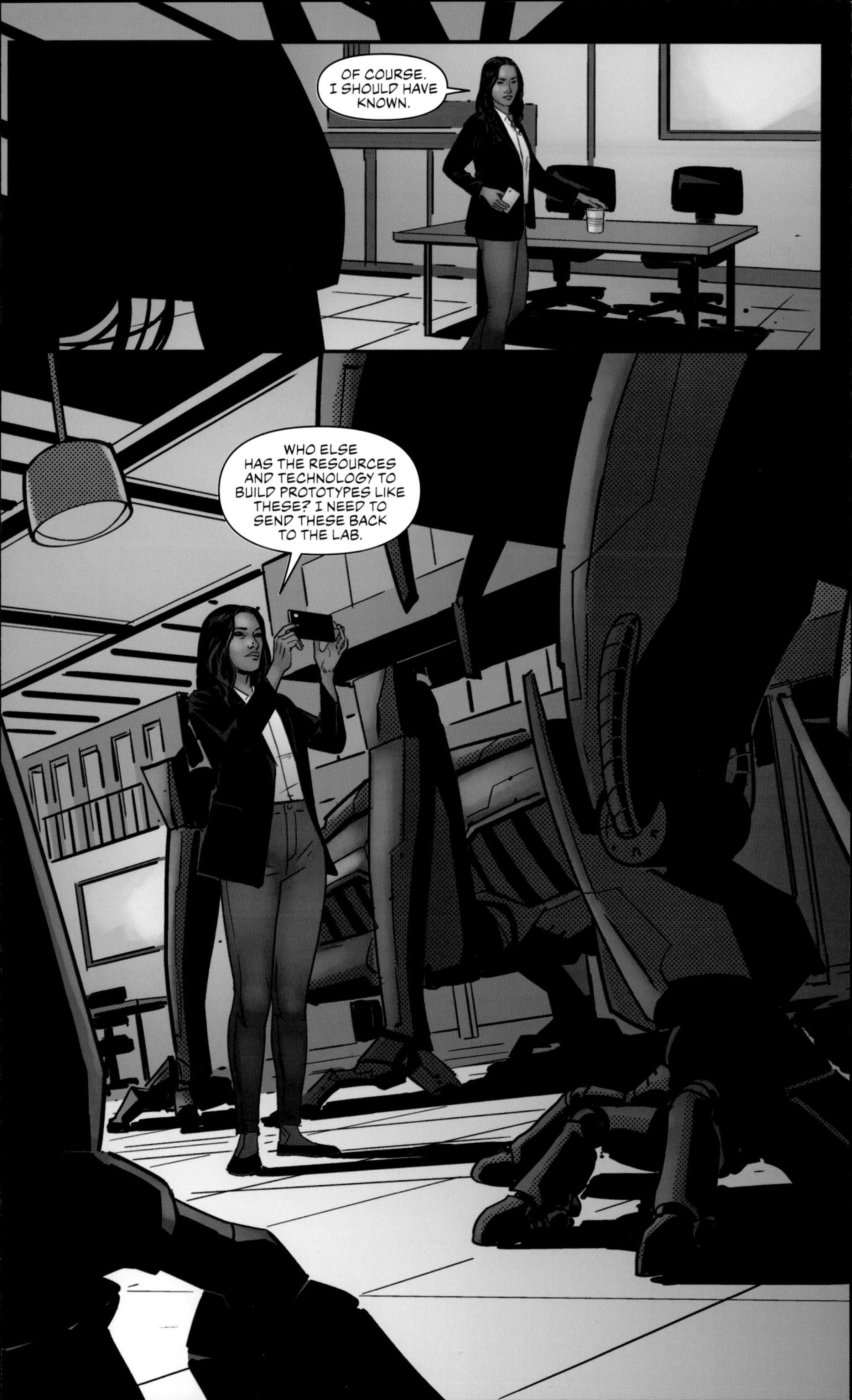
OF COURSE. I SHOULD HAVE KNOWN.
WHO ELSE HAS THE RESOURCES AND TECHNOLOGY TO BUILD PROTOTYPES LIKE THESE? I NEED TO SEND THESE BACK TO THE LAB.

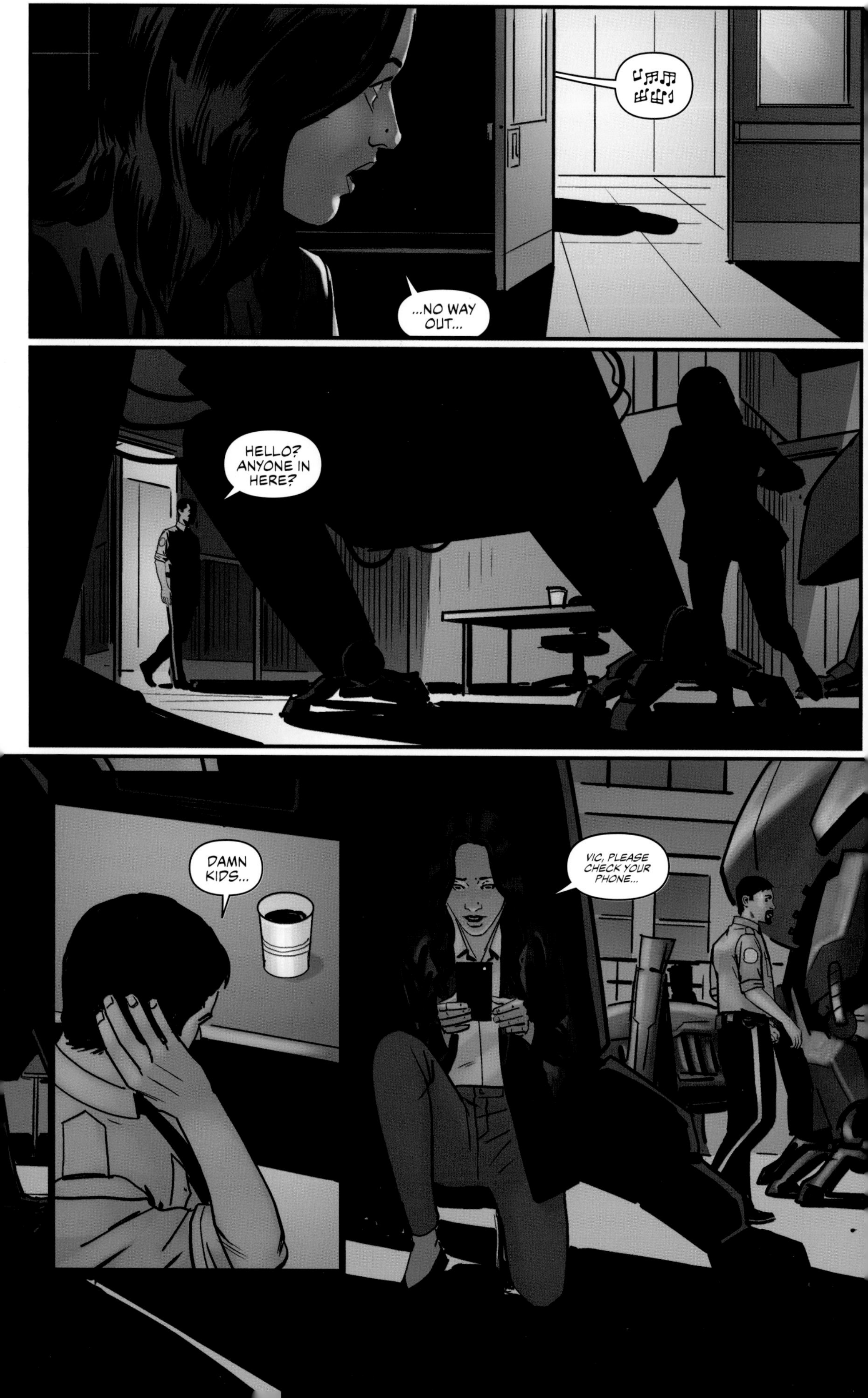
...NO WAY OUT...
HELLO? ANYONE IN HERE?
DAMN KIDS...
VIC, PLEASE CHECK YOUR PHONE...

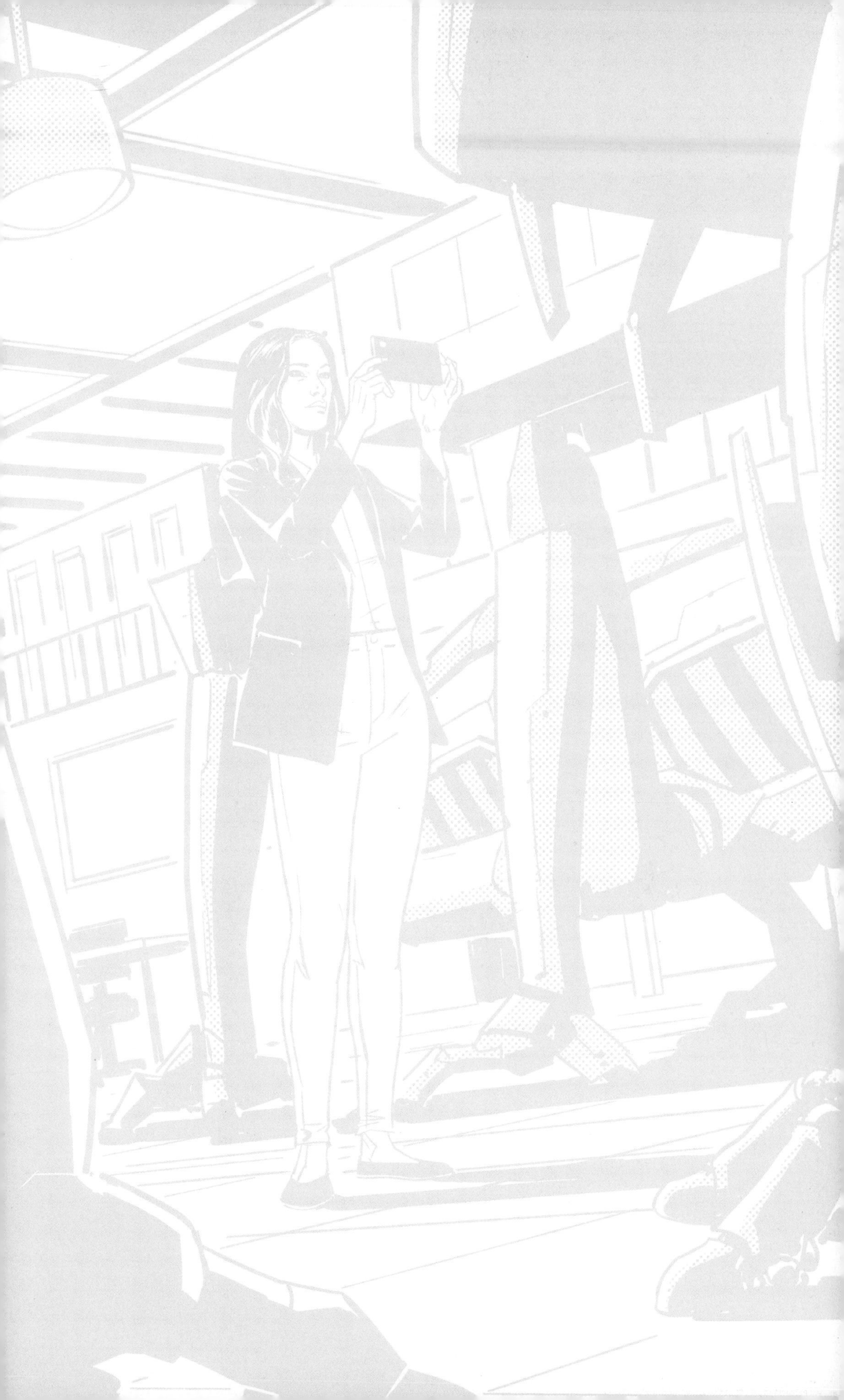

CHAPTER FOUR

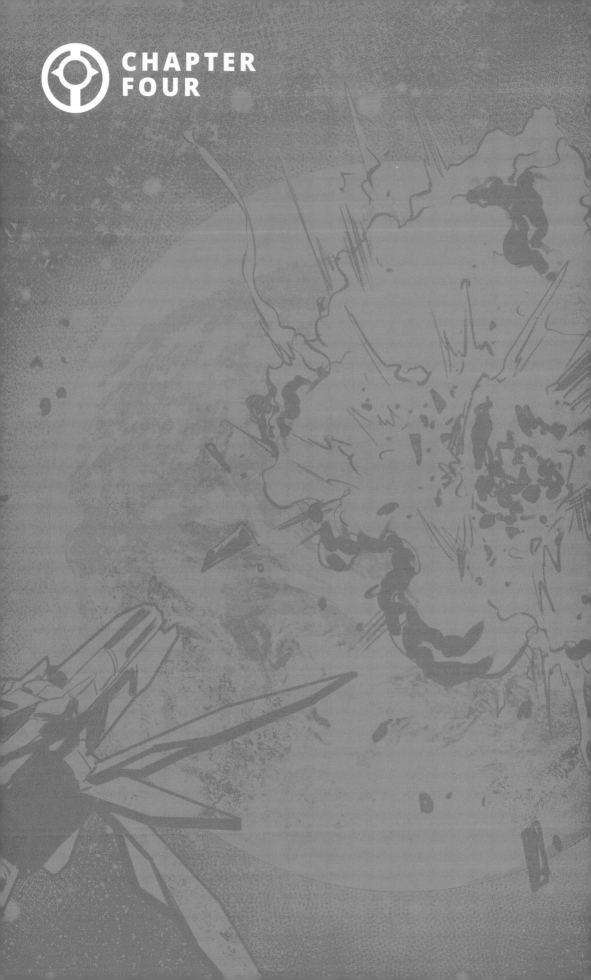

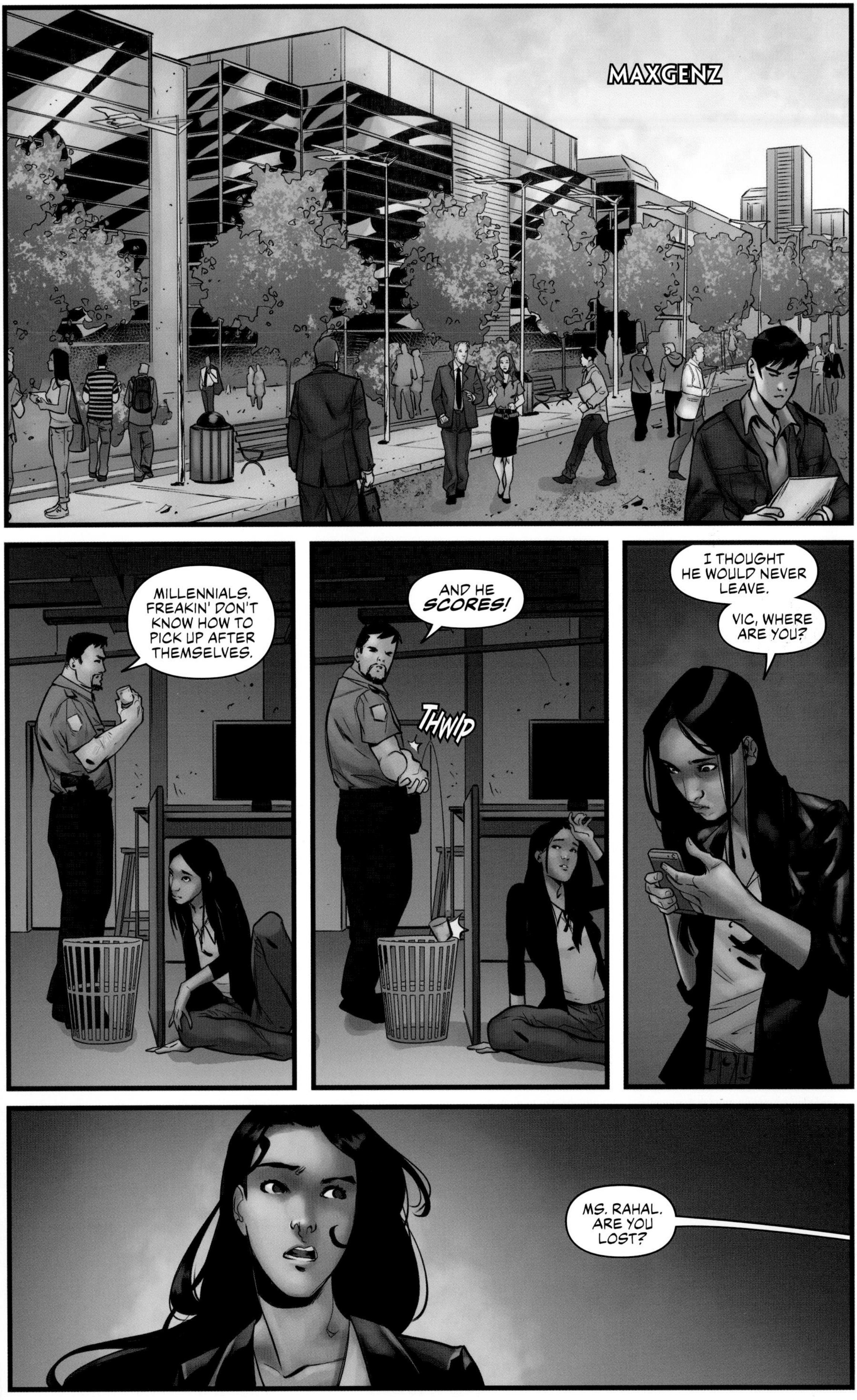
MAXGENZ
MILLENNIALS. FREAKIN' DON'T KNOW HOW TO PICK UP AFTER THEMSELVES.
AND HE SCORES!
THWIP
I THOUGHT HE WOULD NEVER LEAVE.
VIC, WHERE ARE YOU?
MS. RAHAL. ARE YOU LOST?

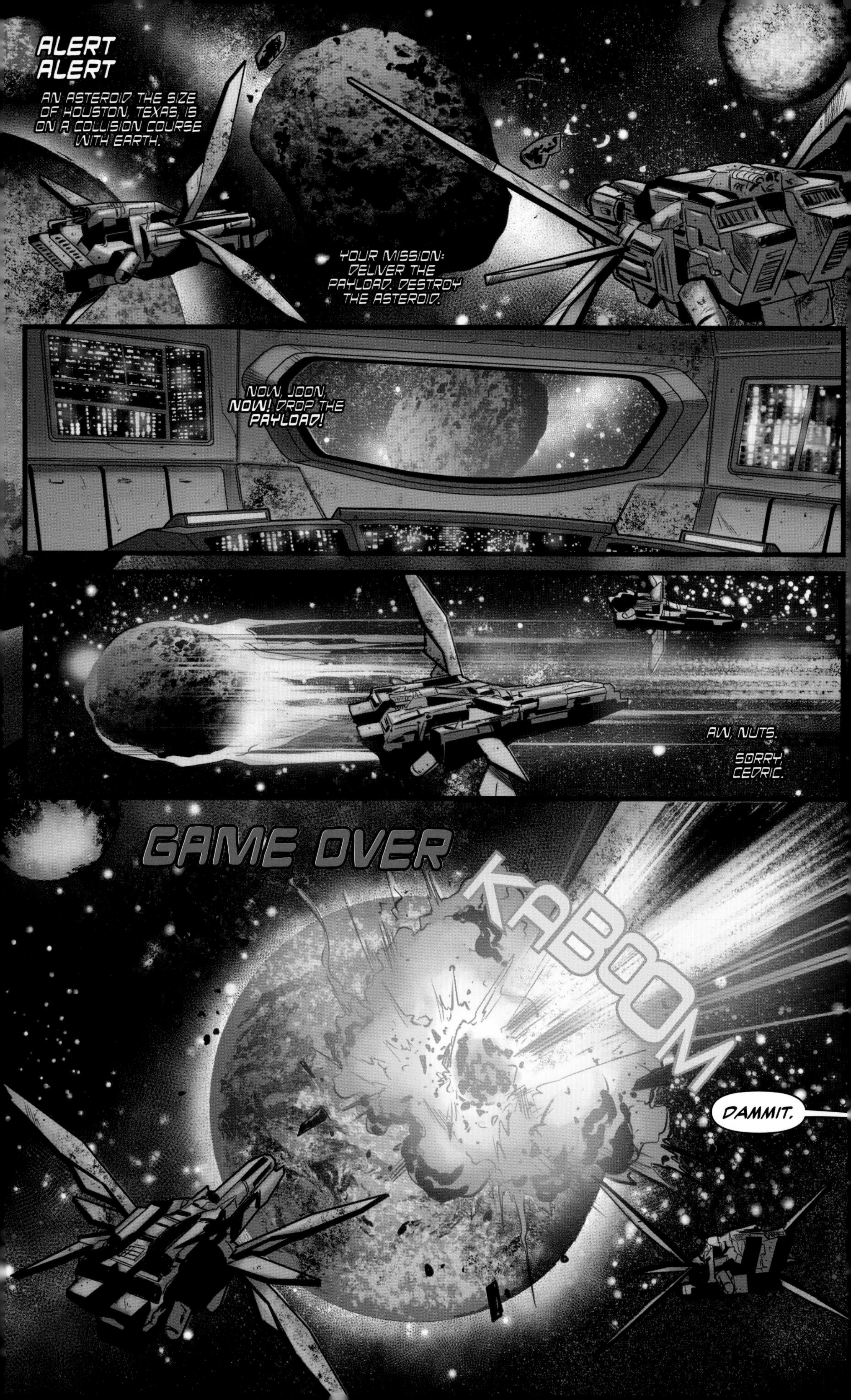
ALERT
ALERT
AN ASTEROID THE SIZE OF HOUSTON, TEXAS, IS ON A COLLISION COURSE WITH EARTH.
YOUR MISSION: DELIVER THE PAYLOAD. DESTROY THE ASTEROID.
NOW, JOON, NOW! DROP THE PAYLOAD!
AW, NUTS.
SORRY, CEDRIC.
GAME OVER
KABOOM
DAMMIT.

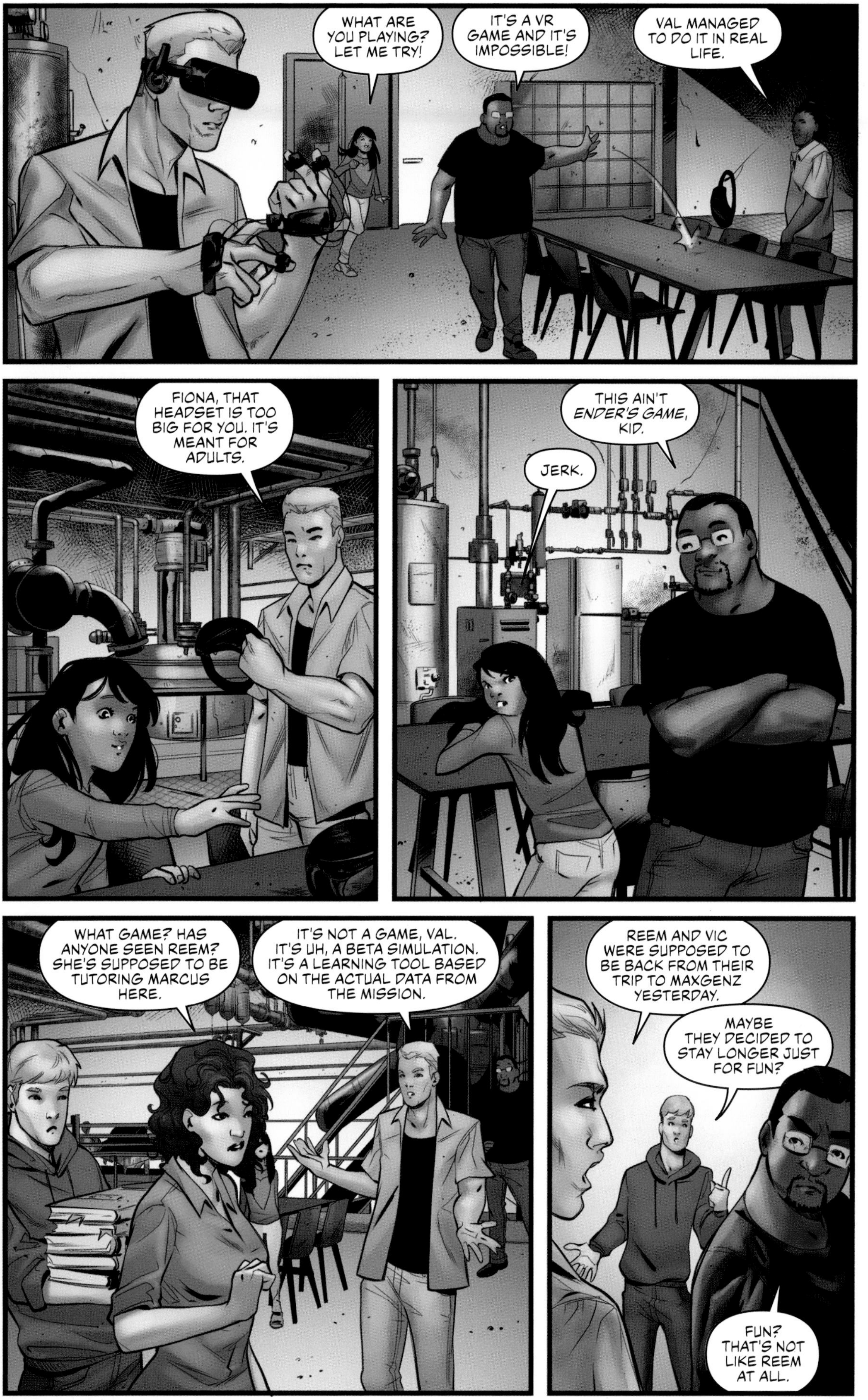
WHAT ARE YOU PLAYING? LET ME TRY!
IT'S A VR GAME AND IT'S IMPOSSIBLE!
VAL MANAGED TO DO IT IN REAL LIFE.
FIONA, THAT HEADSET IS TOO BIG FOR YOU. IT'S MEANT FOR ADULTS.
THIS AIN'T *ENDER'S GAME*, KID.
JERK.
WHAT GAME? HAS ANYONE SEEN REEM? SHE'S SUPPOSED TO BE TUTORING MARCUS HERE.
IT'S NOT A GAME, VAL. IT'S UH, A BETA SIMULATION. IT'S A LEARNING TOOL BASED ON THE ACTUAL DATA FROM THE MISSION.
REEM AND VIC WERE SUPPOSED TO BE BACK FROM THEIR TRIP TO MAXGENZ YESTERDAY.
MAYBE THEY DECIDED TO STAY LONGER JUST FOR FUN?
FUN? THAT'S NOT LIKE REEM AT ALL.

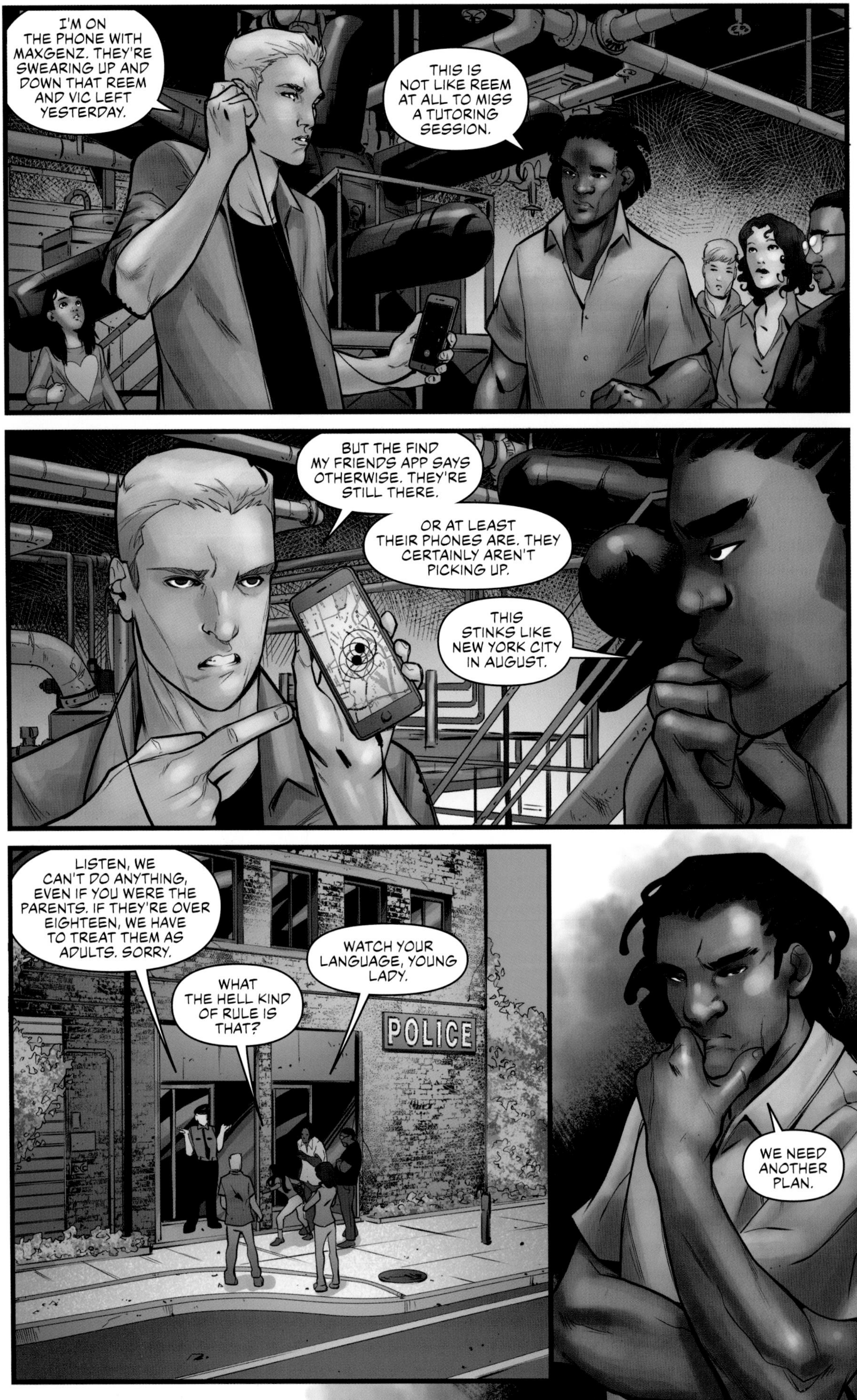
I'M ON THE PHONE WITH MAXGENZ. THEY'RE SWEARING UP AND DOWN THAT REEM AND VIC LEFT YESTERDAY.
THIS IS NOT LIKE REEM AT ALL TO MISS A TUTORING SESSION.
BUT THE FIND MY FRIENDS APP SAYS OTHERWISE. THEY'RE STILL THERE.
OR AT LEAST THEIR PHONES ARE. THEY CERTAINLY AREN'T PICKING UP.
THIS STINKS LIKE NEW YORK CITY IN AUGUST.
LISTEN, WE CAN'T DO ANYTHING, EVEN IF YOU WERE THE PARENTS. IF THEY'RE OVER EIGHTEEN, WE HAVE TO TREAT THEM AS ADULTS. SORRY.
WHAT THE HELL KIND OF RULE IS THAT?
WATCH YOUR LANGUAGE, YOUNG LADY.
POLICE
WE NEED ANOTHER PLAN.

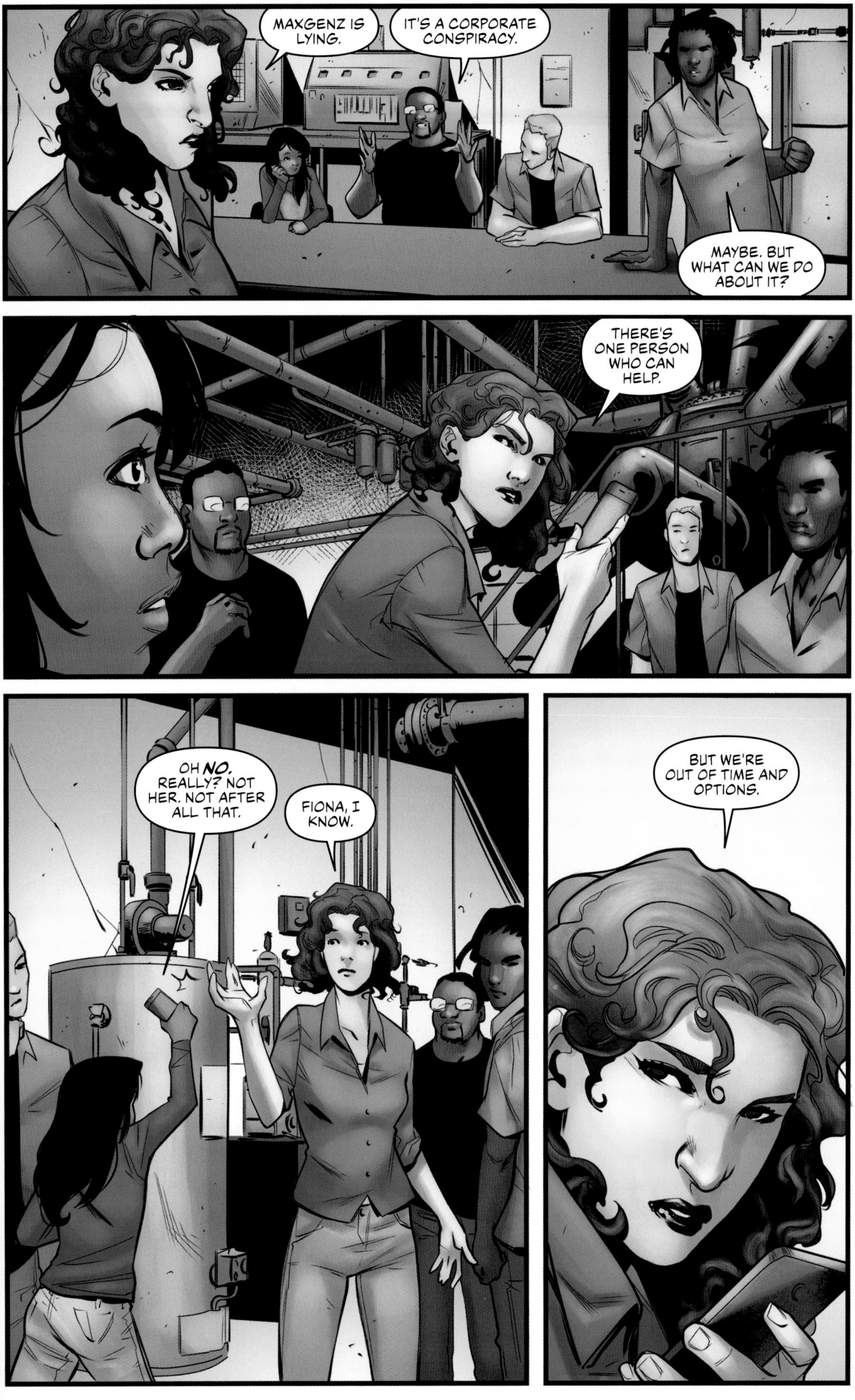
MAXGENZ IS LYING.
IT'S A CORPORATE CONSPIRACY.
MAYBE. BUT WHAT CAN WE DO ABOUT IT?
THERE'S ONE PERSON WHO CAN HELP.
OH NO. REALLY? NOT HER. NOT AFTER ALL THAT.
FIONA, I KNOW.
BUT WE'RE OUT OF TIME AND OPTIONS.

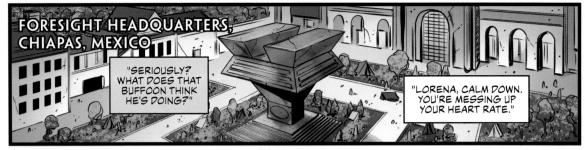

FORESIGHT HEADQUARTERS, CHIAPAS, MEXICO

"SERIOUSLY? WHAT DOES THAT BUFFOON THINK HE'S DOING?"

"LORENA, CALM DOWN. YOU'RE MESSING UP YOUR HEART RATE."

IF THERE'S A WALL GOING UP, IT'LL BE MY WALL, MY TERMS...

ASSHOLE.

UH, LORENA--

GET MY BROKER ON THE LINE.

ELIAS, YOU THERE? I WANT YOU TO SHORT 50,000 SHARES...YOU HEARD ME. NO, MAKE THAT 80,000 OF THAT PIECE OF $#!'S STOCK.

SORRY TO INTERRUPT, LORENA, BUT YOU HAVE A CALL.

≈UFF≈

JOSITA, NOT NOW. CAN'T YOU SEE I'M BUSY?

I THINK YOU'LL WANT TO TAKE THIS ONE.

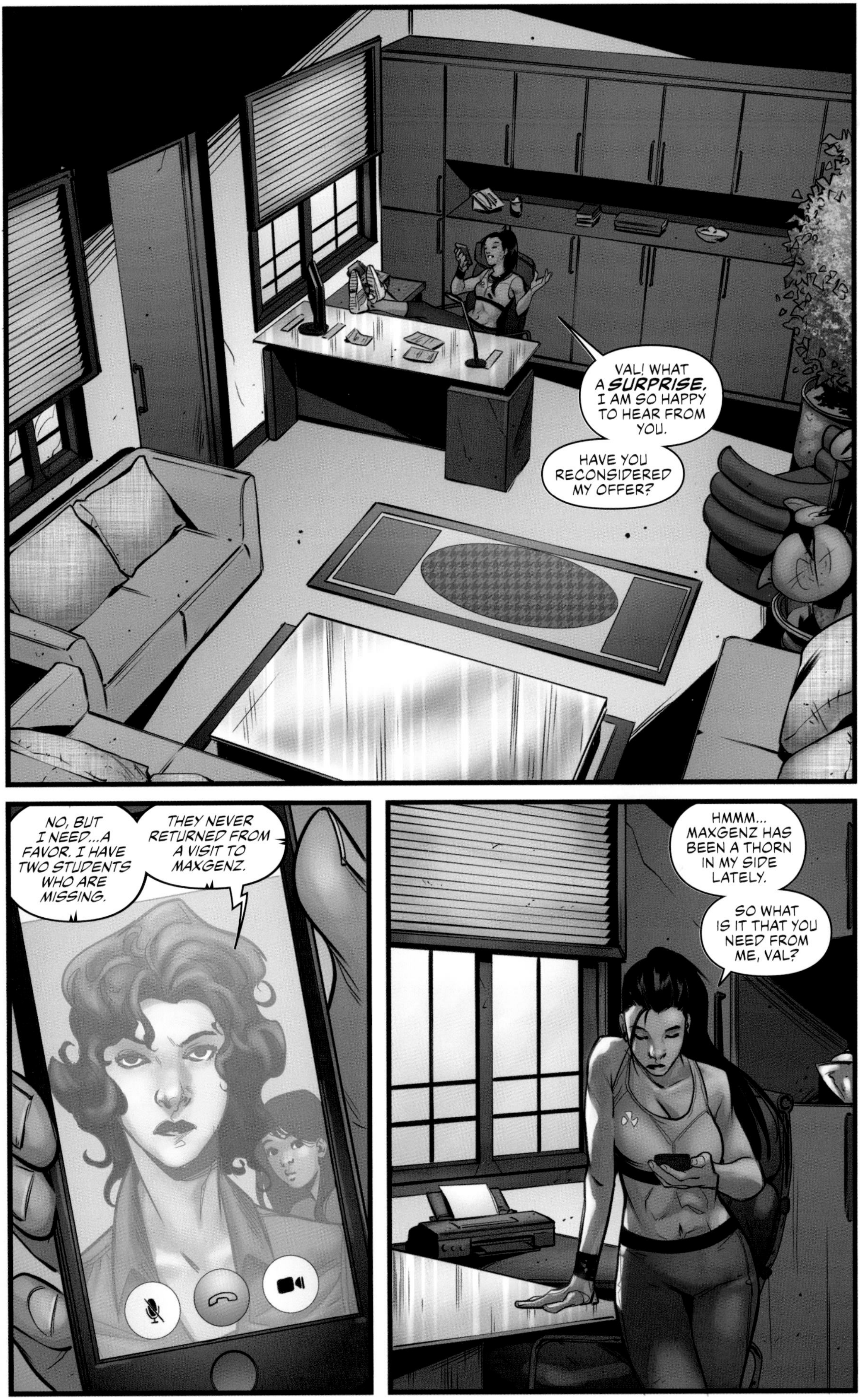
VAL! WHAT A SURPRISE. I AM SO HAPPY TO HEAR FROM YOU.
HAVE YOU RECONSIDERED MY OFFER?
NO, BUT I NEED...A FAVOR. I HAVE TWO STUDENTS WHO ARE MISSING.
THEY NEVER RETURNED FROM A VISIT TO MAXGENZ.
HMMM... MAXGENZ HAS BEEN A THORN IN MY SIDE LATELY.
SO WHAT IS IT THAT YOU NEED FROM ME, VAL?

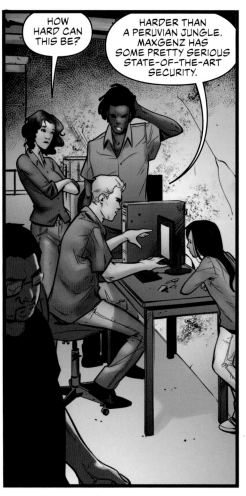

HOW HARD CAN THIS BE?

HARDER THAN A PERUVIAN JUNGLE. MAXGENZ HAS SOME PRETTY SERIOUS STATE-OF-THE-ART SECURITY.

BUT EVERY SECURITY SYSTEM HAS ITS WEAKNESSES.

THEY'RE NOT EXPECTING SOMEONE WHO COULD PULVERIZE A WALL IN SECONDS. WITH A DISTRACTION IN THE FRONT, A PERSON WITH SUCH POWERS SHOULD BE ABLE TO SLIP IN HERE THROUGH THE BACK OF THE R&D WING.

I'LL DO IT! I'M GOOD AT BEING A DISTRACTION!

NO WAY, FIONA. NOT WHEN I'M YOUR GUARDIAN. I NEED AN ADULT.

I'M IN, MAN. JUST TELL ME WHAT TO DO.

HE SAID AN ADULT, CEDRIC.

HA HA. I CAN BE ONE WHEN I WANT TO.

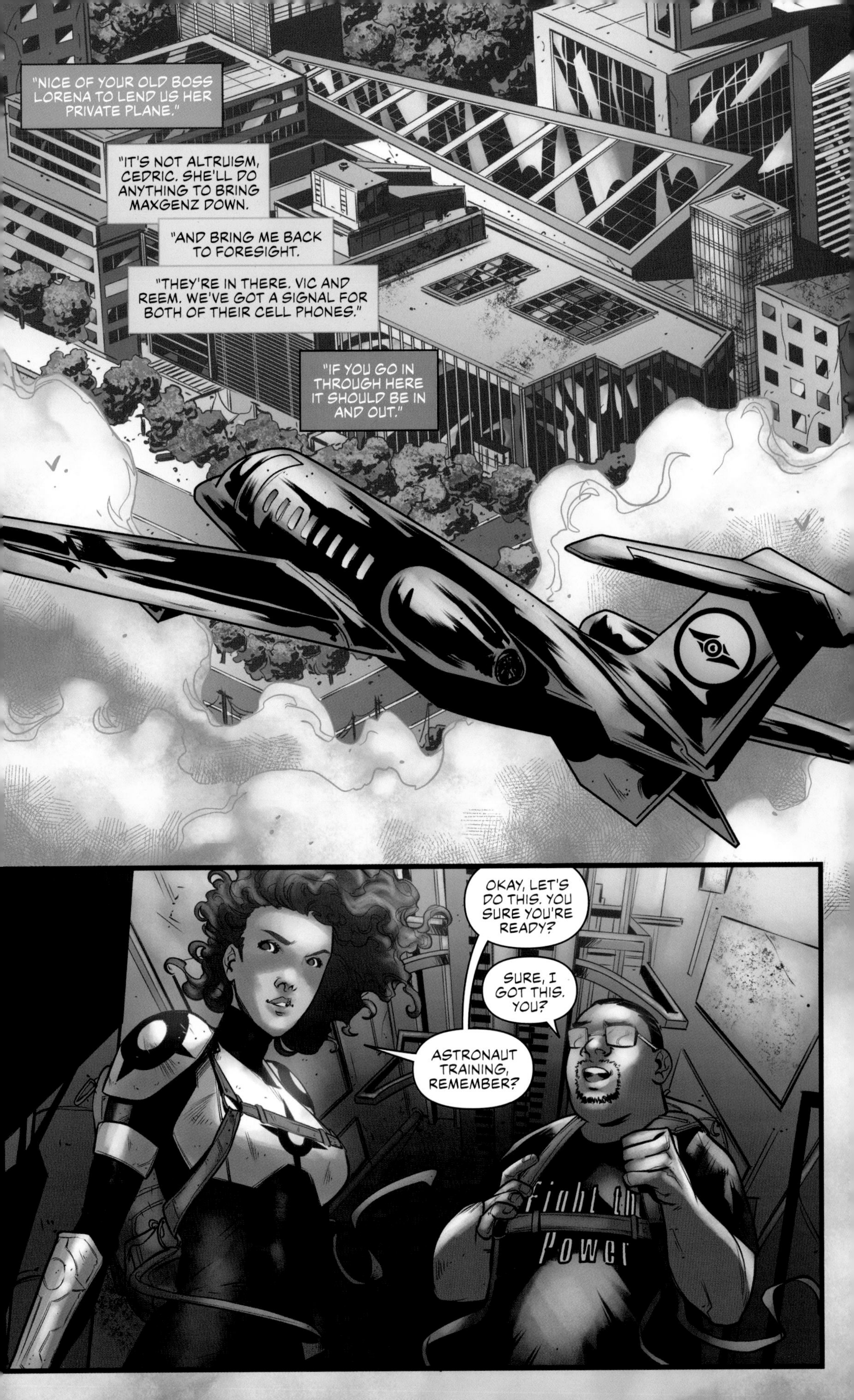
"NICE OF YOUR OLD BOSS LORENA TO LEND US HER PRIVATE PLANE."
"IT'S NOT ALTRUISM, CEDRIC. SHE'LL DO ANYTHING TO BRING MAXGENZ DOWN.
"AND BRING ME BACK TO FORESIGHT.
"THEY'RE IN THERE. VIC AND REEM. WE'VE GOT A SIGNAL FOR BOTH OF THEIR CELL PHONES."
"IF YOU GO IN THROUGH HERE IT SHOULD BE IN AND OUT."
OKAY, LET'S DO THIS. YOU SURE YOU'RE READY?
SURE, I GOT THIS. YOU?
ASTRONAUT TRAINING, REMEMBER?
Fight the Power

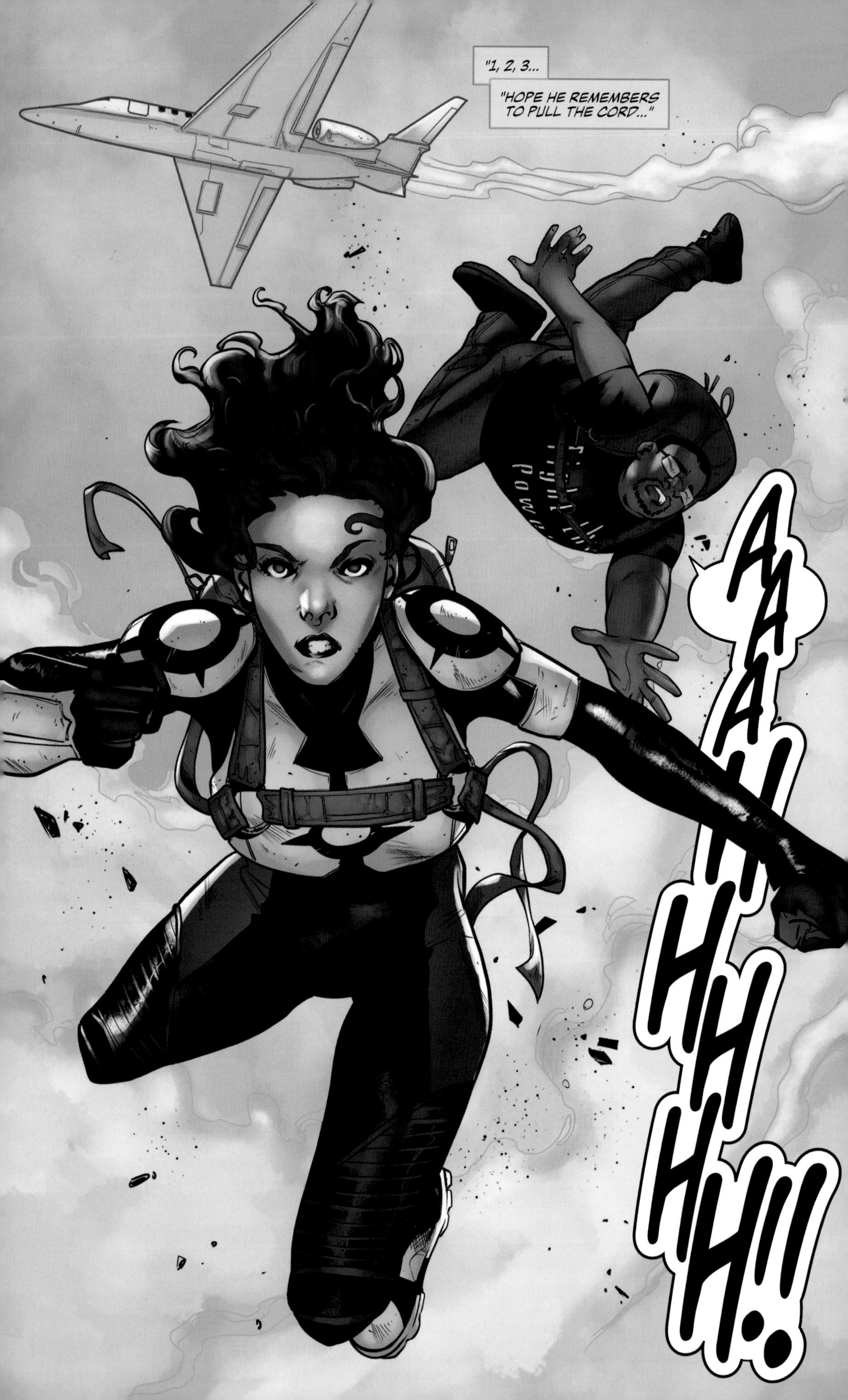
"1, 2, 3...
"HOPE HE REMEMBERS TO PULL THE CORD..."
AAAAHHHHHHH!!

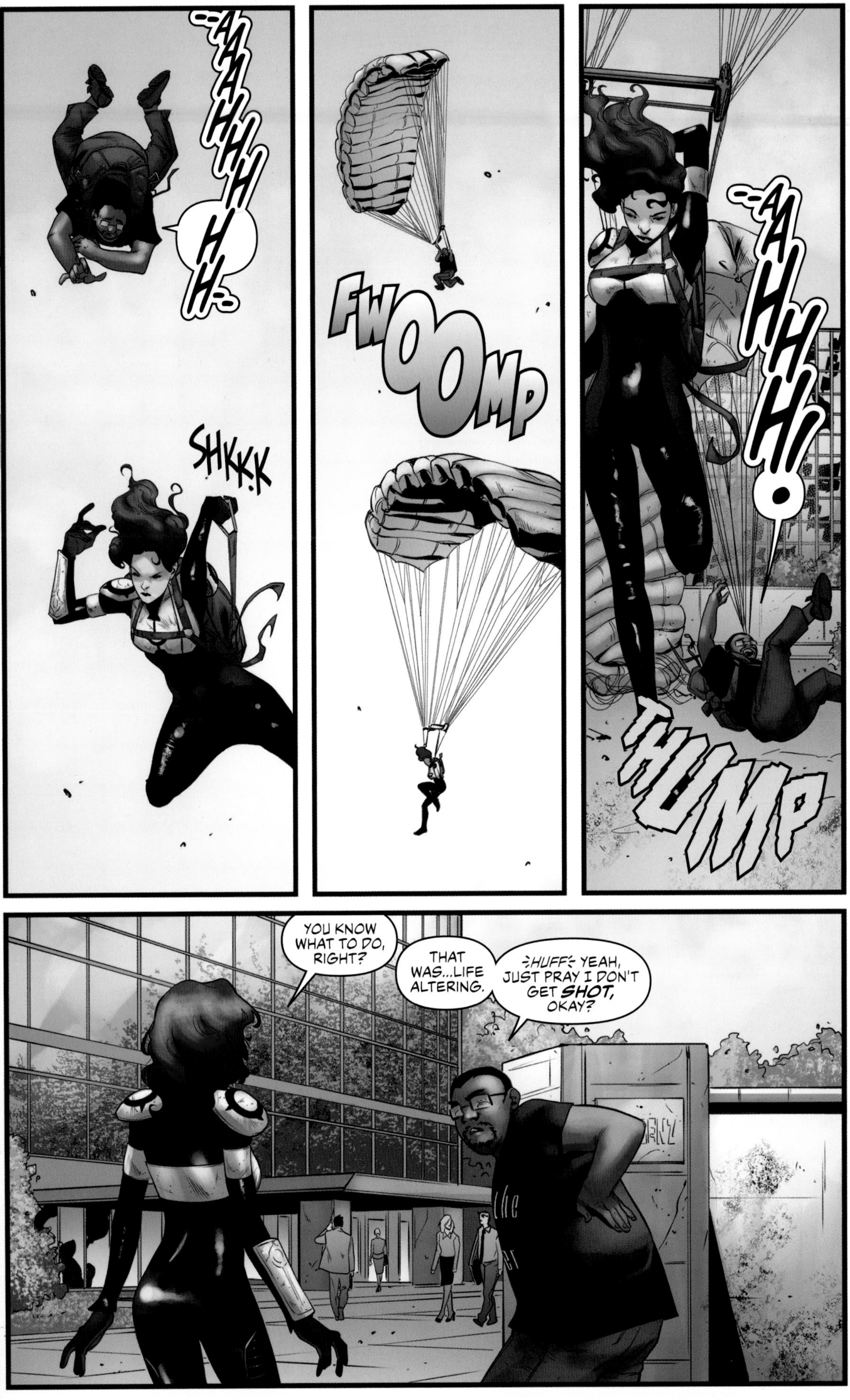
--AAAHHHHHH--
SHKKK
FWOOOMP
--AAHHHH!!
THUMP
YOU KNOW WHAT TO DO, RIGHT?
THAT WAS...LIFE ALTERING.
-HUFF- YEAH, JUST PRAY I DON'T GET SHOT, OKAY?

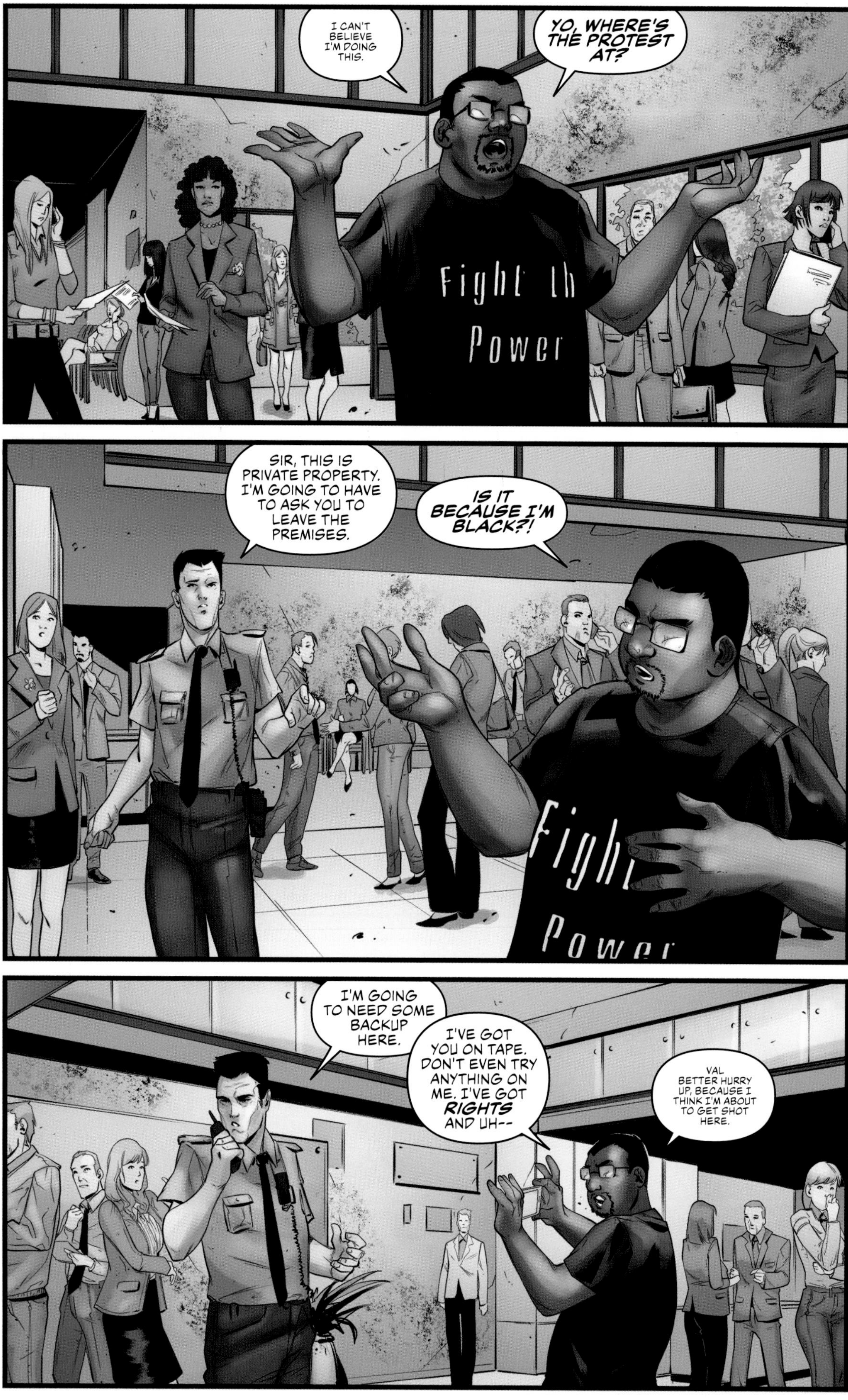
I CAN'T BELIEVE I'M DOING THIS.
YO, WHERE'S THE PROTEST AT?
SIR, THIS IS PRIVATE PROPERTY. I'M GOING TO HAVE TO ASK YOU TO LEAVE THE PREMISES.
IS IT BECAUSE I'M BLACK?!
I'M GOING TO NEED SOME BACKUP HERE.
I'VE GOT YOU ON TAPE. DON'T EVEN TRY ANYTHING ON ME. I'VE GOT RIGHTS AND UH--
VAL BETTER HURRY UP, BECAUSE I THINK I'M ABOUT TO GET SHOT HERE.

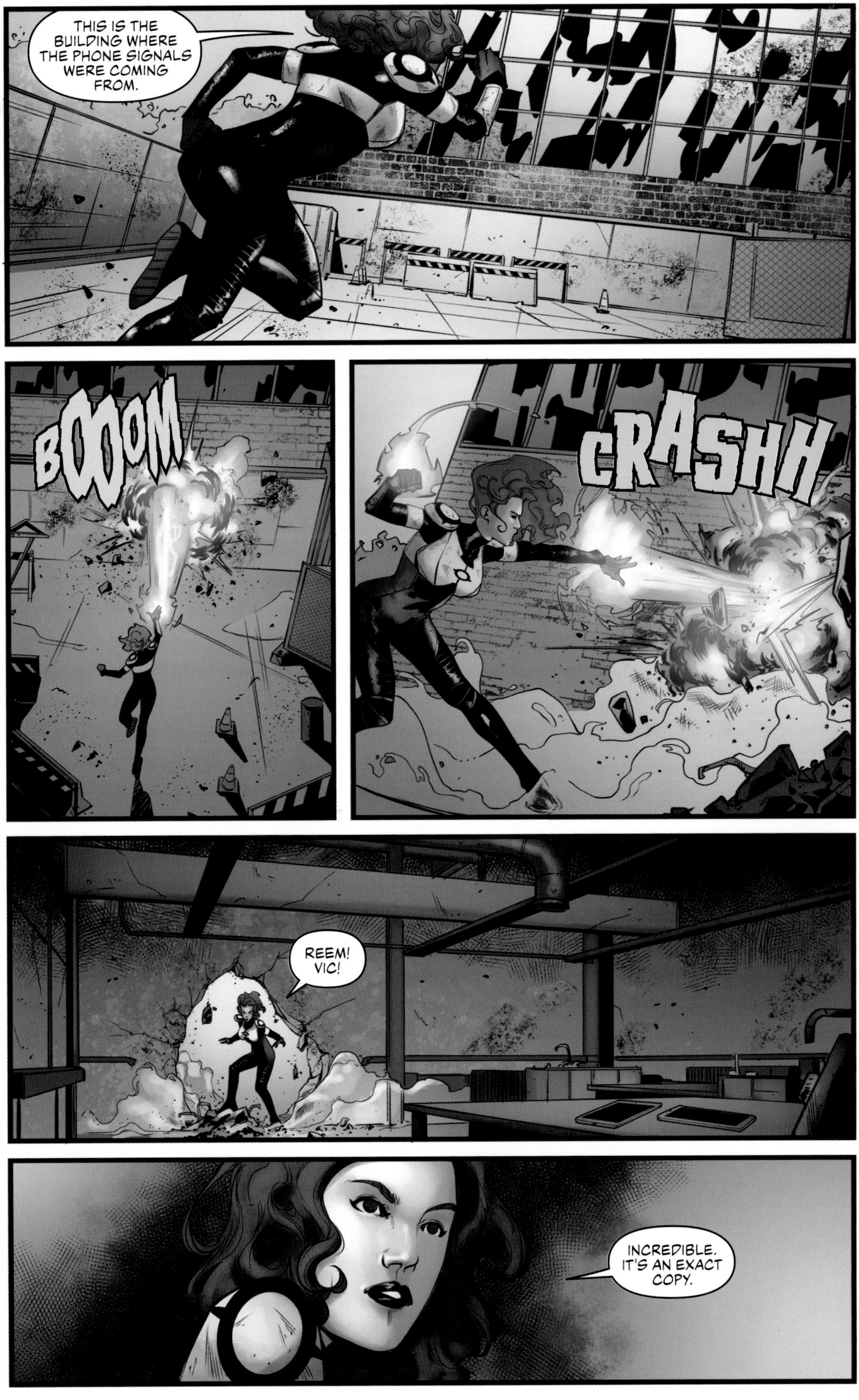
THIS IS THE BUILDING WHERE THE PHONE SIGNALS WERE COMING FROM.
BOOOM
CRASHH
REEM! VIC!
INCREDIBLE. IT'S AN EXACT COPY.

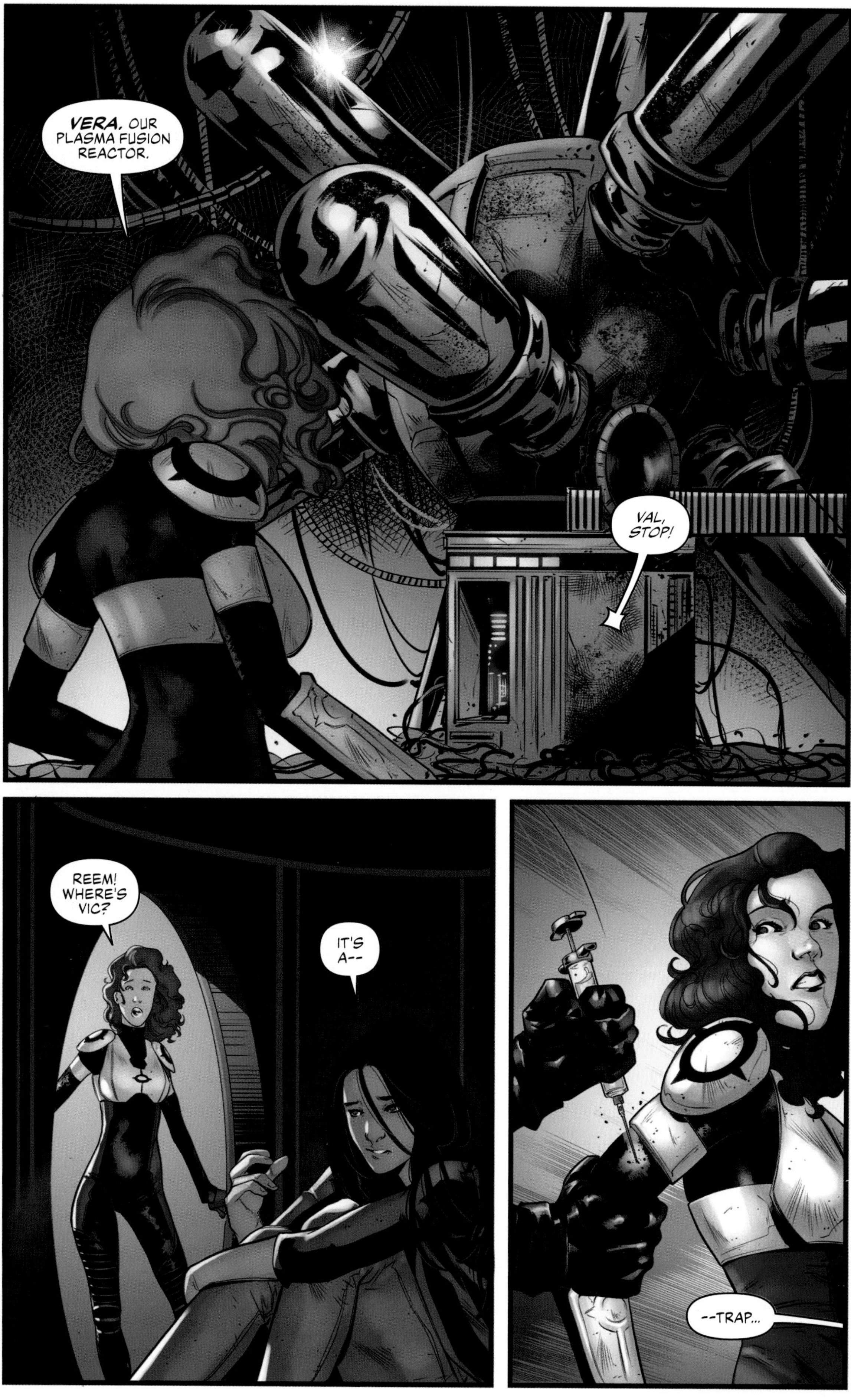
VERA, OUR PLASMA FUSION REACTOR.
VAL, STOP!
REEM! WHERE'S VIC?
IT'S A--
--TRAP...

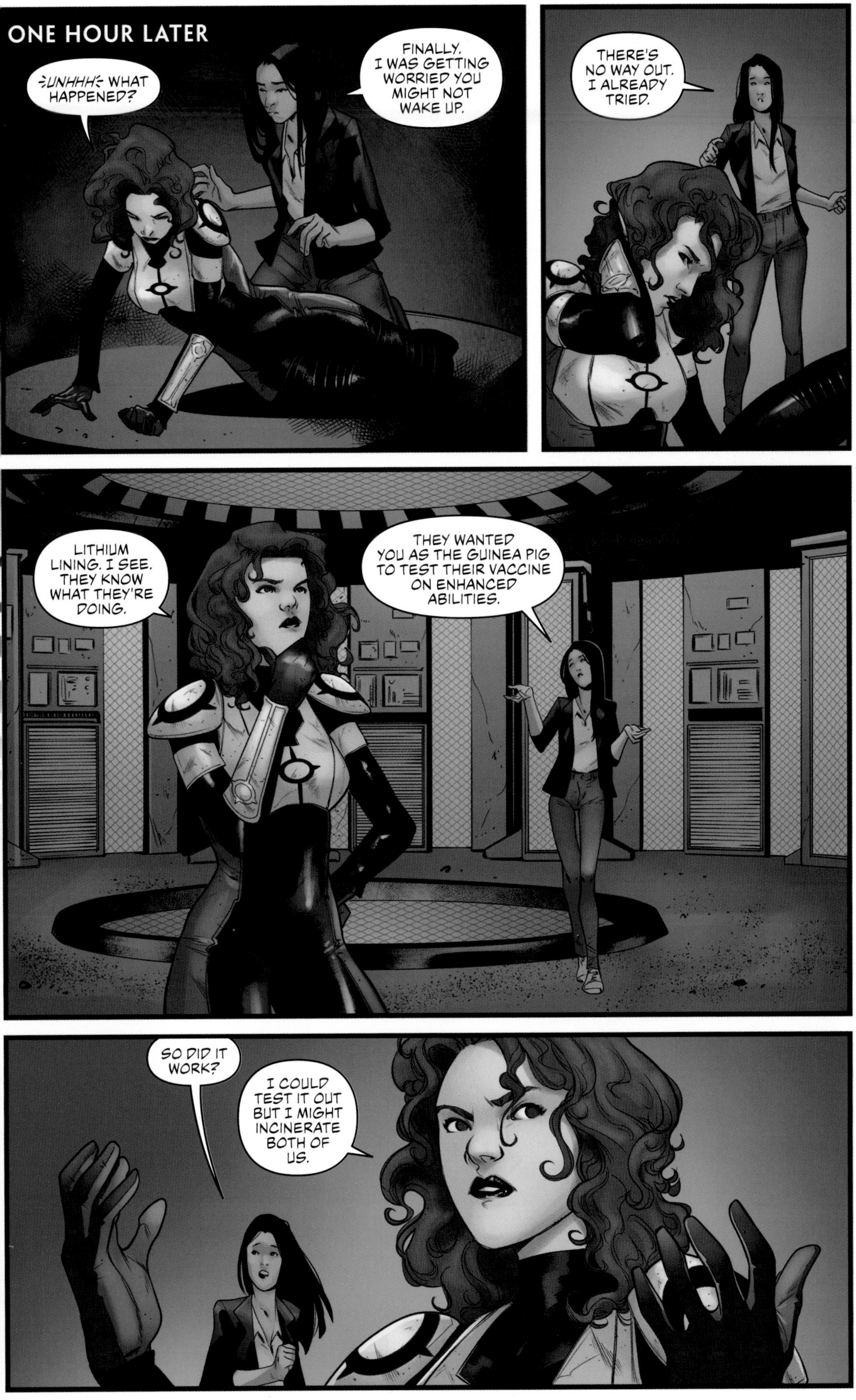
ONE HOUR LATER
-UNHHH- WHAT HAPPENED?
FINALLY. I WAS GETTING WORRIED YOU MIGHT NOT WAKE UP.
THERE'S NO WAY OUT. I ALREADY TRIED.
LITHIUM LINING. I SEE. THEY KNOW WHAT THEY'RE DOING.
THEY WANTED YOU AS THE GUINEA PIG TO TEST THEIR VACCINE ON ENHANCED ABILITIES.
SO DID IT WORK?
I COULD TEST IT OUT BUT I MIGHT INCINERATE BOTH OF US.

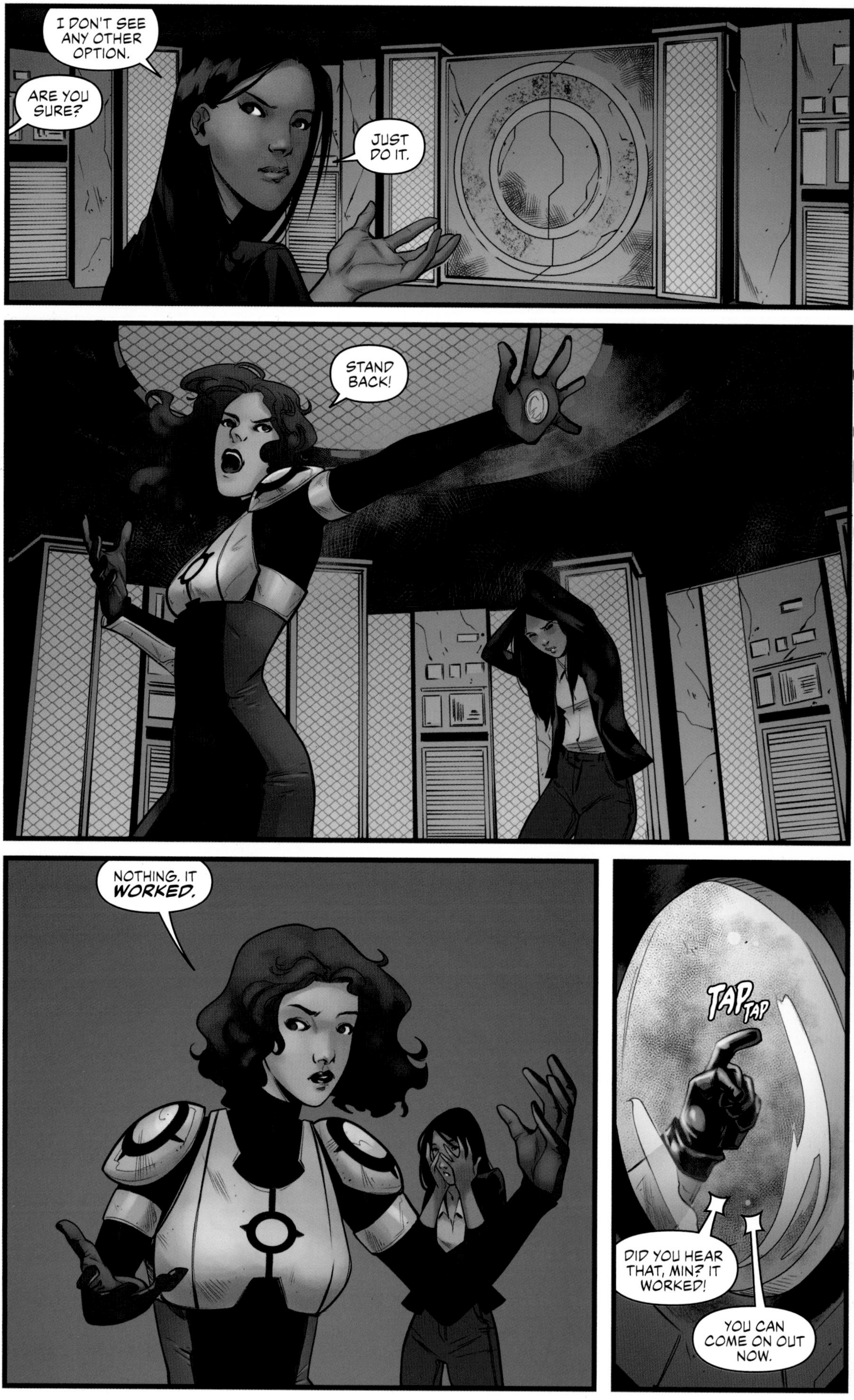
I DON'T SEE ANY OTHER OPTION.
ARE YOU SURE?
JUST DO IT.
STAND BACK!
NOTHING. IT *WORKED.*
TAP TAP
DID YOU HEAR THAT, MIN? IT WORKED!
YOU CAN COME ON OUT NOW.

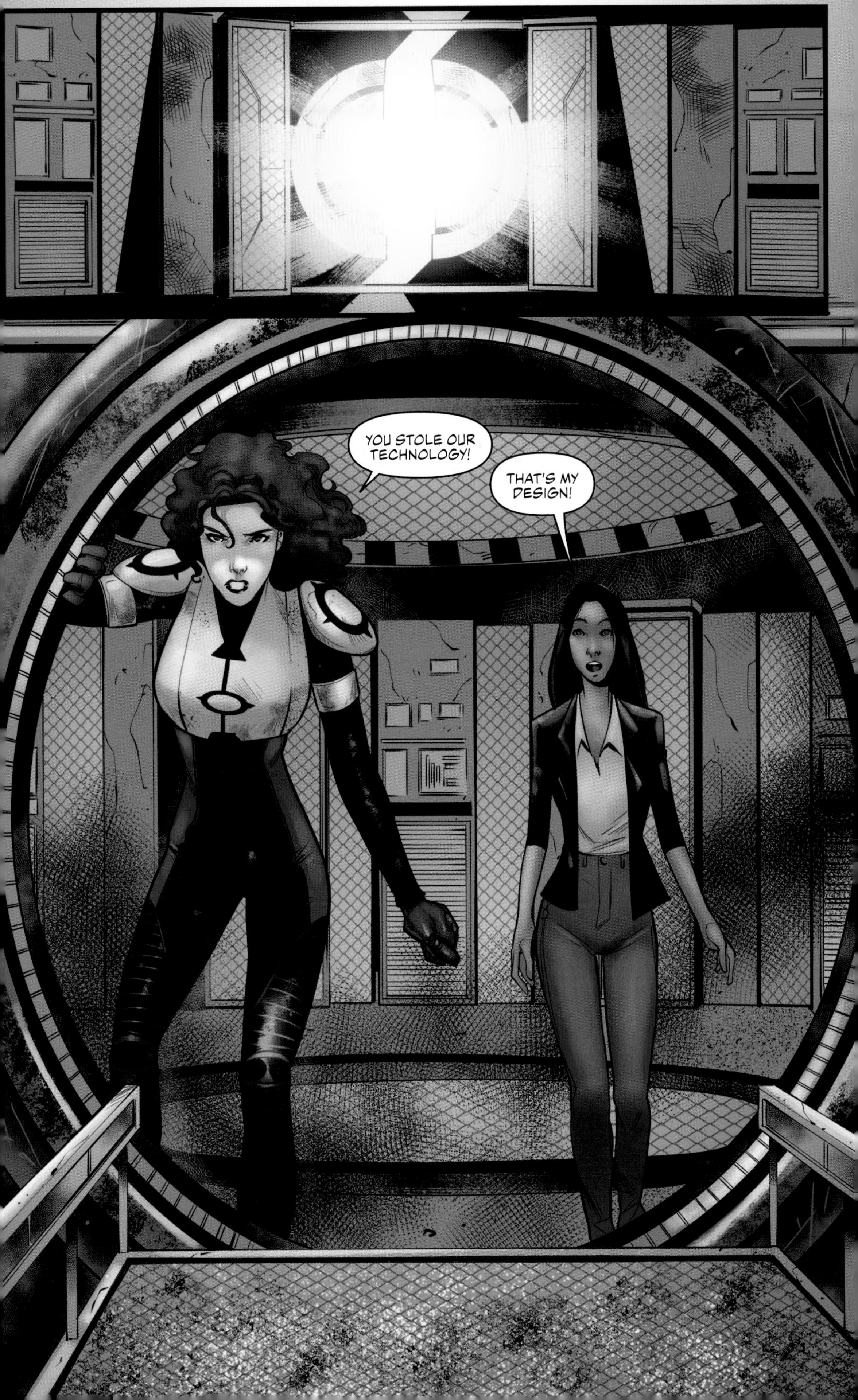
YOU STOLE OUR TECHNOLOGY!
THAT'S MY DESIGN!

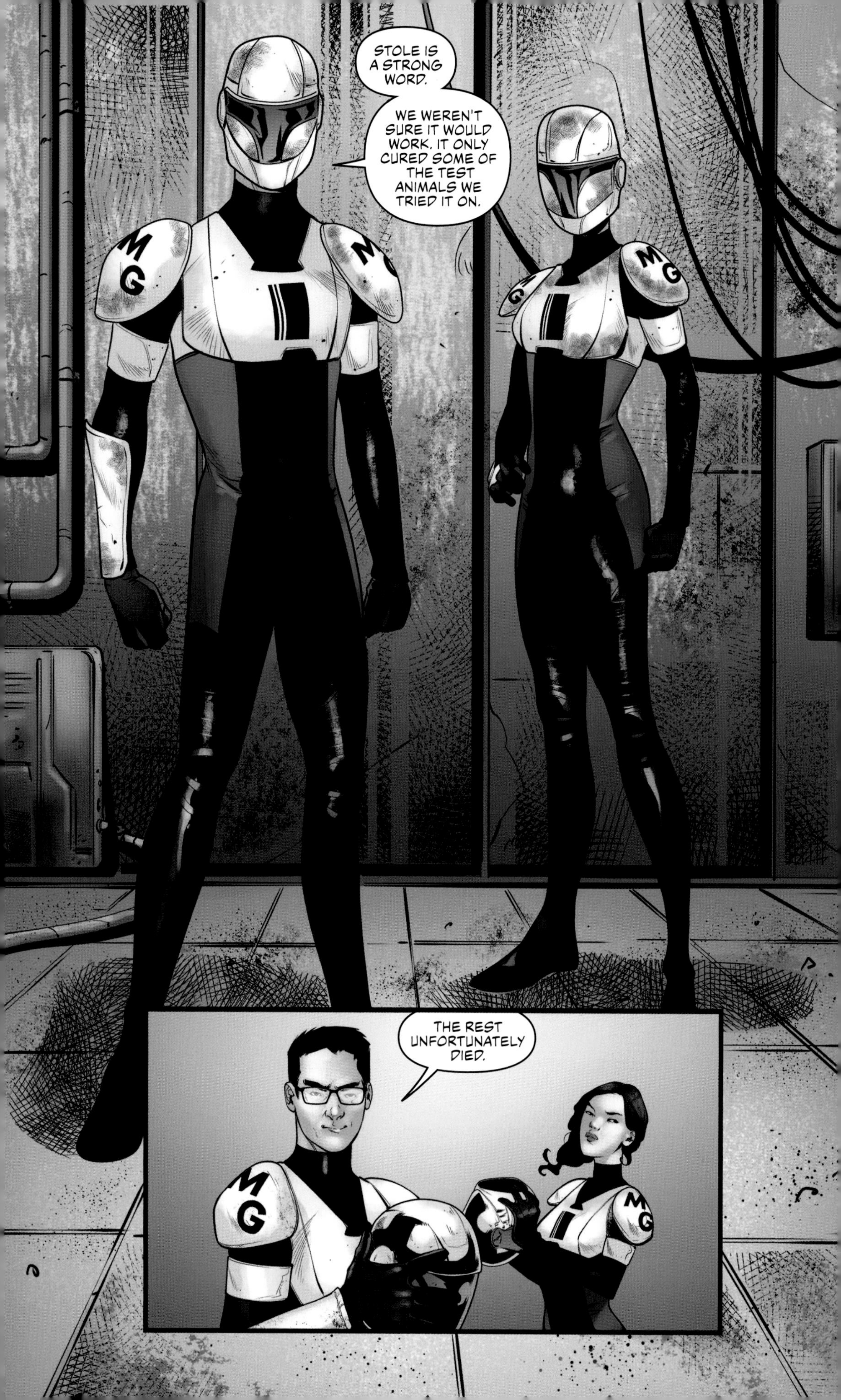
STOLE IS A STRONG WORD.
WE WEREN'T SURE IT WOULD WORK. IT ONLY CURED SOME OF THE TEST ANIMALS WE TRIED IT ON.
MG
MG
MG
THE REST UNFORTUNATELY DIED.
MG
MG

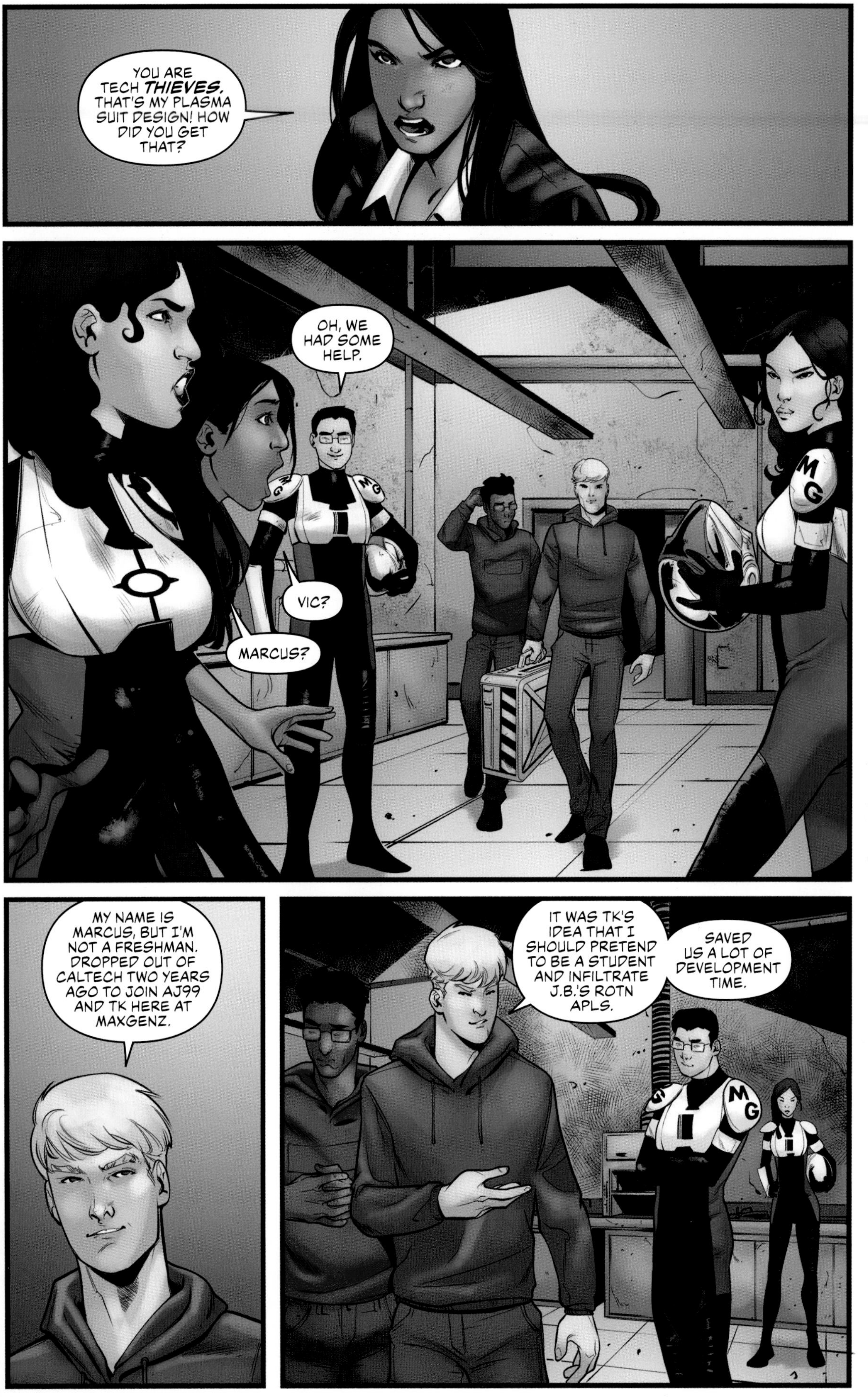

YOU ARE TECH THIEVES. THAT'S MY PLASMA SUIT DESIGN! HOW DID YOU GET THAT?
OH, WE HAD SOME HELP.
VIC?
MARCUS?
MY NAME IS MARCUS, BUT I'M NOT A FRESHMAN. DROPPED OUT OF CALTECH TWO YEARS AGO TO JOIN AJ99 AND TK HERE AT MAXGENZ.
IT WAS TK'S IDEA THAT I SHOULD PRETEND TO BE A STUDENT AND INFILTRATE J.B.'S ROTN APLS.
SAVED US A LOT OF DEVELOPMENT TIME.

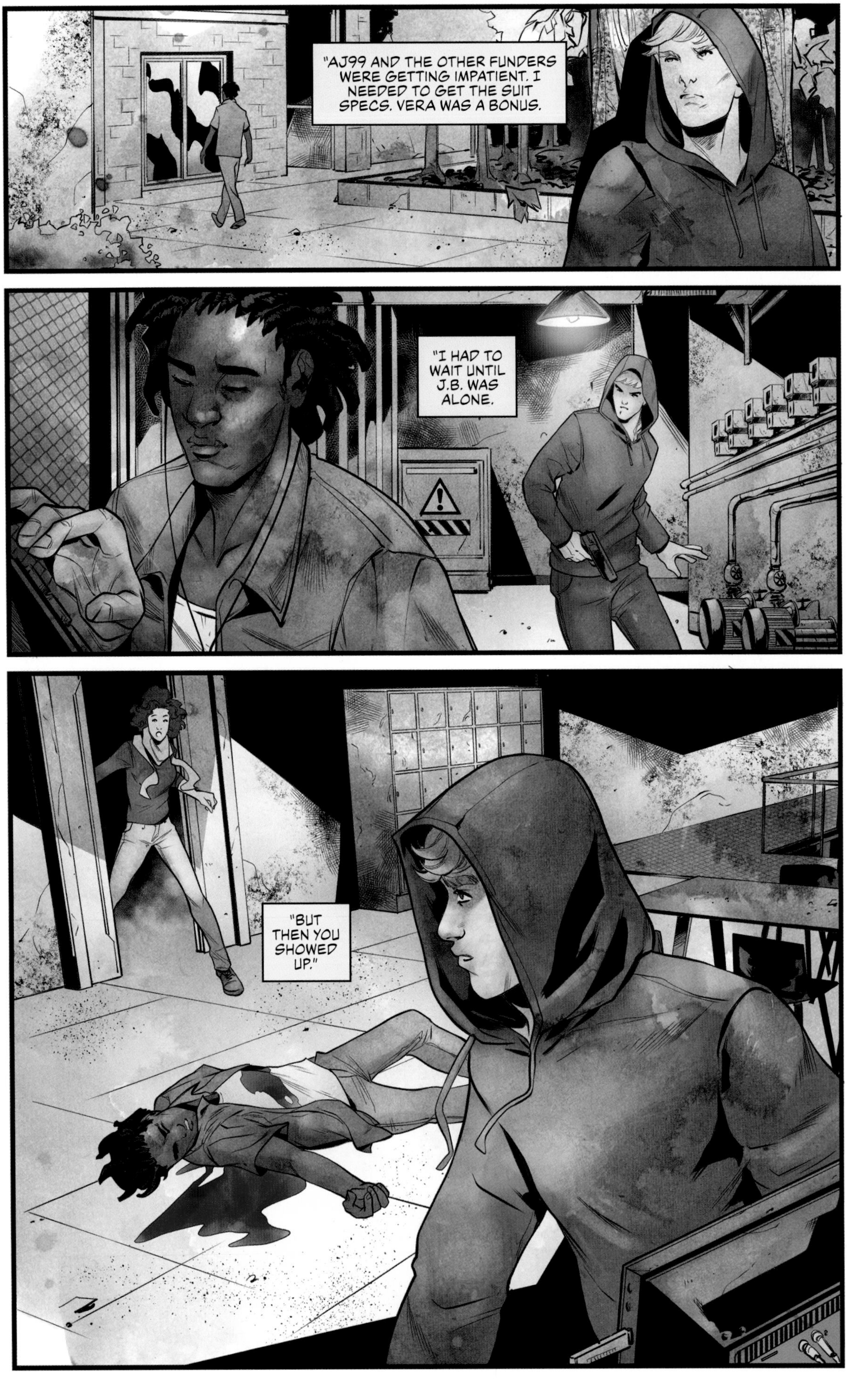
"AJ99 AND THE OTHER FUNDERS WERE GETTING IMPATIENT. I NEEDED TO GET THE SUIT SPECS. VERA WAS A BONUS.
"I HAD TO WAIT UNTIL J.B. WAS ALONE.
"BUT THEN YOU SHOWED UP."

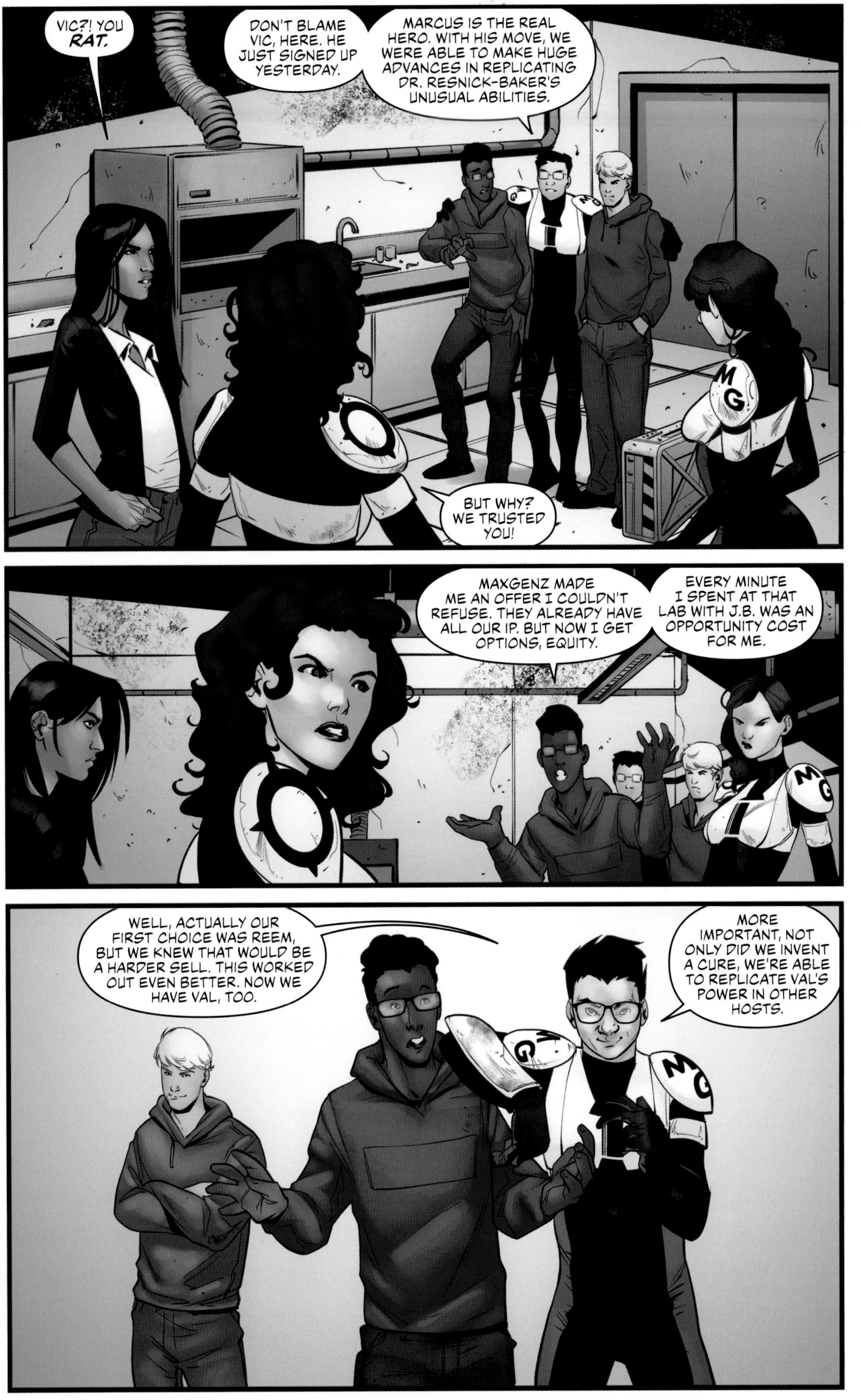
VIC?! YOU RAT.
DON'T BLAME VIC, HERE. HE JUST SIGNED UP YESTERDAY.
MARCUS IS THE REAL HERO. WITH HIS MOVE, WE WERE ABLE TO MAKE HUGE ADVANCES IN REPLICATING DR. RESNICK-BAKER'S UNUSUAL ABILITIES.
BUT WHY? WE TRUSTED YOU!
MAXGENZ MADE ME AN OFFER I COULDN'T REFUSE. THEY ALREADY HAVE ALL OUR IP. BUT NOW I GET OPTIONS, EQUITY.
EVERY MINUTE I SPENT AT THAT LAB WITH J.B. WAS AN OPPORTUNITY COST FOR ME.
WELL, ACTUALLY OUR FIRST CHOICE WAS REEM, BUT WE KNEW THAT WOULD BE A HARDER SELL. THIS WORKED OUT EVEN BETTER. NOW WE HAVE VAL, TOO.
MORE IMPORTANT, NOT ONLY DID WE INVENT A CURE, WE'RE ABLE TO REPLICATE VAL'S POWER IN OTHER HOSTS.

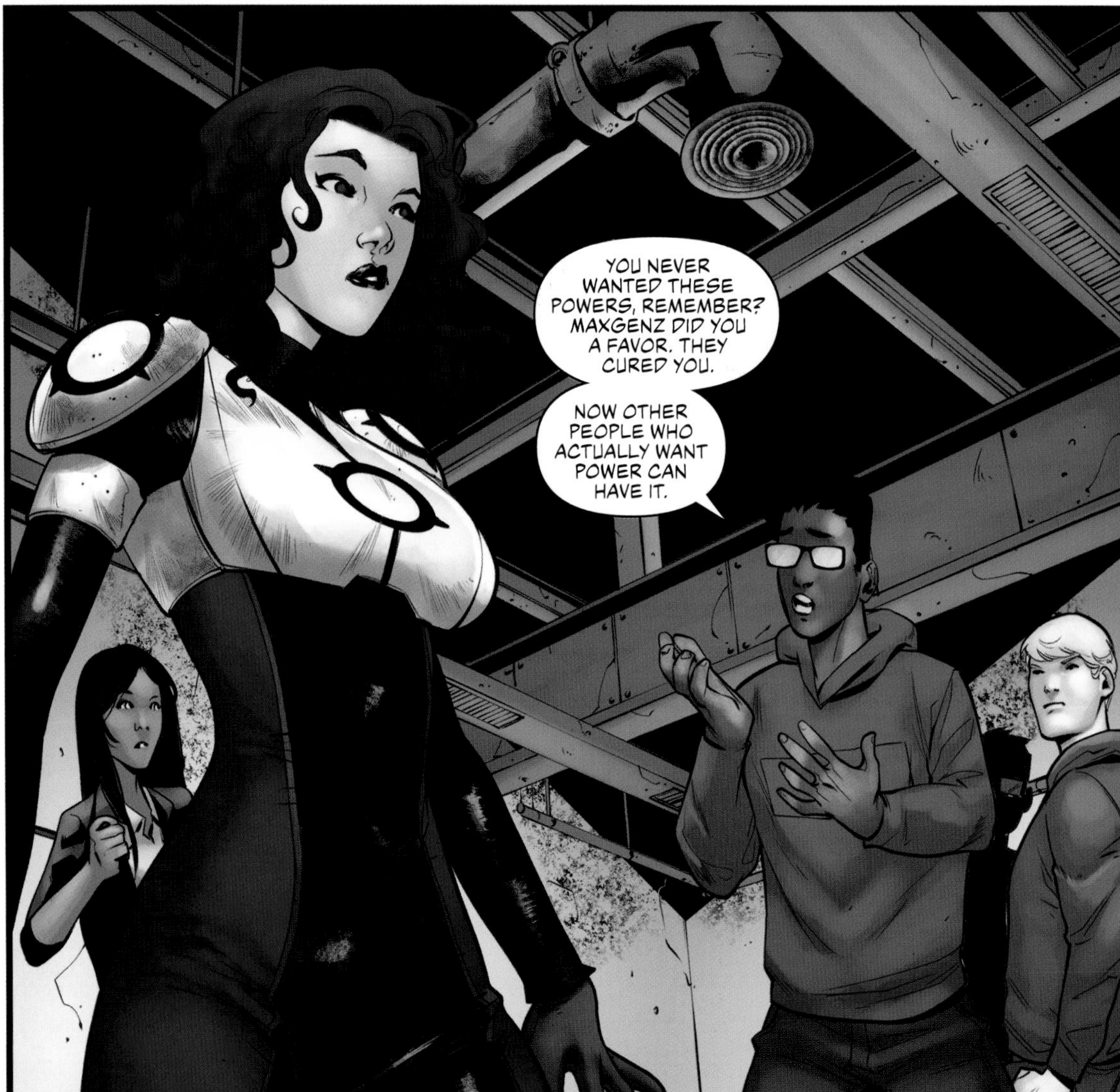
YOU NEVER WANTED THESE POWERS, REMEMBER? MAXGENZ DID YOU A FAVOR. THEY CURED YOU.
NOW OTHER PEOPLE WHO ACTUALLY WANT POWER CAN HAVE IT.

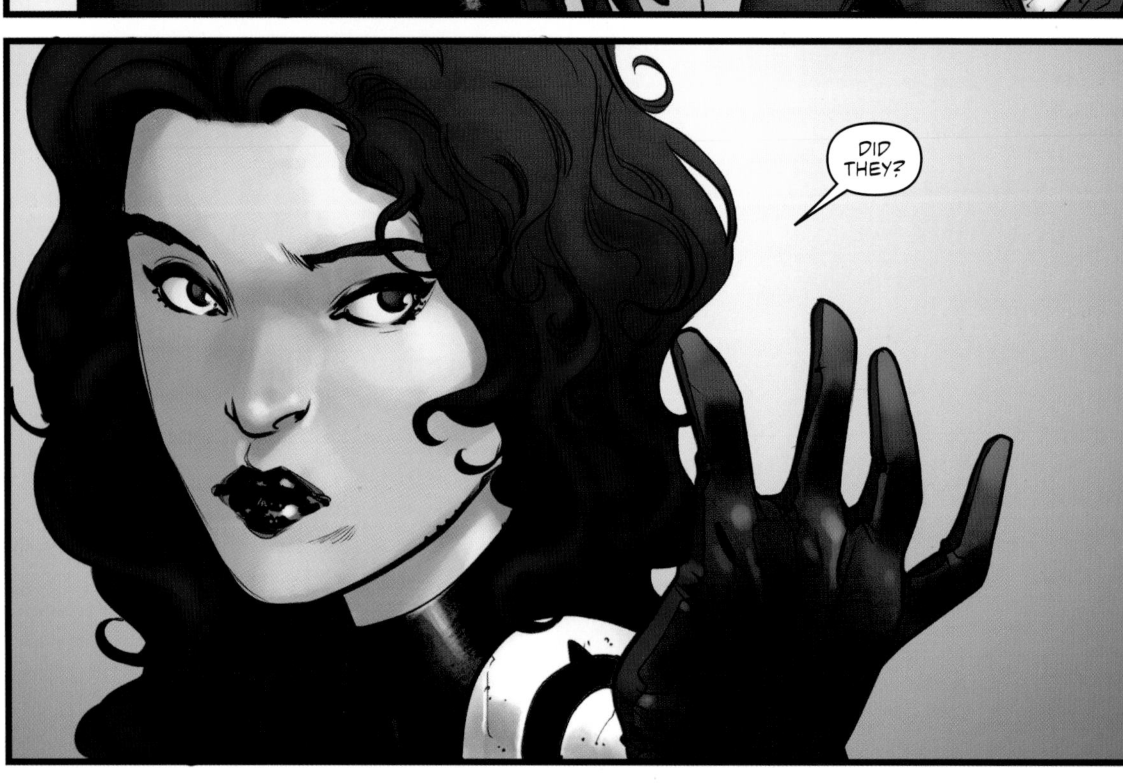
DID THEY?

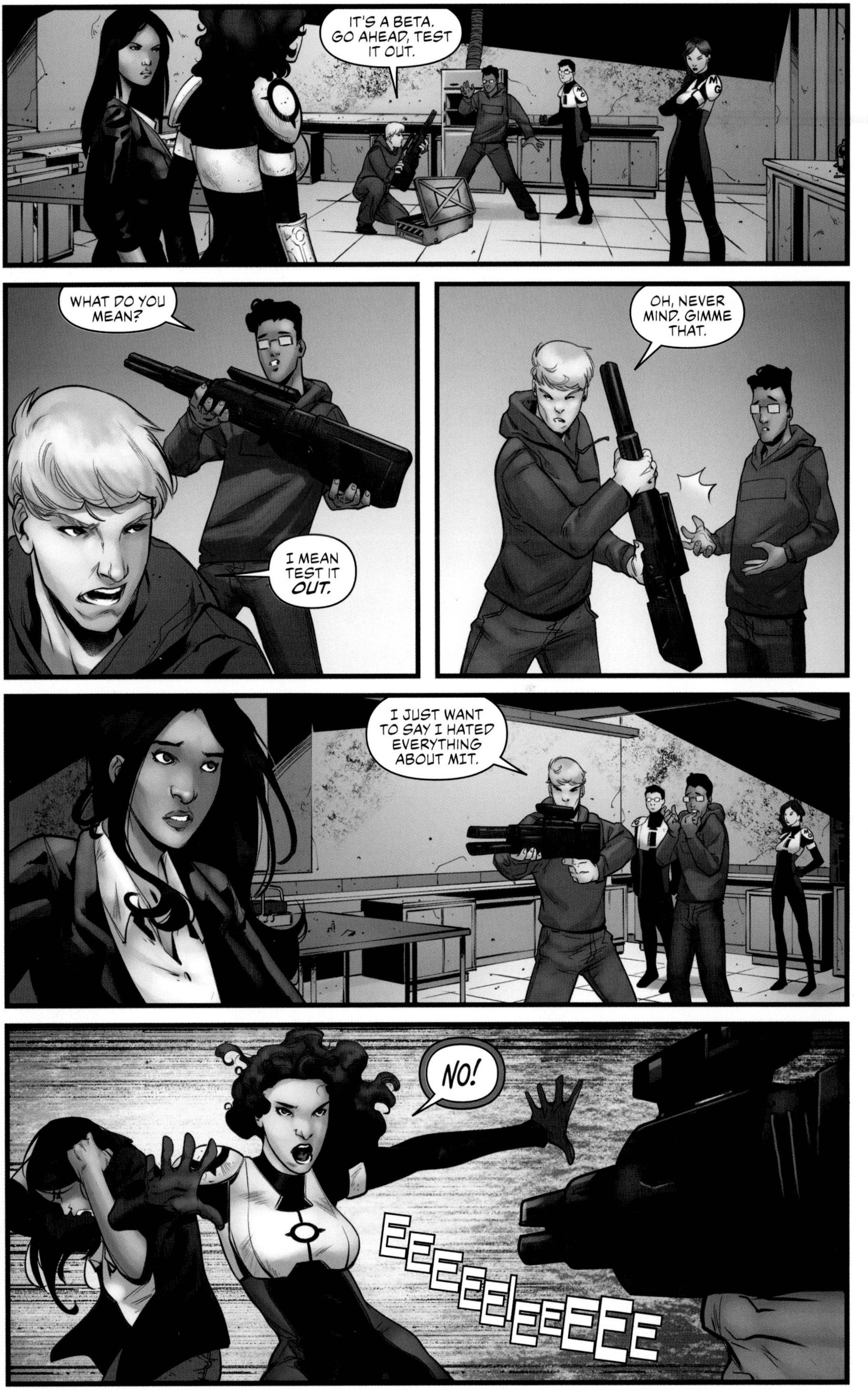
IT'S A BETA. GO AHEAD, TEST IT OUT.
WHAT DO YOU MEAN?
I MEAN TEST IT OUT.
OH, NEVER MIND. GIMME THAT.
I JUST WANT TO SAY I HATED EVERYTHING ABOUT MIT.
NO!
EEEEEEEEEEE

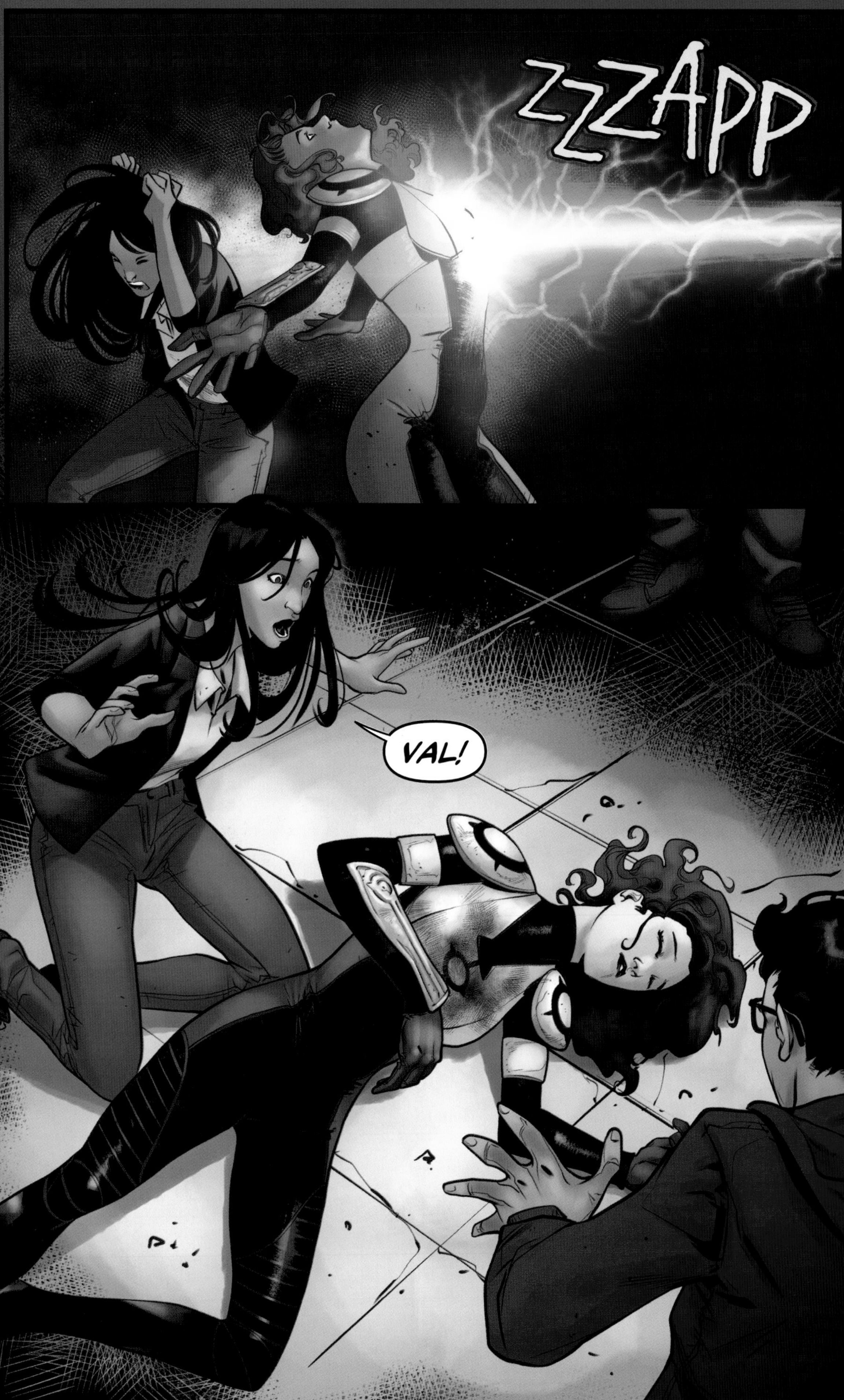
ZZZAPP
VAL!

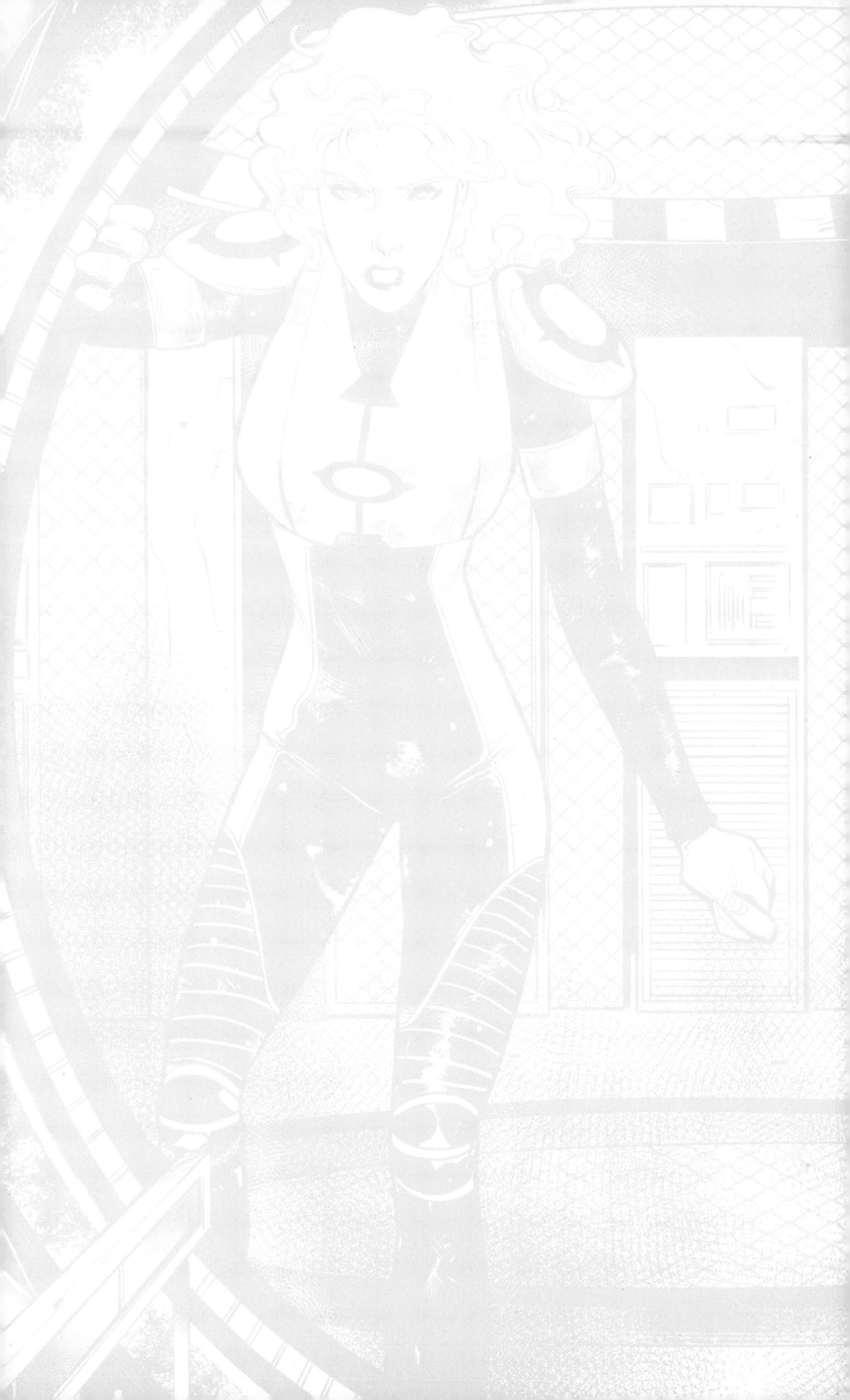

CHAPTER FIVE

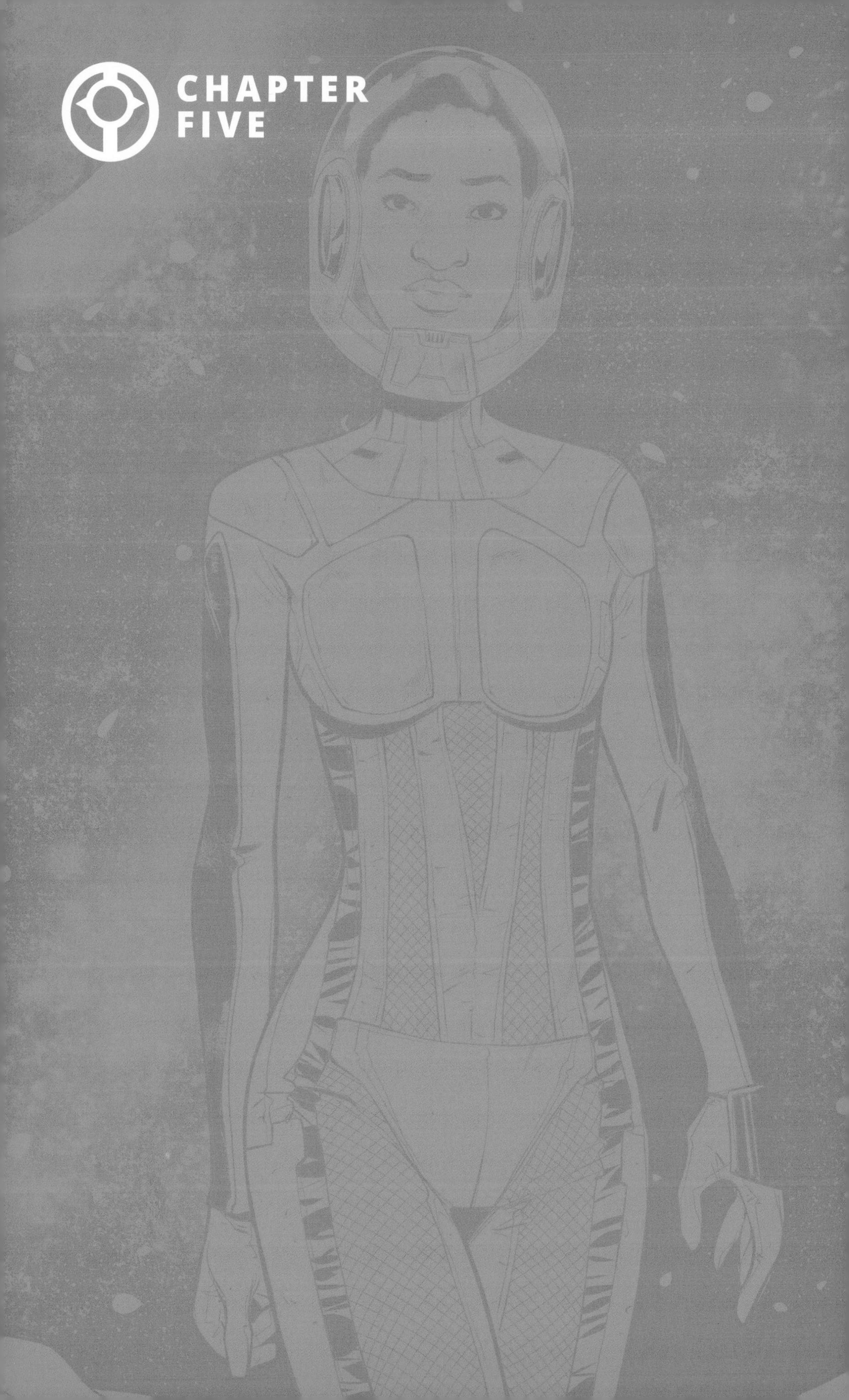

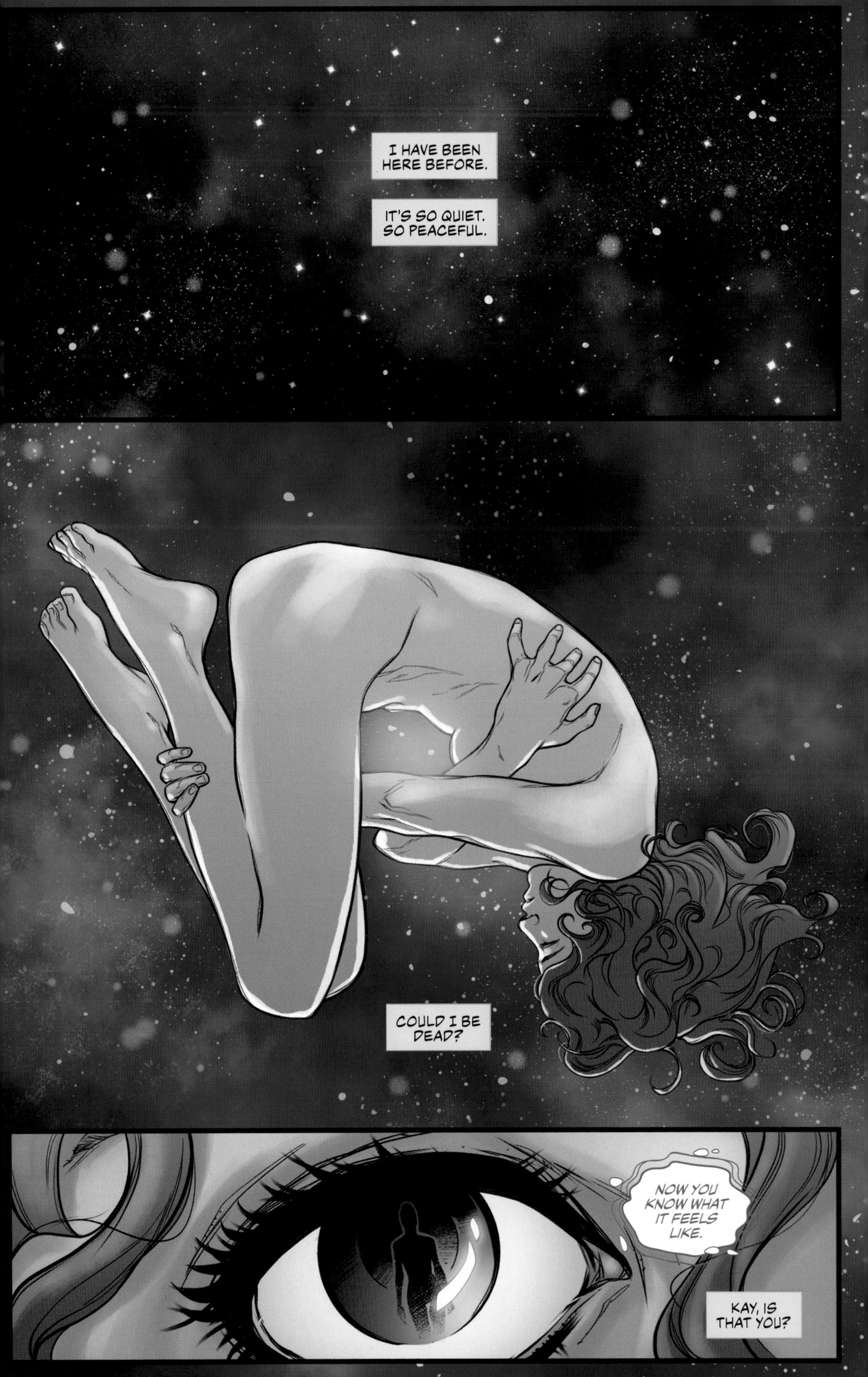
I HAVE BEEN HERE BEFORE.
IT'S SO QUIET. SO PEACEFUL.
COULD I BE DEAD?
NOW YOU KNOW WHAT IT FEELS LIKE.
KAY, IS THAT YOU?

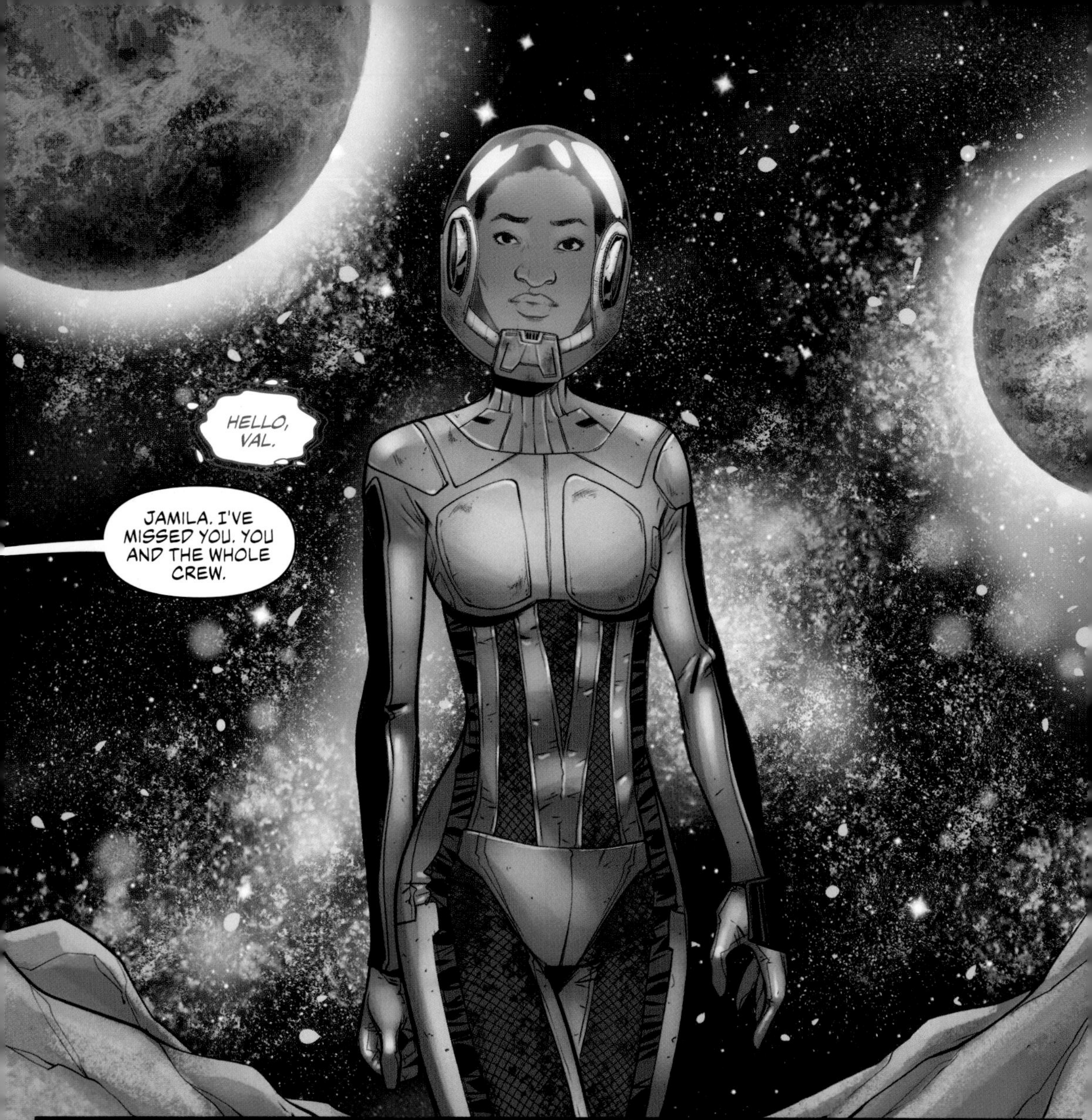
HELLO, VAL.
JAMILA. I'VE MISSED YOU. YOU AND THE WHOLE CREW.

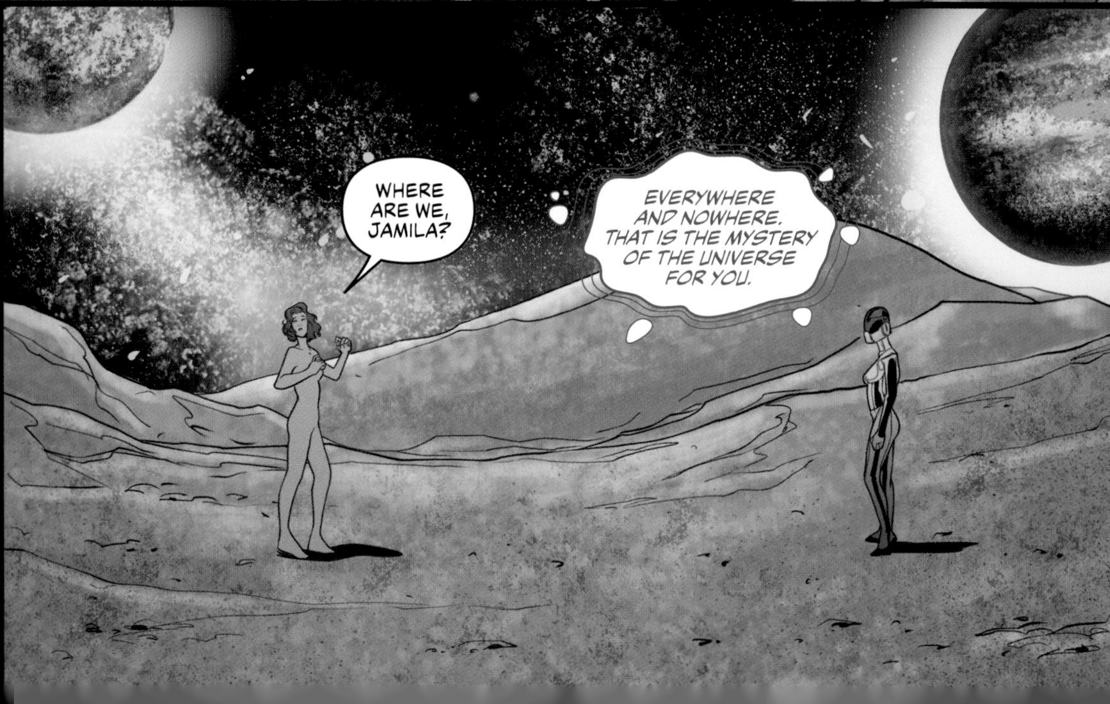
WHERE ARE WE, JAMILA?
EVERYWHERE AND NOWHERE. THAT IS THE MYSTERY OF THE UNIVERSE FOR YOU.

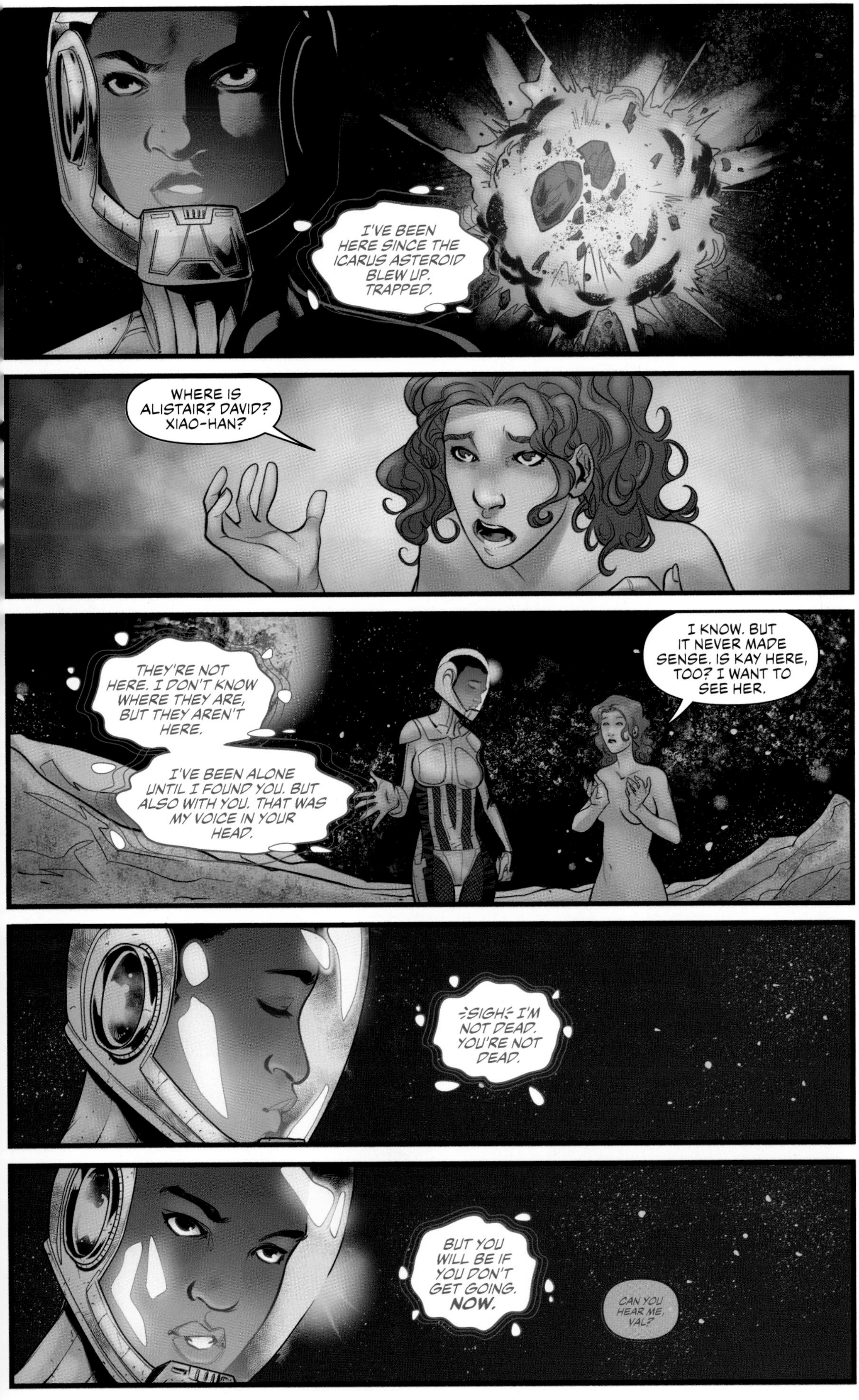
I'VE BEEN HERE SINCE THE ICARUS ASTEROID BLEW UP. TRAPPED.
WHERE IS ALISTAIR? DAVID? XIAO-HAN?
THEY'RE NOT HERE. I DON'T KNOW WHERE THEY ARE, BUT THEY AREN'T HERE.
I'VE BEEN ALONE UNTIL I FOUND YOU. BUT ALSO WITH YOU. THAT WAS MY VOICE IN YOUR HEAD.
I KNOW. BUT IT NEVER MADE SENSE. IS KAY HERE, TOO? I WANT TO SEE HER.
=SIGH= I'M NOT DEAD. YOU'RE NOT DEAD.
BUT YOU WILL BE IF YOU DON'T GET GOING. **NOW.**
CAN YOU HEAR ME, VAL?

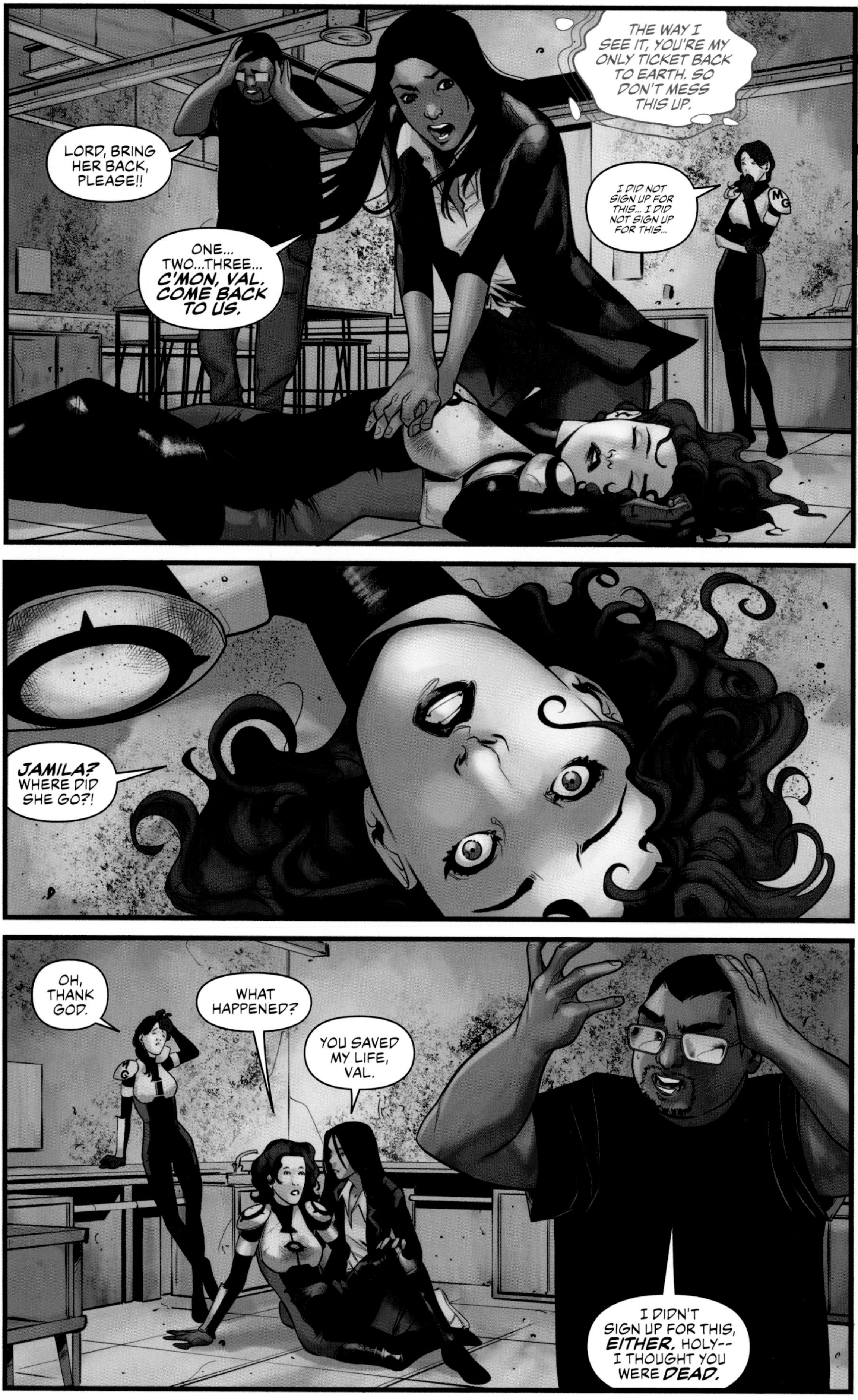
THE WAY I SEE IT, YOU'RE MY ONLY TICKET BACK TO EARTH. SO DON'T MESS THIS UP.
LORD, BRING HER BACK, PLEASE!!
I DID NOT SIGN UP FOR THIS... I DID NOT SIGN UP FOR THIS...
ONE... TWO...THREE... C'MON, VAL, COME BACK TO US.
JAMILA? WHERE DID SHE GO?!
OH, THANK GOD.
WHAT HAPPENED?
YOU SAVED MY LIFE, VAL.
I DIDN'T SIGN UP FOR THIS, EITHER. HOLY-- I THOUGHT YOU WERE DEAD.

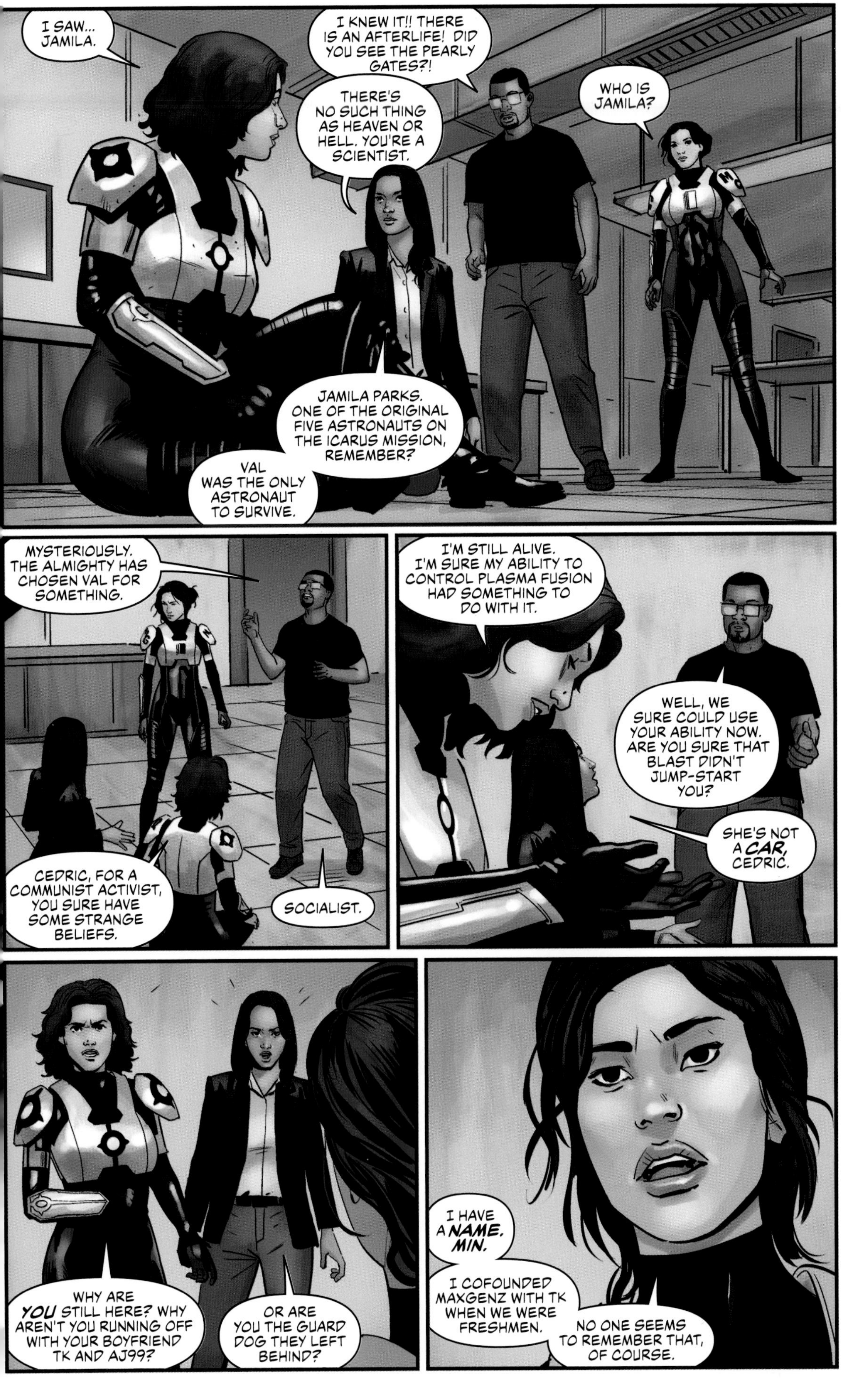
I SAW... JAMILA.
I KNEW IT!! THERE IS AN AFTERLIFE! DID YOU SEE THE PEARLY GATES?!
THERE'S NO SUCH THING AS HEAVEN OR HELL. YOU'RE A SCIENTIST.
WHO IS JAMILA?
JAMILA PARKS. ONE OF THE ORIGINAL FIVE ASTRONAUTS ON THE ICARUS MISSION, REMEMBER?
VAL WAS THE ONLY ASTRONAUT TO SURVIVE.
MYSTERIOUSLY. THE ALMIGHTY HAS CHOSEN VAL FOR SOMETHING.
CEDRIC, FOR A COMMUNIST ACTIVIST, YOU SURE HAVE SOME STRANGE BELIEFS.
SOCIALIST.
I'M STILL ALIVE. I'M SURE MY ABILITY TO CONTROL PLASMA FUSION HAD SOMETHING TO DO WITH IT.
WELL, WE SURE COULD USE YOUR ABILITY NOW. ARE YOU SURE THAT BLAST DIDN'T JUMP-START YOU?
SHE'S NOT A ***CAR,*** CEDRIC.
WHY ARE ***YOU*** STILL HERE? WHY AREN'T YOU RUNNING OFF WITH YOUR BOYFRIEND TK AND AJ99?
OR ARE YOU THE GUARD DOG THEY LEFT BEHIND?
I HAVE A ***NAME, MIN.***
I COFOUNDED MAXGENZ WITH TK WHEN WE WERE FRESHMEN.
NO ONE SEEMS TO REMEMBER THAT, OF COURSE.

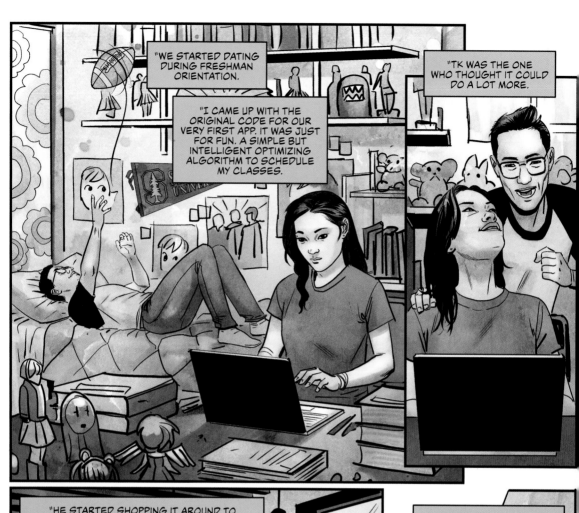

"WE STARTED DATING DURING FRESHMAN ORIENTATION.

"I CAME UP WITH THE ORIGINAL CODE FOR OUR VERY FIRST APP. IT WAS JUST FOR FUN. A SIMPLE BUT INTELLIGENT OPTIMIZING ALGORITHM TO SCHEDULE MY CLASSES.

"TK WAS THE ONE WHO THOUGHT IT COULD DO A LOT MORE.

"HE STARTED SHOPPING IT AROUND TO VENTURE CAPITALISTS. AJ99 AGREED TO A MEETING. I WAS NERVOUS, SO TK WENT ALONE. HE WAS WORRIED I WOULD GET IN THE WAY.

"TURNED OUT AJ99 WAS IMPRESSED. HE THOUGHT IT WAS TK'S IDEA AND GAVE THE INITIAL SEED FUNDING TO GET MAXGENZ GOING. I WENT ALONG WITH IT BECAUSE I DIDN'T WANT TO SCREW THE DEAL UP."

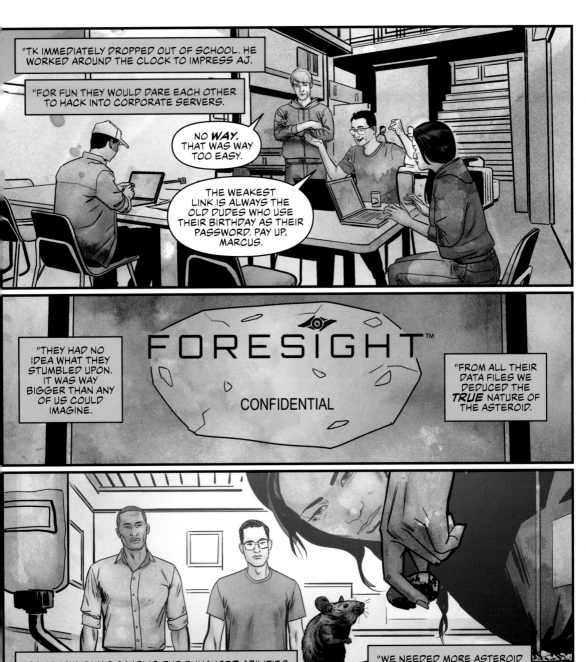

"TK IMMEDIATELY DROPPED OUT OF SCHOOL. HE WORKED AROUND THE CLOCK TO IMPRESS AJ.

"FOR FUN THEY WOULD DARE EACH OTHER TO HACK INTO CORPORATE SERVERS.

NO **WAY.** THAT WAS WAY TOO EASY.

THE WEAKEST LINK IS ALWAYS THE OLD DUDES WHO USE THEIR BIRTHDAY AS THEIR PASSWORD. PAY UP, MARCUS.

FORESIGHT™

CONFIDENTIAL

"THEY HAD NO IDEA WHAT THEY STUMBLED UPON. IT WAS WAY BIGGER THAN ANY OF US COULD IMAGINE.

"FROM ALL THEIR DATA FILES WE DEDUCED THE **TRUE** NATURE OF THE ASTEROID.

"SOMEHOW IT WAS CAUSING THE ENHANCED ABILITIES WE SAW AROUND THE WORLD. AND THAT'S WHY LORENA WAS CORNERING THE MARKET IN SECRET.

"WE NEEDED MORE ASTEROID MATERIAL. AJ99 AND TK WERE OBSESSED WITH BEATING LORENA AT THIS GAME.

"MARCUS FIGURED OUT THE EASIEST WAY WAS TO STEAL IT. HE LOVED THE CLOAK-AND-DAGGER STUFF.

"I DIDN'T LIKE WHAT HE WAS DOING, BUT TK AND AJ99 DIDN'T CARE HOW THINGS WERE DONE AS LONG AS THEY WERE GETTING WHAT THEY WANTED."

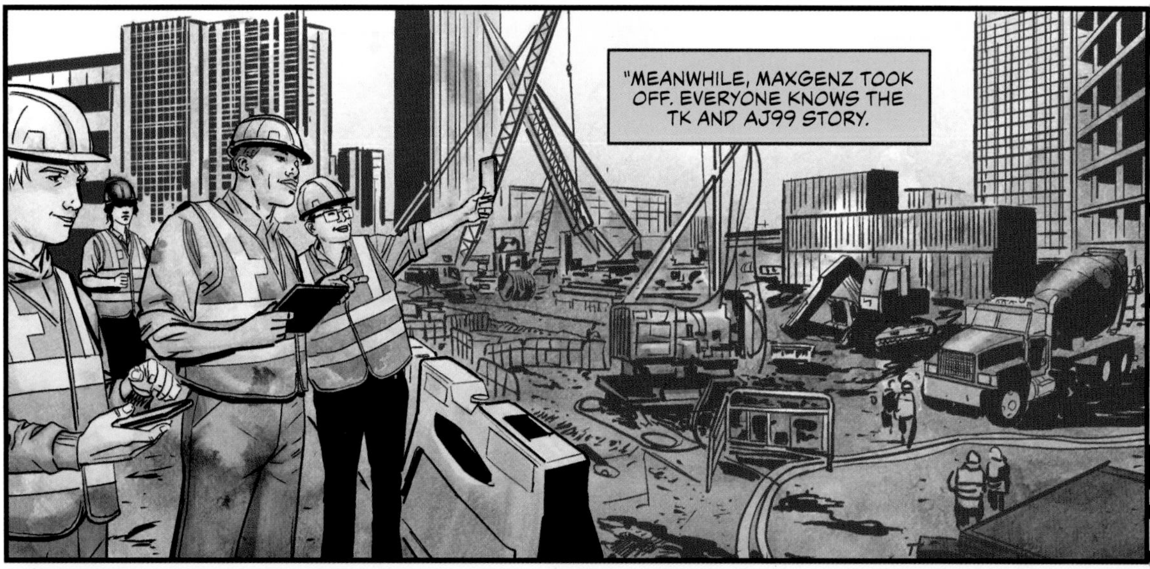
"MEANWHILE, MAXGENZ TOOK OFF. EVERYONE KNOWS THE TK AND AJ99 STORY.

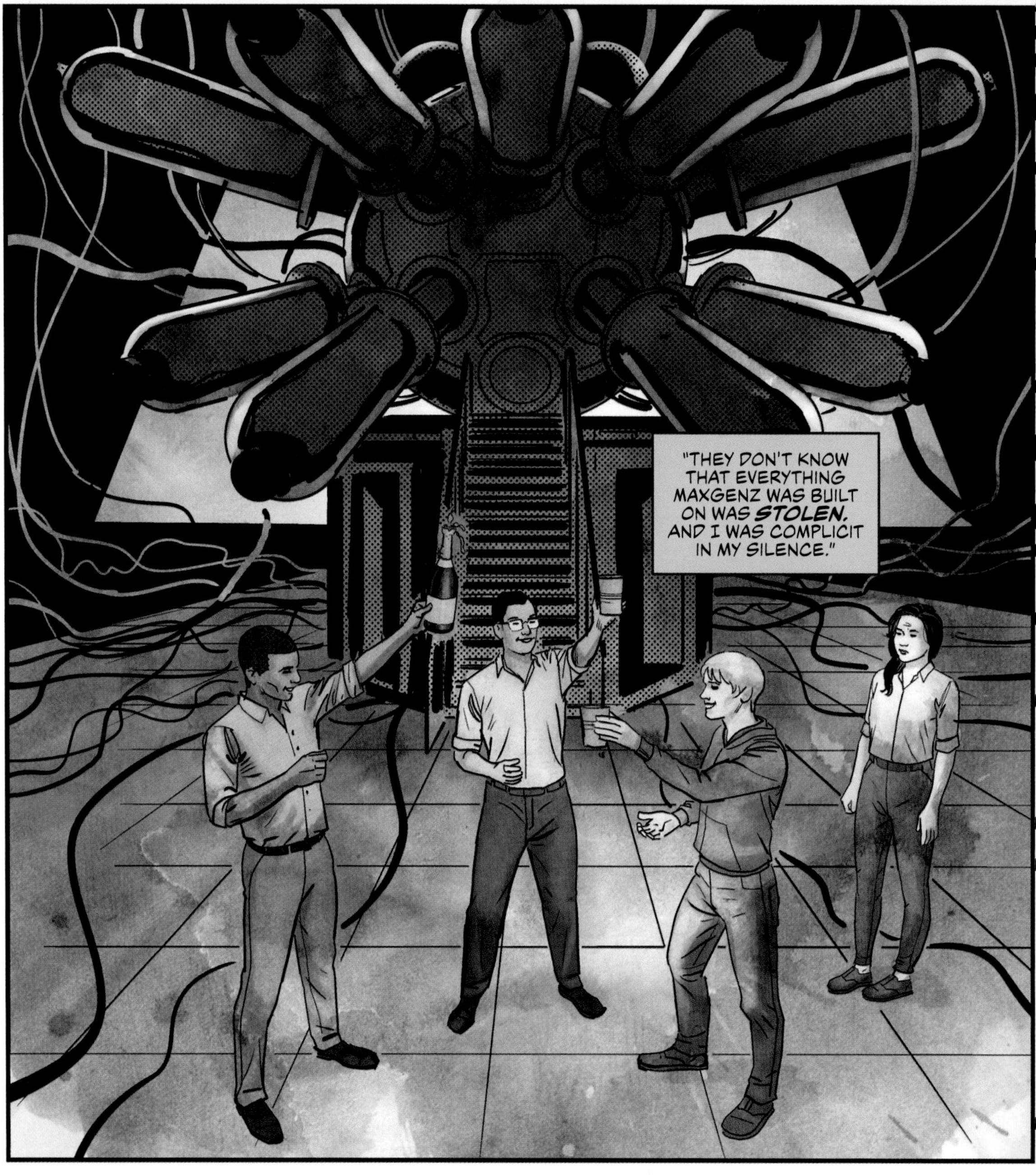
"THEY DON'T KNOW THAT EVERYTHING MAXGENZ WAS BUILT ON WAS ***STOLEN,*** AND I WAS COMPLICIT IN MY SILENCE."

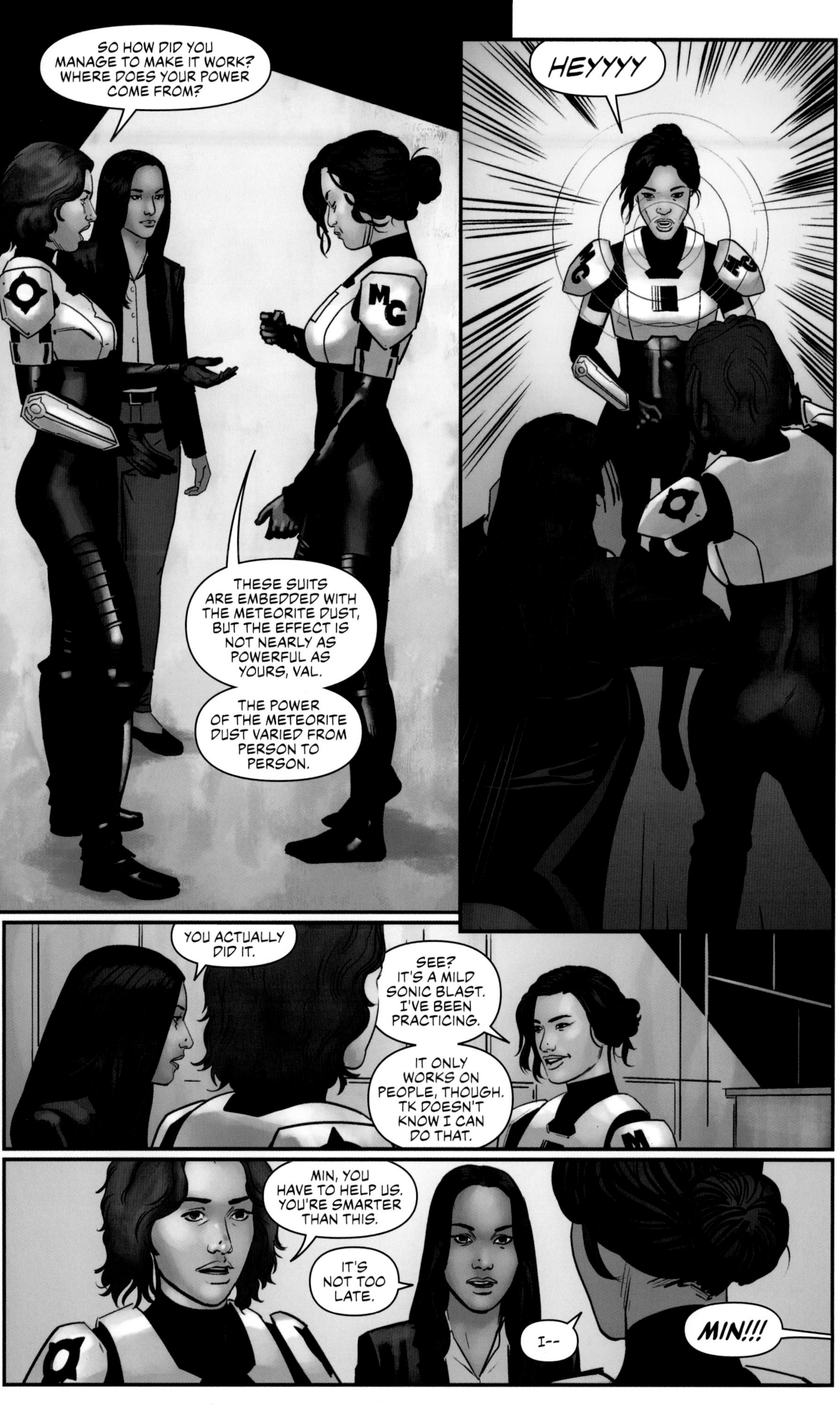

SO HOW DID YOU MANAGE TO MAKE IT WORK? WHERE DOES YOUR POWER COME FROM?
THESE SUITS ARE EMBEDDED WITH THE METEORITE DUST, BUT THE EFFECT IS NOT NEARLY AS POWERFUL AS YOURS, VAL.
THE POWER OF THE METEORITE DUST VARIED FROM PERSON TO PERSON.
HEYYYY
YOU ACTUALLY DID IT.
SEE? IT'S A MILD SONIC BLAST. I'VE BEEN PRACTICING.
IT ONLY WORKS ON PEOPLE, THOUGH. TK DOESN'T KNOW I CAN DO THAT.
MIN, YOU HAVE TO HELP US. YOU'RE SMARTER THAN THIS.
IT'S NOT TOO LATE.
I--
MIN!!!

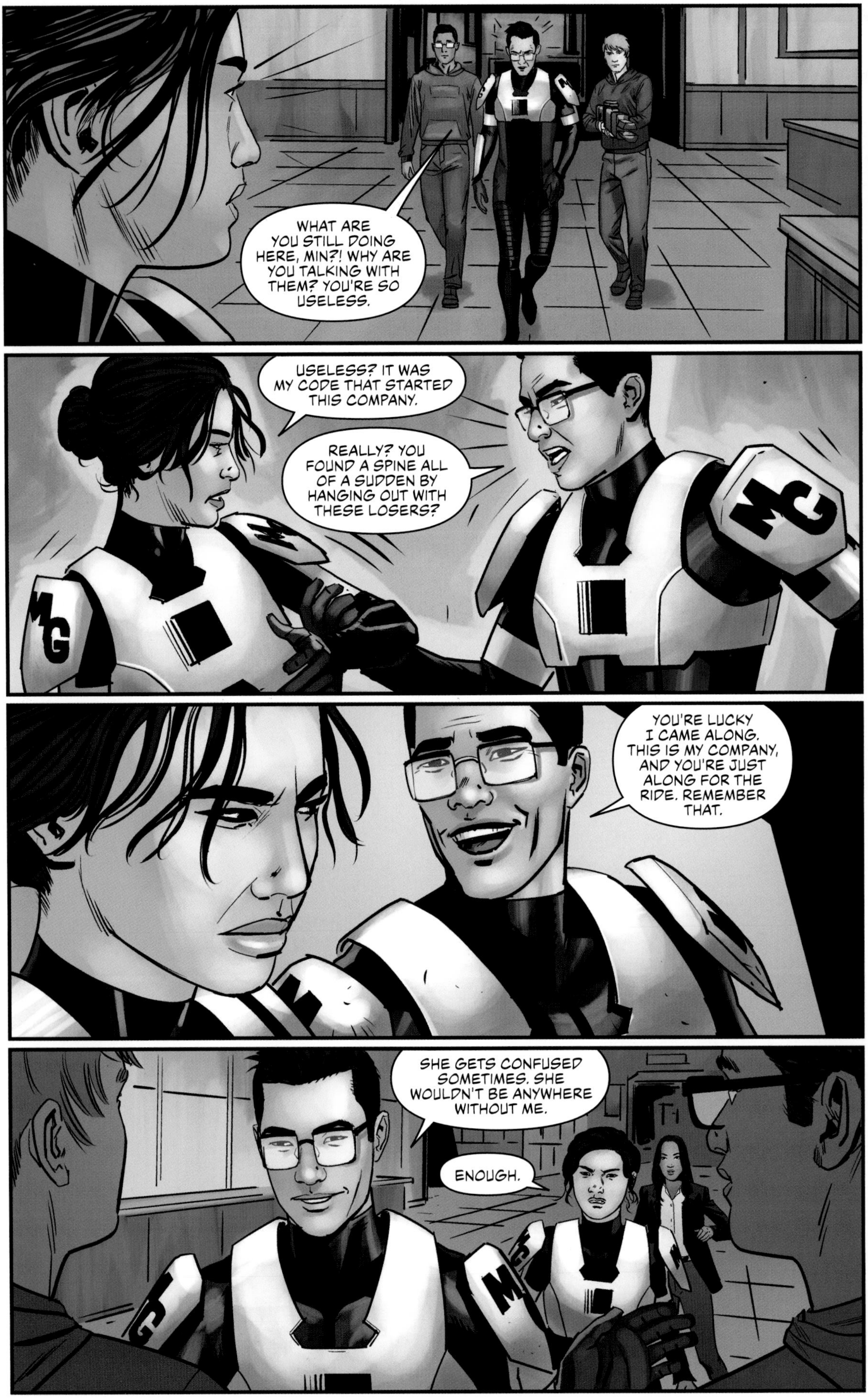
WHAT ARE YOU STILL DOING HERE, MIN?! WHY ARE YOU TALKING WITH THEM? YOU'RE SO USELESS.
USELESS? IT WAS MY CODE THAT STARTED THIS COMPANY.
REALLY? YOU FOUND A SPINE ALL OF A SUDDEN BY HANGING OUT WITH THESE LOSERS?
YOU'RE LUCKY I CAME ALONG. THIS IS MY COMPANY, AND YOU'RE JUST ALONG FOR THE RIDE. REMEMBER THAT.
SHE GETS CONFUSED SOMETIMES. SHE WOULDN'T BE ANYWHERE WITHOUT ME.
ENOUGH.

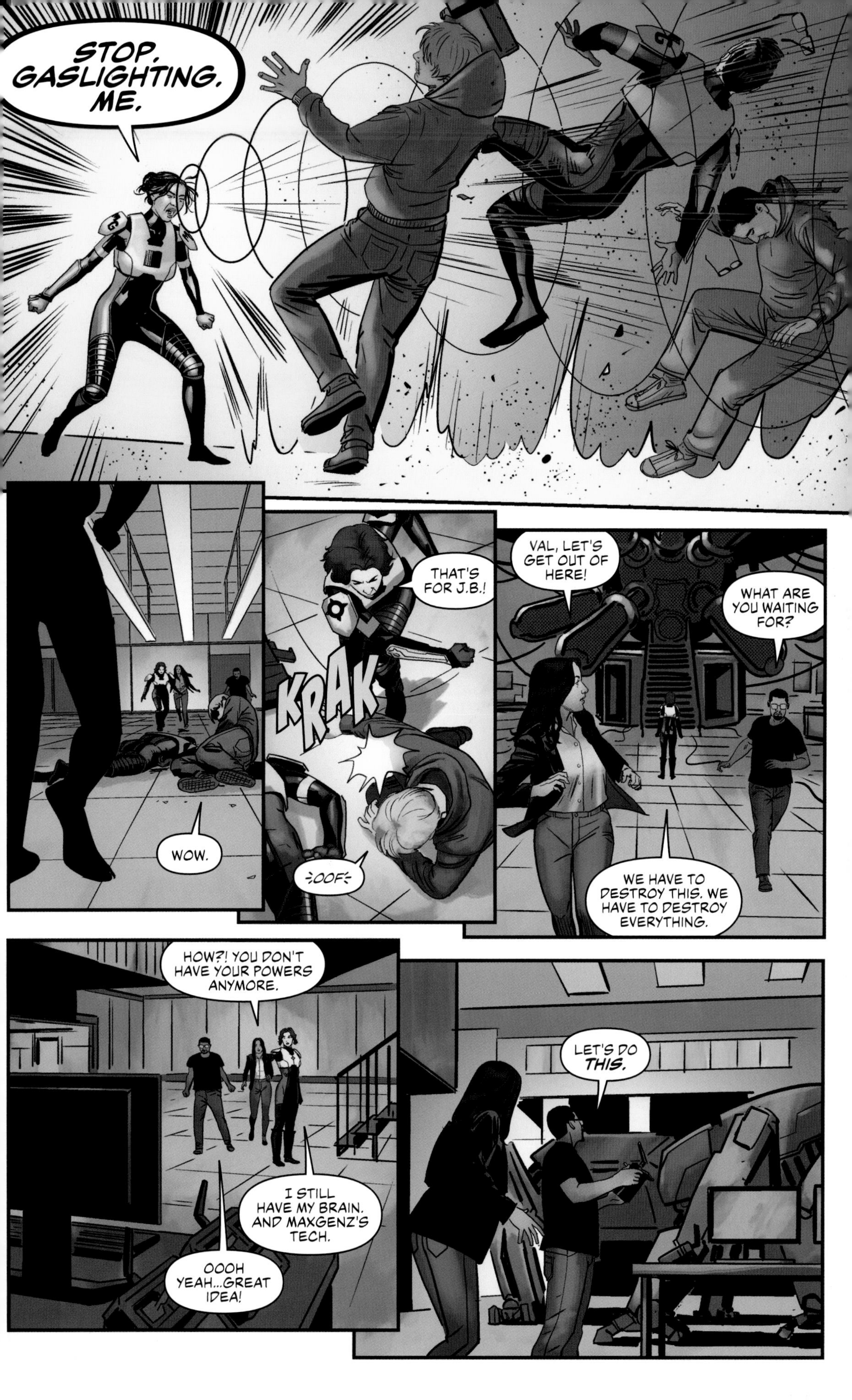
STOP. GASLIGHTING. ME.
WOW.
THAT'S FOR J.B.!
KRAK
OOF
VAL, LET'S GET OUT OF HERE!
WHAT ARE YOU WAITING FOR?
WE HAVE TO DESTROY THIS. WE HAVE TO DESTROY EVERYTHING.
HOW?! YOU DON'T HAVE YOUR POWERS ANYMORE.
I STILL HAVE MY BRAIN. AND MAXGENZ'S TECH.
OOOH YEAH...GREAT IDEA!
LET'S DO THIS.

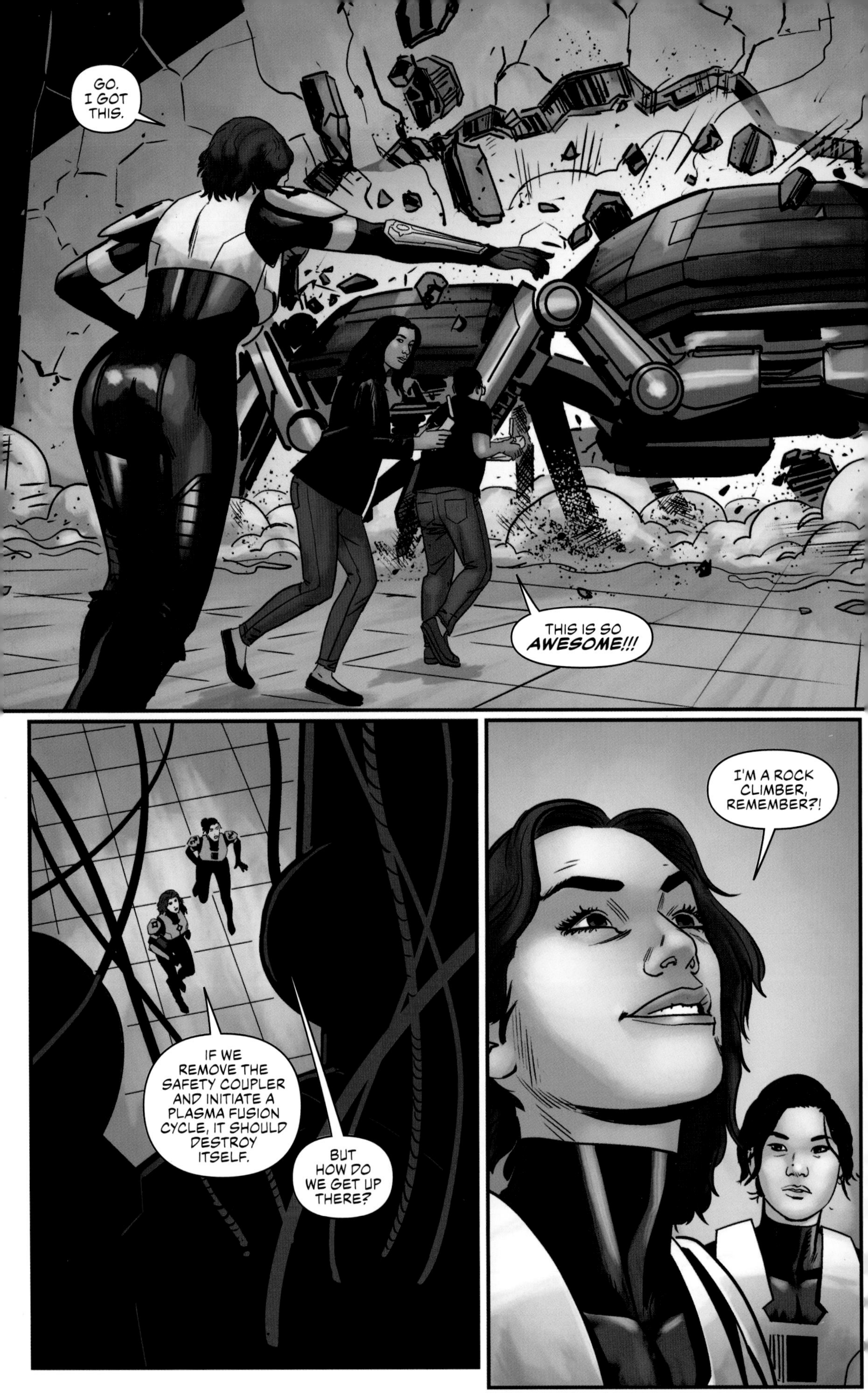
GO. I GOT THIS.
THIS IS SO AWESOME!!!
IF WE REMOVE THE SAFETY COUPLER AND INITIATE A PLASMA FUSION CYCLE, IT SHOULD DESTROY ITSELF.
BUT HOW DO WE GET UP THERE?
I'M A ROCK CLIMBER, REMEMBER?!

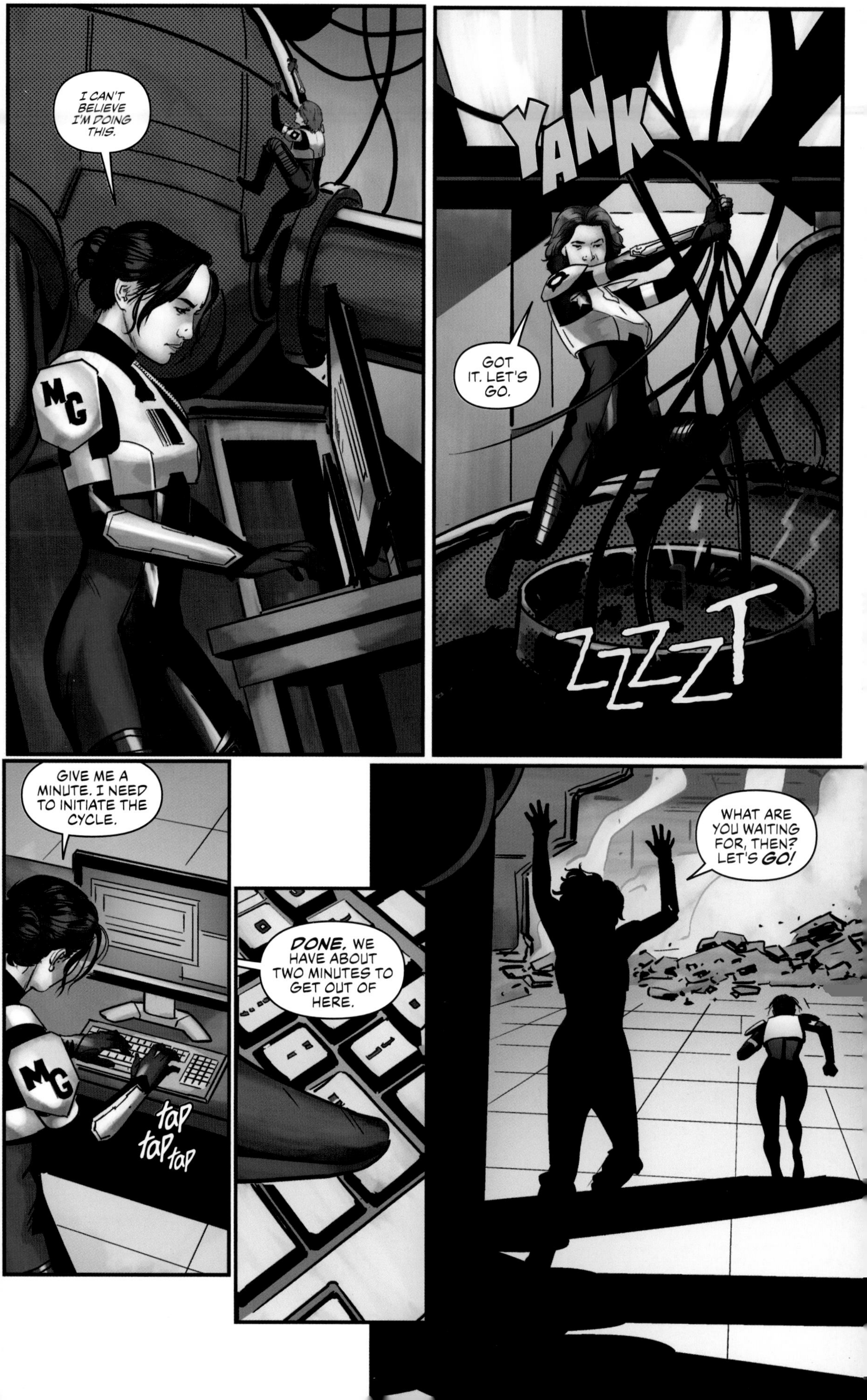
I CAN'T BELIEVE I'M DOING THIS.
YANK
GOT IT. LET'S GO.
ZZZZT
GIVE ME A MINUTE. I NEED TO INITIATE THE CYCLE.
tap tap tap
DONE. WE HAVE ABOUT TWO MINUTES TO GET OUT OF HERE.
WHAT ARE YOU WAITING FOR, THEN? LET'S GO!

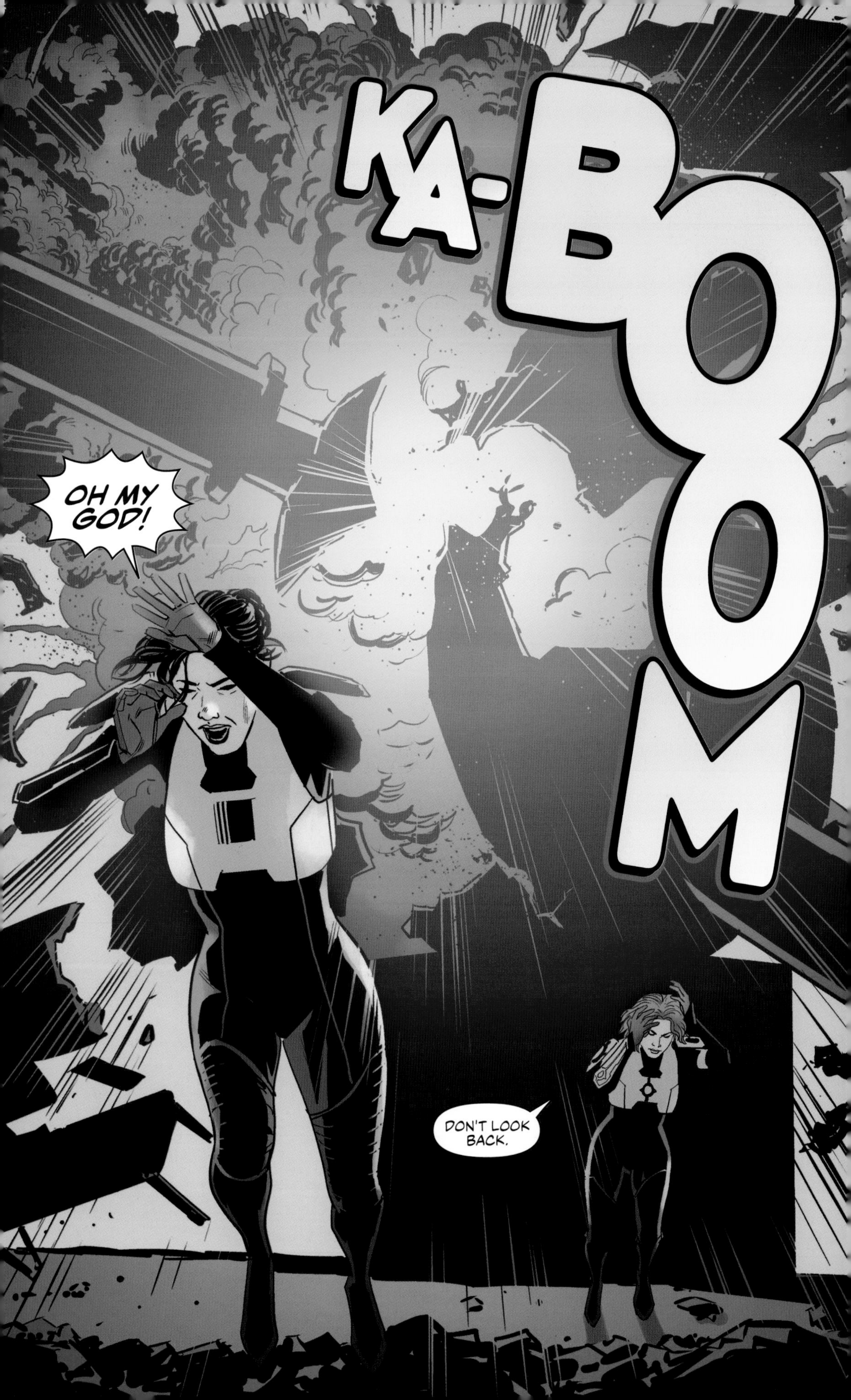
KA-BOOM
OH MY GOD!
DON'T LOOK BACK.

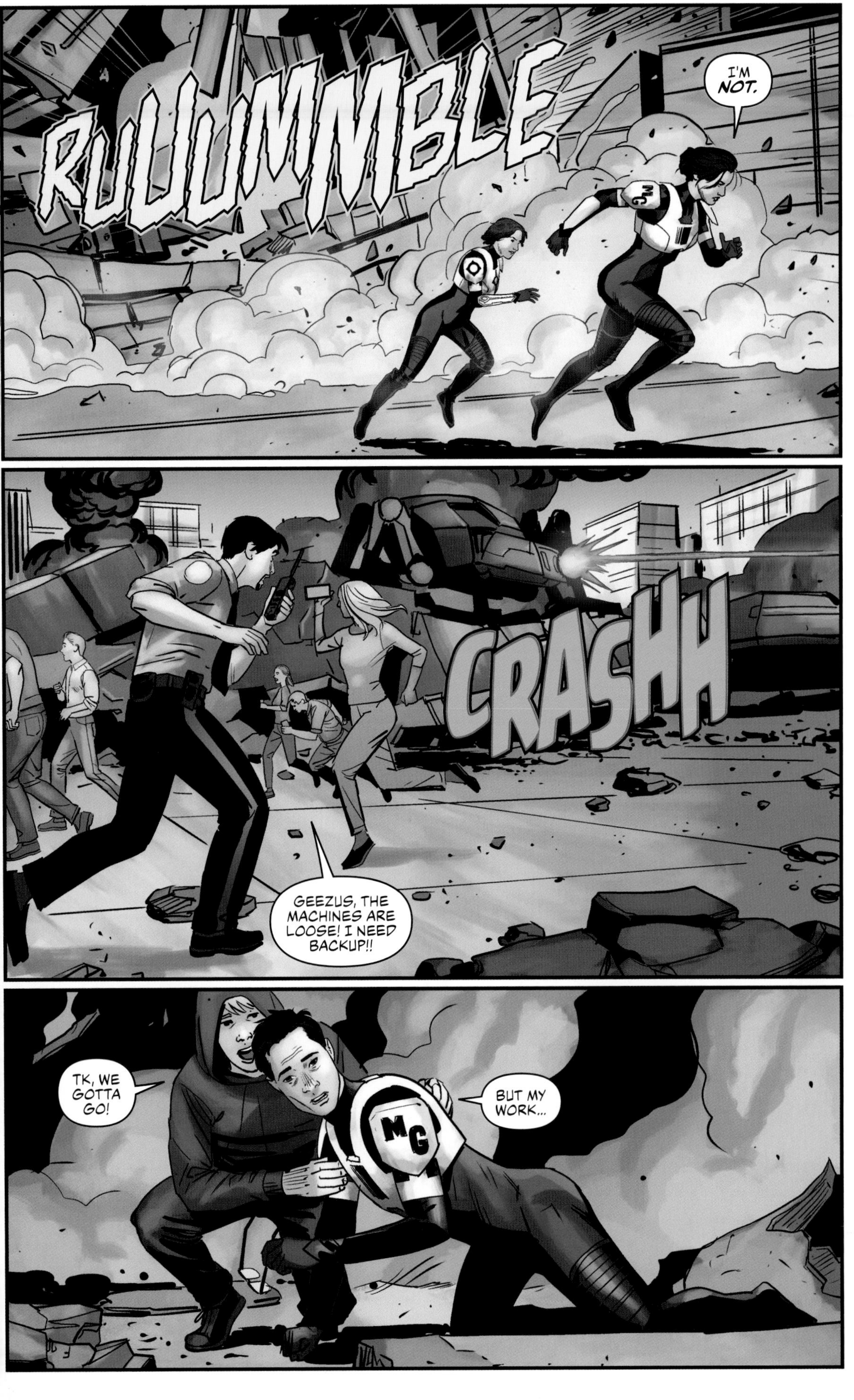
RUUMMBLE
I'M NOT.
CRASHH
GEEZUS, THE MACHINES ARE LOOSE! I NEED BACKUP!!
MG
TK, WE GOTTA GO!
BUT MY WORK...

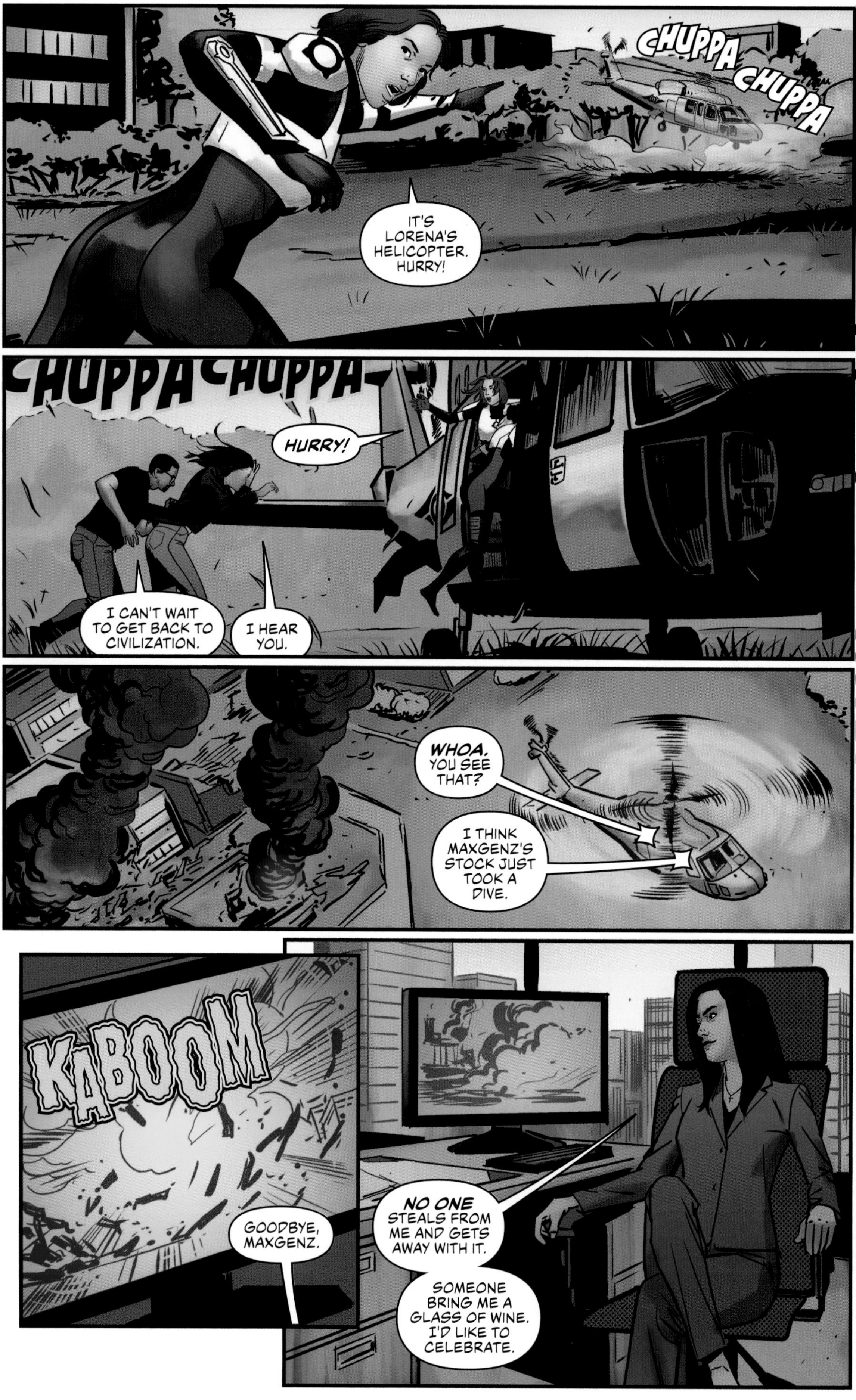
CHUPPA CHUPPA
IT'S LORENA'S HELICOPTER. HURRY!
CHUPPA CHUPPA
HURRY!
I CAN'T WAIT TO GET BACK TO CIVILIZATION.
I HEAR YOU.
WHOA. YOU SEE THAT?
I THINK MAXGENZ'S STOCK JUST TOOK A DIVE.
KABOOM
GOODBYE, MAXGENZ.
NO ONE STEALS FROM ME AND GETS AWAY WITH IT.
SOMEONE BRING ME A GLASS OF WINE. I'D LIKE TO CELEBRATE.

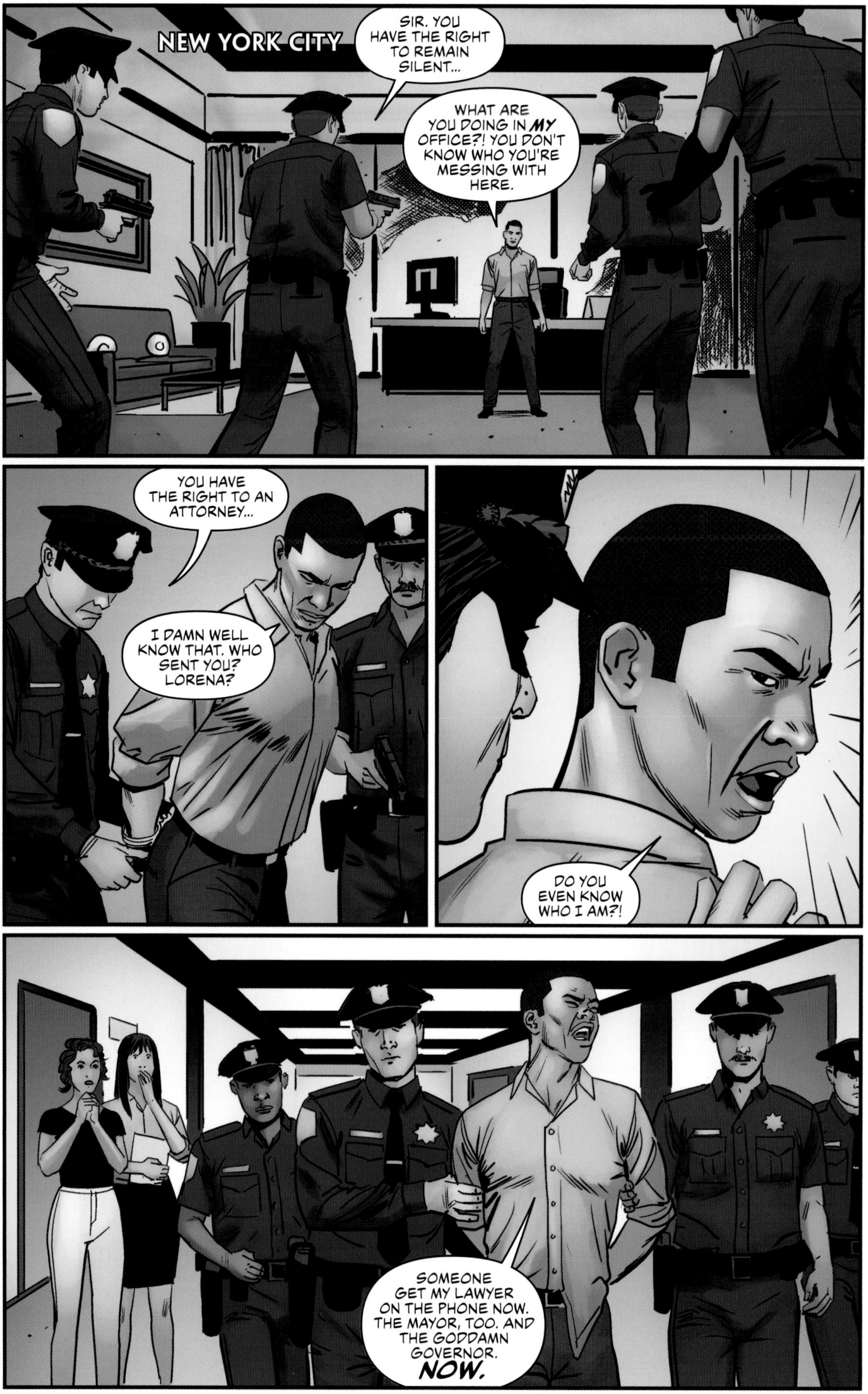
NEW YORK CITY
SIR. YOU HAVE THE RIGHT TO REMAIN SILENT...
WHAT ARE YOU DOING IN MY OFFICE?! YOU DON'T KNOW WHO YOU'RE MESSING WITH HERE.
YOU HAVE THE RIGHT TO AN ATTORNEY...
I DAMN WELL KNOW THAT. WHO SENT YOU? LORENA?
DO YOU EVEN KNOW WHO I AM?!
SOMEONE GET MY LAWYER ON THE PHONE NOW. THE MAYOR, TOO. AND THE GODDAMN GOVERNOR. NOW.

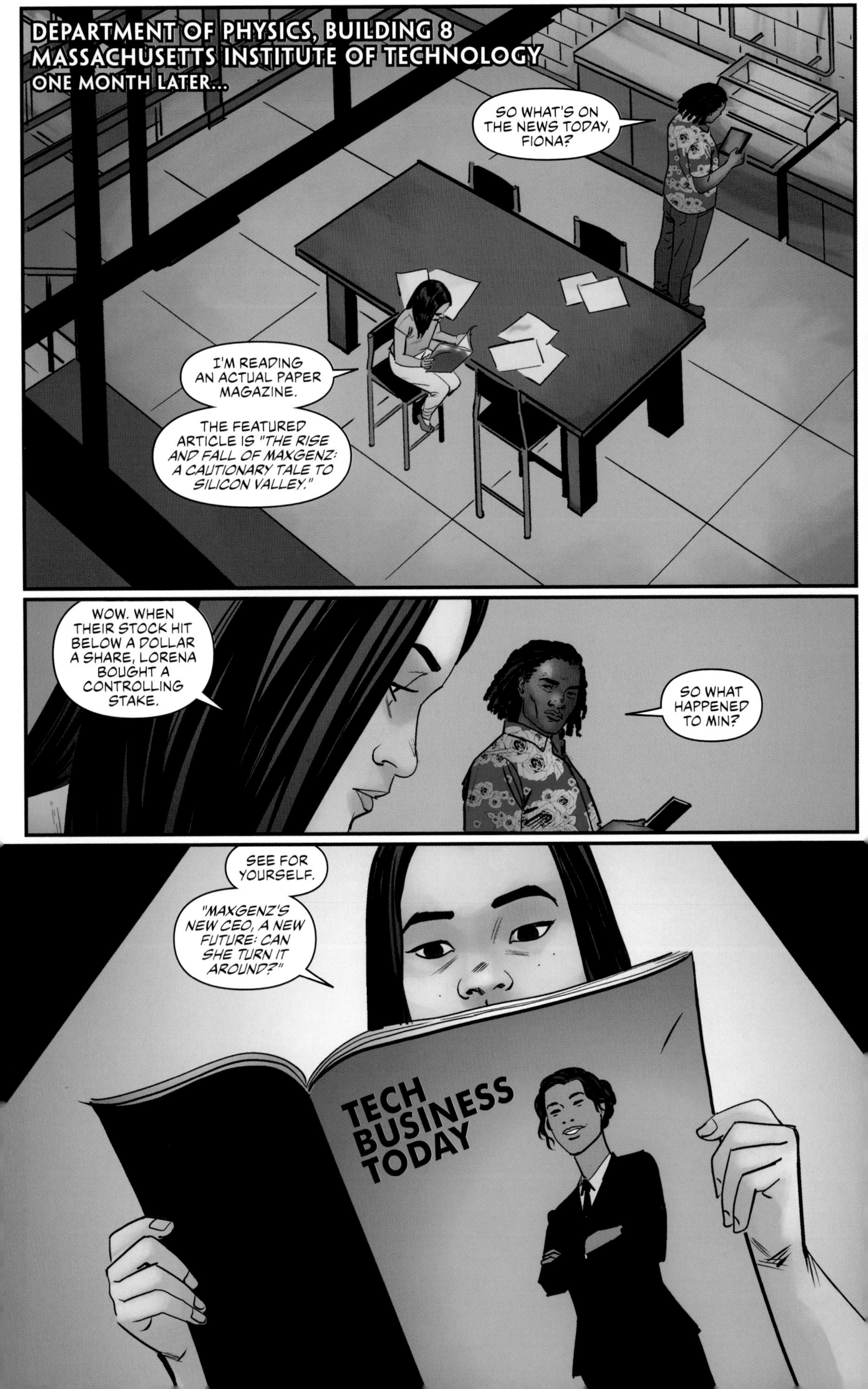
DEPARTMENT OF PHYSICS, BUILDING 8
MASSACHUSETTS INSTITUTE OF TECHNOLOGY
ONE MONTH LATER...
SO WHAT'S ON THE NEWS TODAY, FIONA?
I'M READING AN ACTUAL PAPER MAGAZINE.
THE FEATURED ARTICLE IS "THE RISE AND FALL OF MAXGENZ: A CAUTIONARY TALE TO SILICON VALLEY."
WOW. WHEN THEIR STOCK HIT BELOW A DOLLAR A SHARE, LORENA BOUGHT A CONTROLLING STAKE.
SO WHAT HAPPENED TO MIN?
SEE FOR YOURSELF.
"MAXGENZ'S NEW CEO, A NEW FUTURE: CAN SHE TURN IT AROUND?"
TECH BUSINESS TODAY

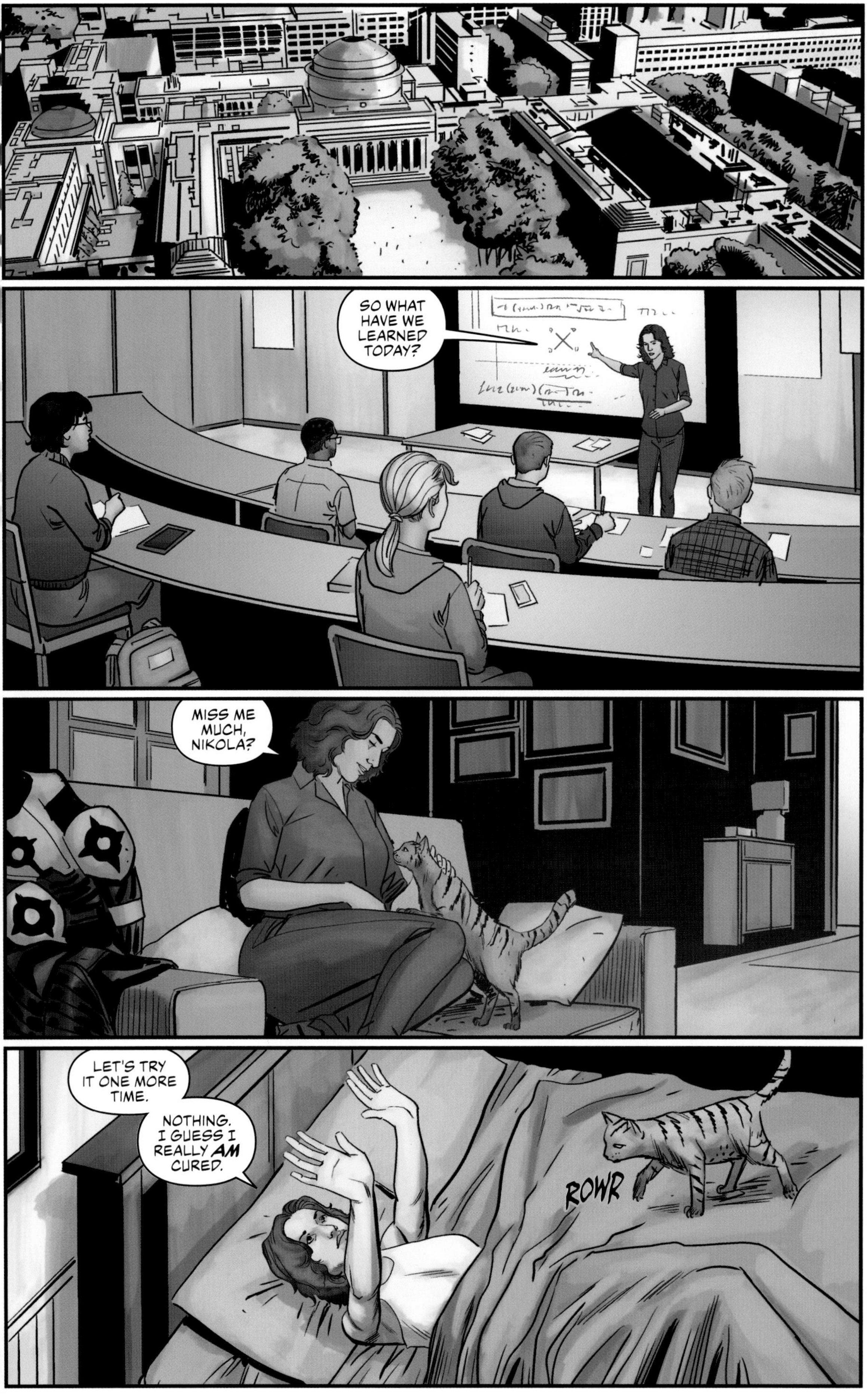
SO WHAT HAVE WE LEARNED TODAY?
MISS ME MUCH, NIKOLA?
LET'S TRY IT ONE MORE TIME.
NOTHING. I GUESS I REALLY AM CURED.
ROWR

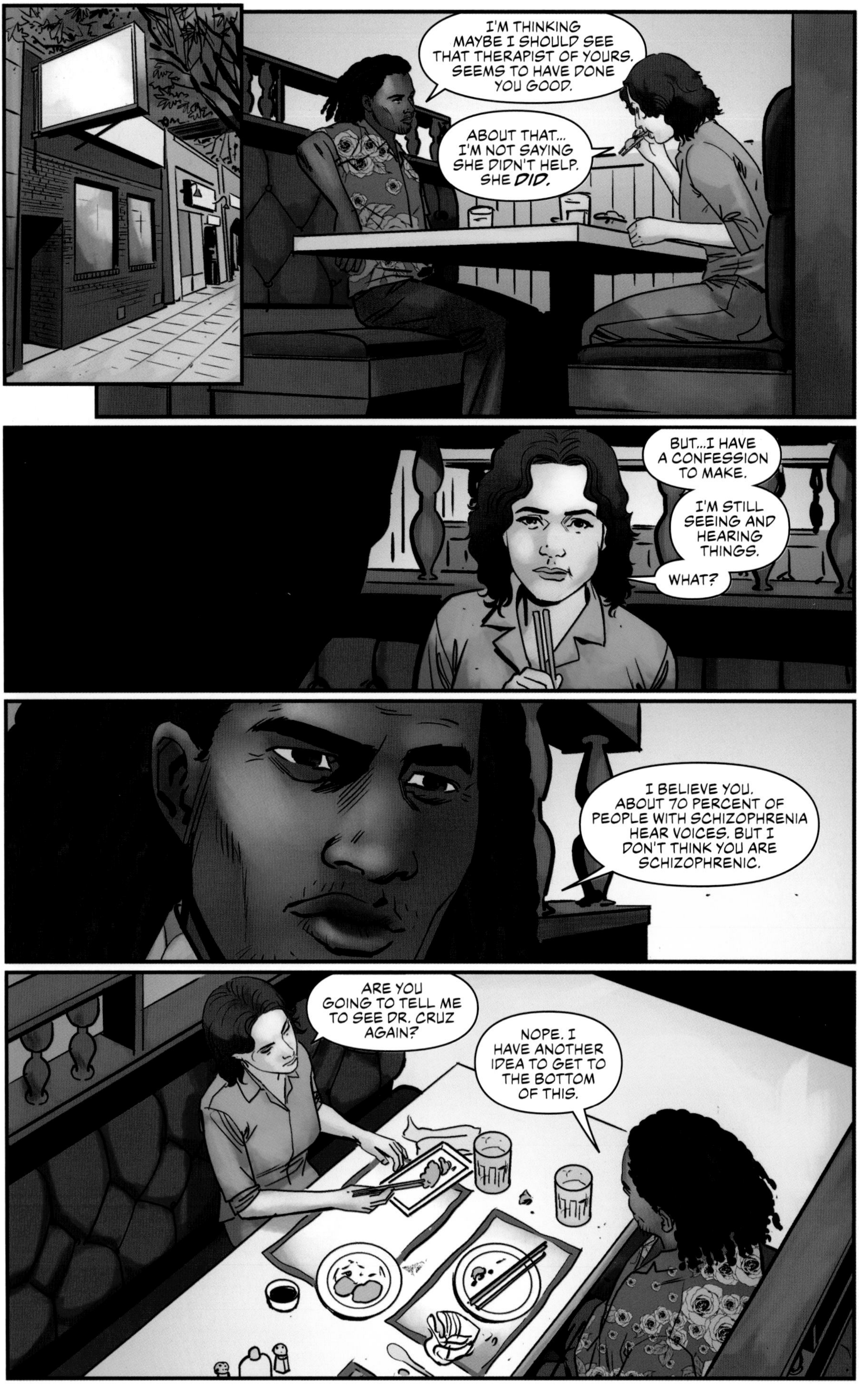
I'M THINKING MAYBE I SHOULD SEE THAT THERAPIST OF YOURS. SEEMS TO HAVE DONE YOU GOOD.
ABOUT THAT... I'M NOT SAYING SHE DIDN'T HELP. SHE DID.
BUT...I HAVE A CONFESSION TO MAKE.
I'M STILL SEEING AND HEARING THINGS.
WHAT?
I BELIEVE YOU. ABOUT 70 PERCENT OF PEOPLE WITH SCHIZOPHRENIA HEAR VOICES. BUT I DON'T THINK YOU ARE SCHIZOPHRENIC.
ARE YOU GOING TO TELL ME TO SEE DR. CRUZ AGAIN?
NOPE. I HAVE ANOTHER IDEA TO GET TO THE BOTTOM OF THIS.

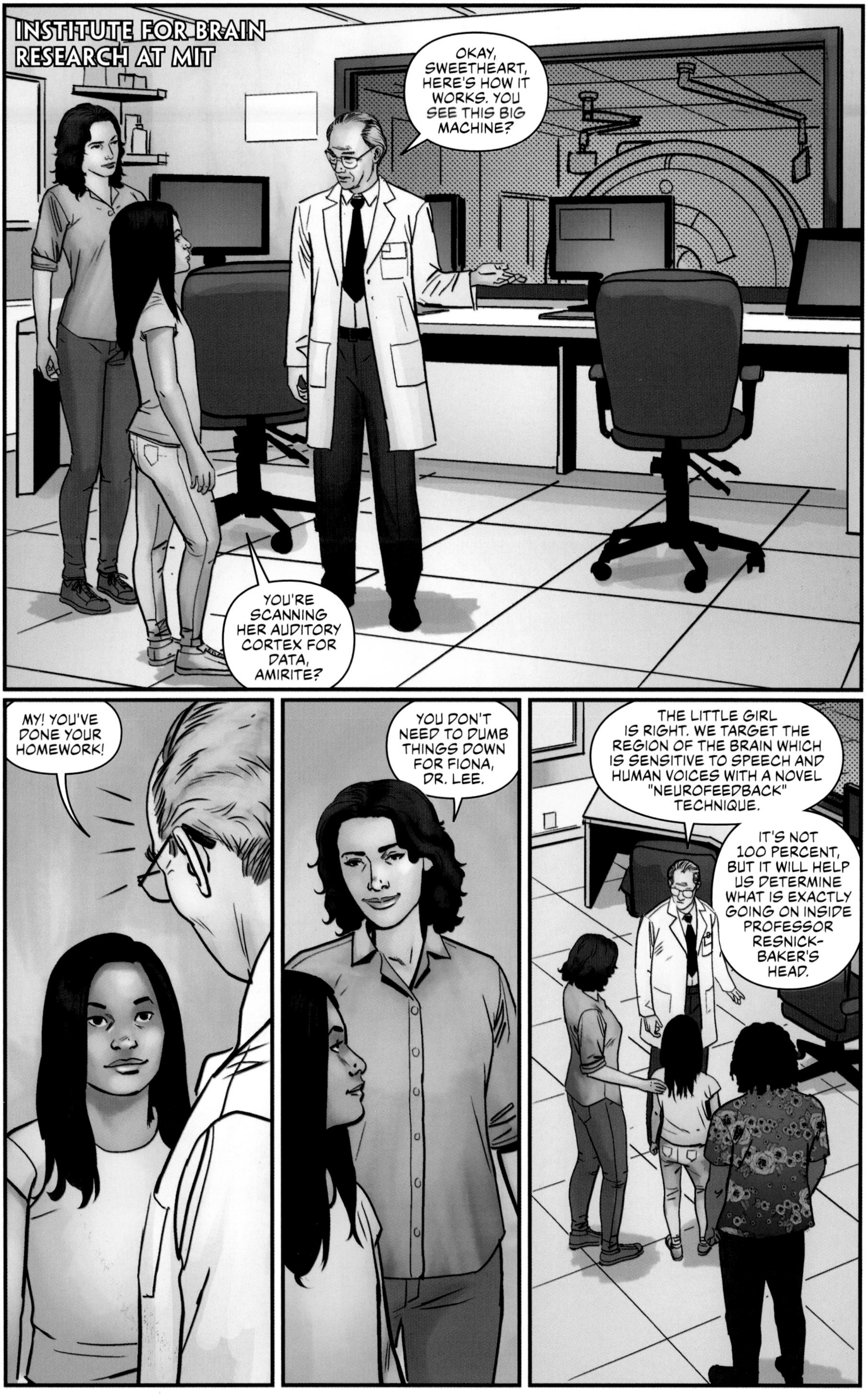
INSTITUTE FOR BRAIN RESEARCH AT MIT
OKAY, SWEETHEART, HERE'S HOW IT WORKS. YOU SEE THIS BIG MACHINE?
YOU'RE SCANNING HER AUDITORY CORTEX FOR DATA, AMIRITE?
MY! YOU'VE DONE YOUR HOMEWORK!
YOU DON'T NEED TO DUMB THINGS DOWN FOR FIONA, DR. LEE.
THE LITTLE GIRL IS RIGHT. WE TARGET THE REGION OF THE BRAIN WHICH IS SENSITIVE TO SPEECH AND HUMAN VOICES WITH A NOVEL "NEUROFEEDBACK" TECHNIQUE.
IT'S NOT 100 PERCENT, BUT IT WILL HELP US DETERMINE WHAT IS EXACTLY GOING ON INSIDE PROFESSOR RESNICK-BAKER'S HEAD.

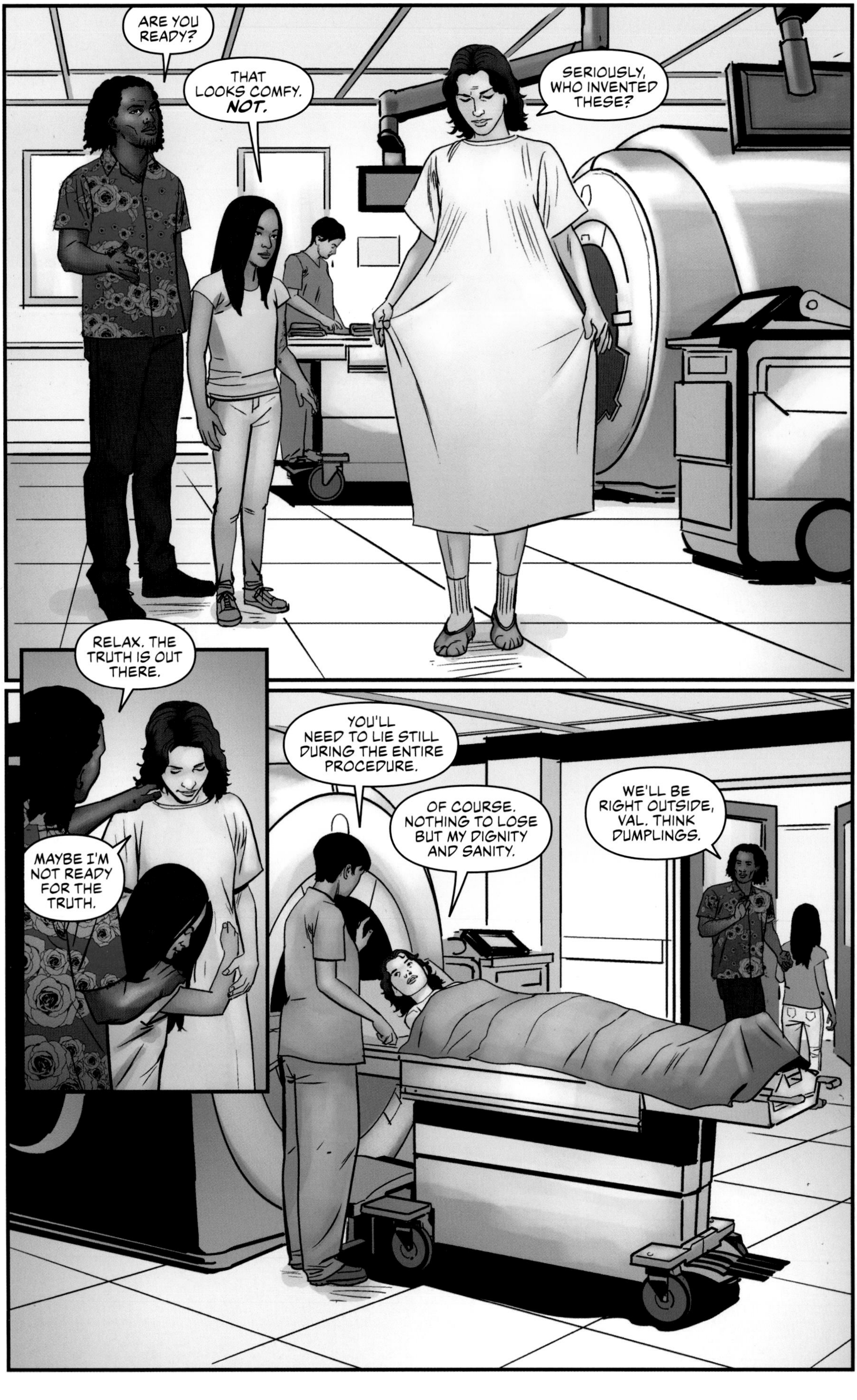
ARE YOU READY?
THAT LOOKS COMFY. NOT.
SERIOUSLY, WHO INVENTED THESE?
RELAX. THE TRUTH IS OUT THERE.
MAYBE I'M NOT READY FOR THE TRUTH.
YOU'LL NEED TO LIE STILL DURING THE ENTIRE PROCEDURE.
OF COURSE. NOTHING TO LOSE BUT MY DIGNITY AND SANITY.
WE'LL BE RIGHT OUTSIDE, VAL. THINK DUMPLINGS.

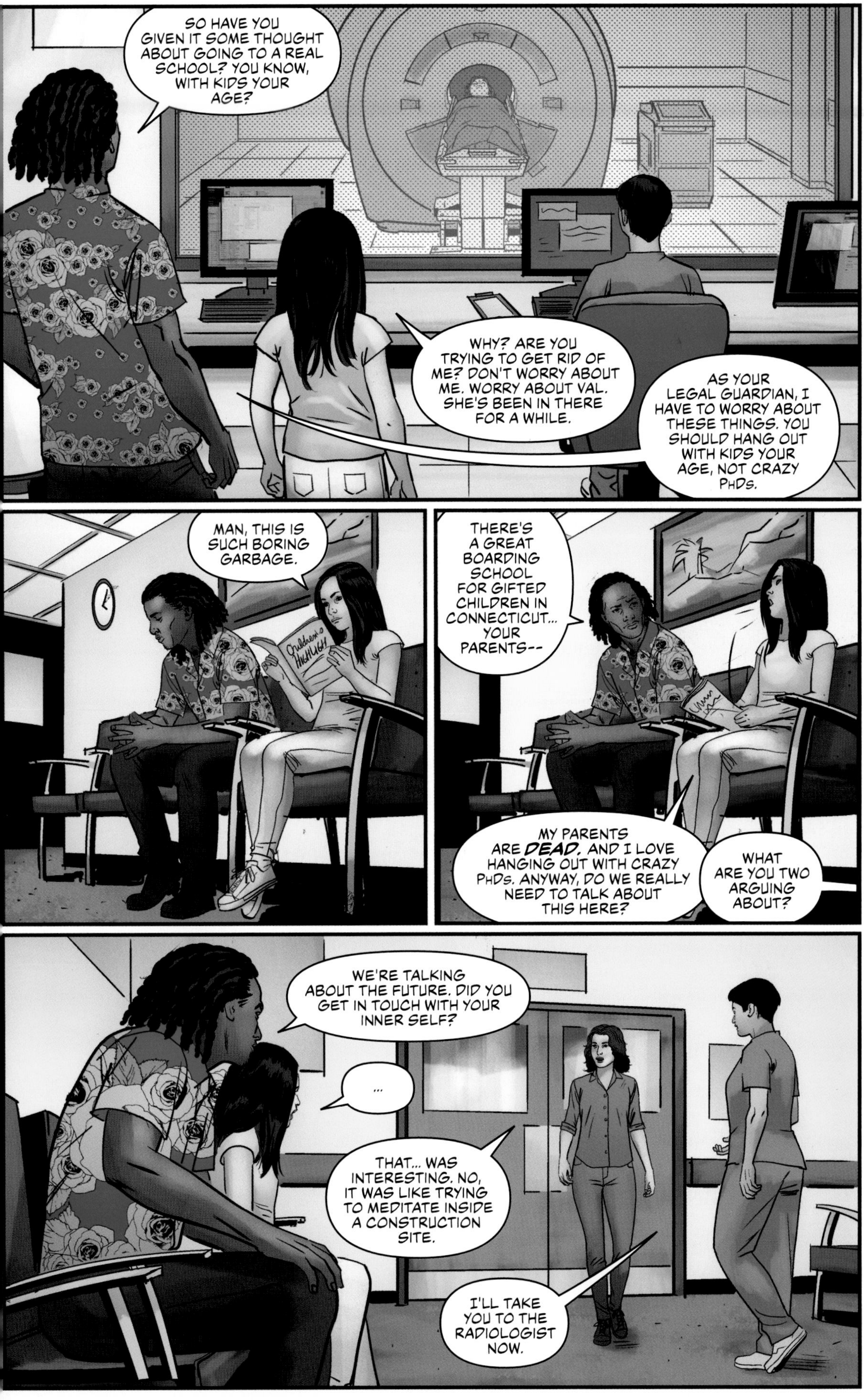
SO HAVE YOU GIVEN IT SOME THOUGHT ABOUT GOING TO A REAL SCHOOL? YOU KNOW, WITH KIDS YOUR AGE?
WHY? ARE YOU TRYING TO GET RID OF ME? DON'T WORRY ABOUT ME. WORRY ABOUT VAL. SHE'S BEEN IN THERE FOR A WHILE.
AS YOUR LEGAL GUARDIAN, I HAVE TO WORRY ABOUT THESE THINGS. YOU SHOULD HANG OUT WITH KIDS YOUR AGE, NOT CRAZY PhDs.
MAN, THIS IS SUCH BORING GARBAGE.
THERE'S A GREAT BOARDING SCHOOL FOR GIFTED CHILDREN IN CONNECTICUT... YOUR PARENTS--
MY PARENTS ARE DEAD. AND I LOVE HANGING OUT WITH CRAZY PhDs. ANYWAY, DO WE REALLY NEED TO TALK ABOUT THIS HERE?
WHAT ARE YOU TWO ARGUING ABOUT?
WE'RE TALKING ABOUT THE FUTURE. DID YOU GET IN TOUCH WITH YOUR INNER SELF?
...
THAT... WAS INTERESTING. NO, IT WAS LIKE TRYING TO MEDITATE INSIDE A CONSTRUCTION SITE.
I'LL TAKE YOU TO THE RADIOLOGIST NOW.

SO, WHAT'S WRONG WITH ME, DR. LEE?

I AM NOT EVEN SURE HOW TO ANSWER THAT. I HAVE NEVER SEEN ANYTHING LIKE THIS IN MY CAREER.

SEE THIS? IT'S HER PRIMARY AUDITORY CORTEX FIRING UP. IT SHOWS THE AUDITORY SENSATION IS *REAL* BUT ORIGINATING IN THE THALAMUS.

IT SEEMS TO INDICATE PROFESSOR RESNICK-BAKER REALLY *IS* HEARING VOICES INSIDE HER HEAD. OR SHALL I SAY, ONE VOICE.

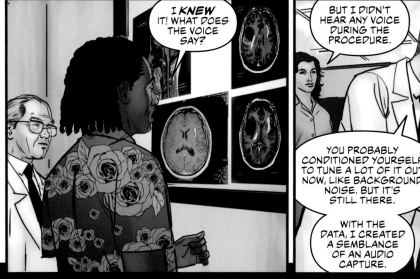

I *KNEW* IT! WHAT DOES THE VOICE SAY?

BUT I DIDN'T HEAR ANY VOICE DURING THE PROCEDURE.

YOU PROBABLY CONDITIONED YOURSELF TO TUNE A LOT OF IT OUT NOW, LIKE BACKGROUND NOISE. BUT IT'S STILL THERE.

WITH THE DATA, I CREATED A SEMBLANCE OF AN AUDIO CAPTURE.

THE SOUND QUALITY WILL BE QUITE GRAINY, BUT IT SHOULD MORE OR LESS MIMIC WHAT'S GOING ON INSIDE VAL'S HEAD.

THAT'S JAMILA'S VOICE!

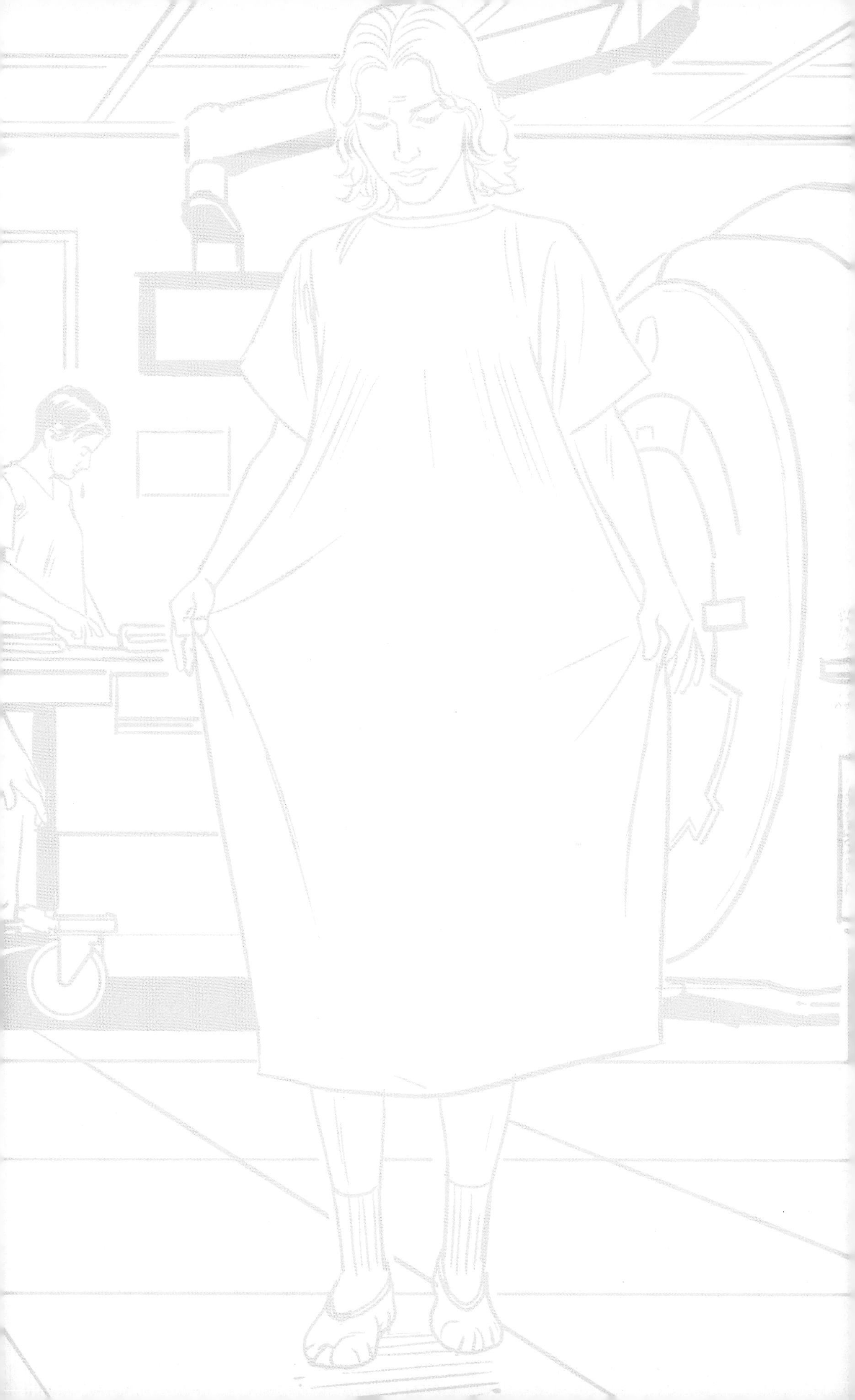

COVER GALLERY

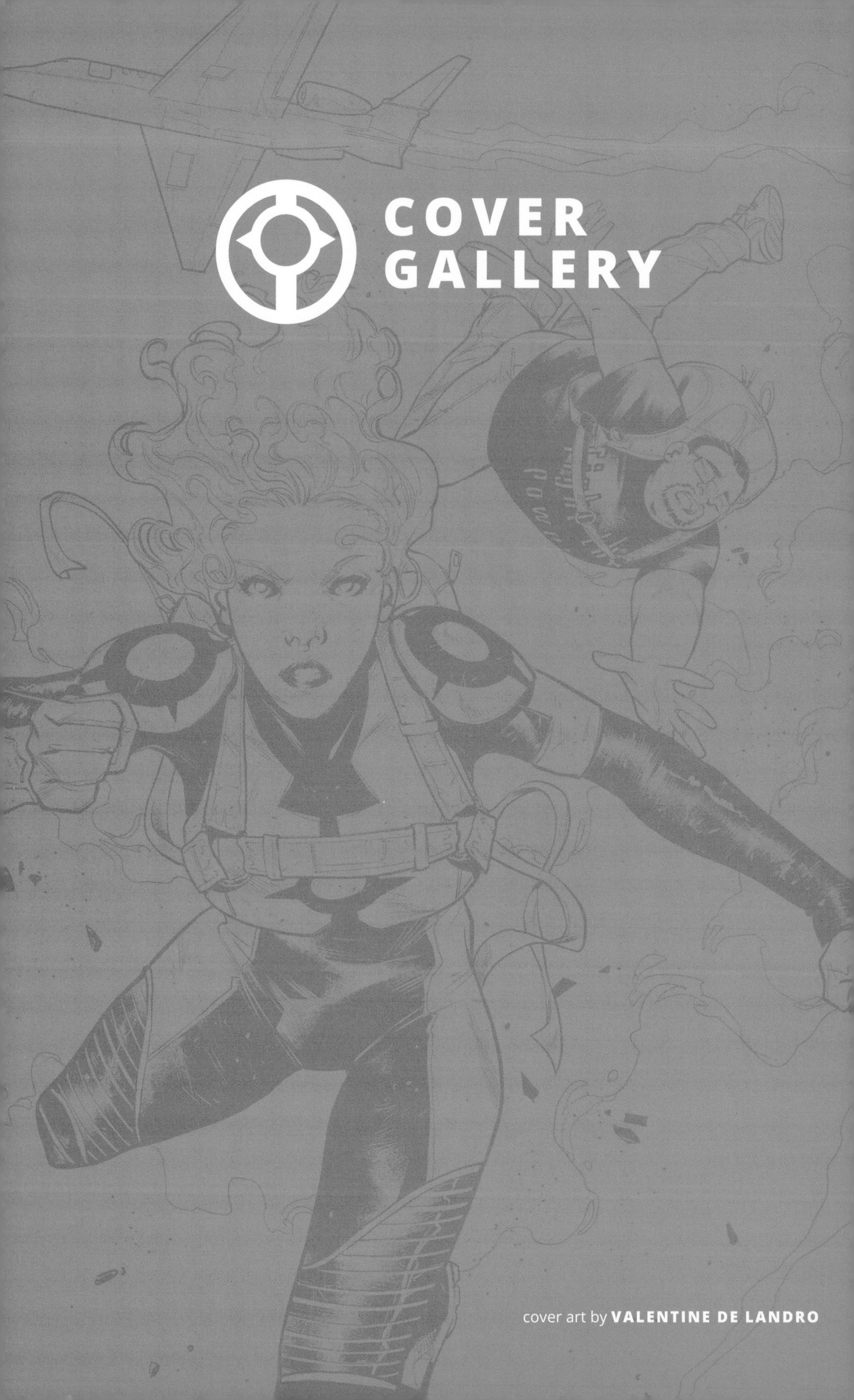

cover art by **VALENTINE DE LANDRO**

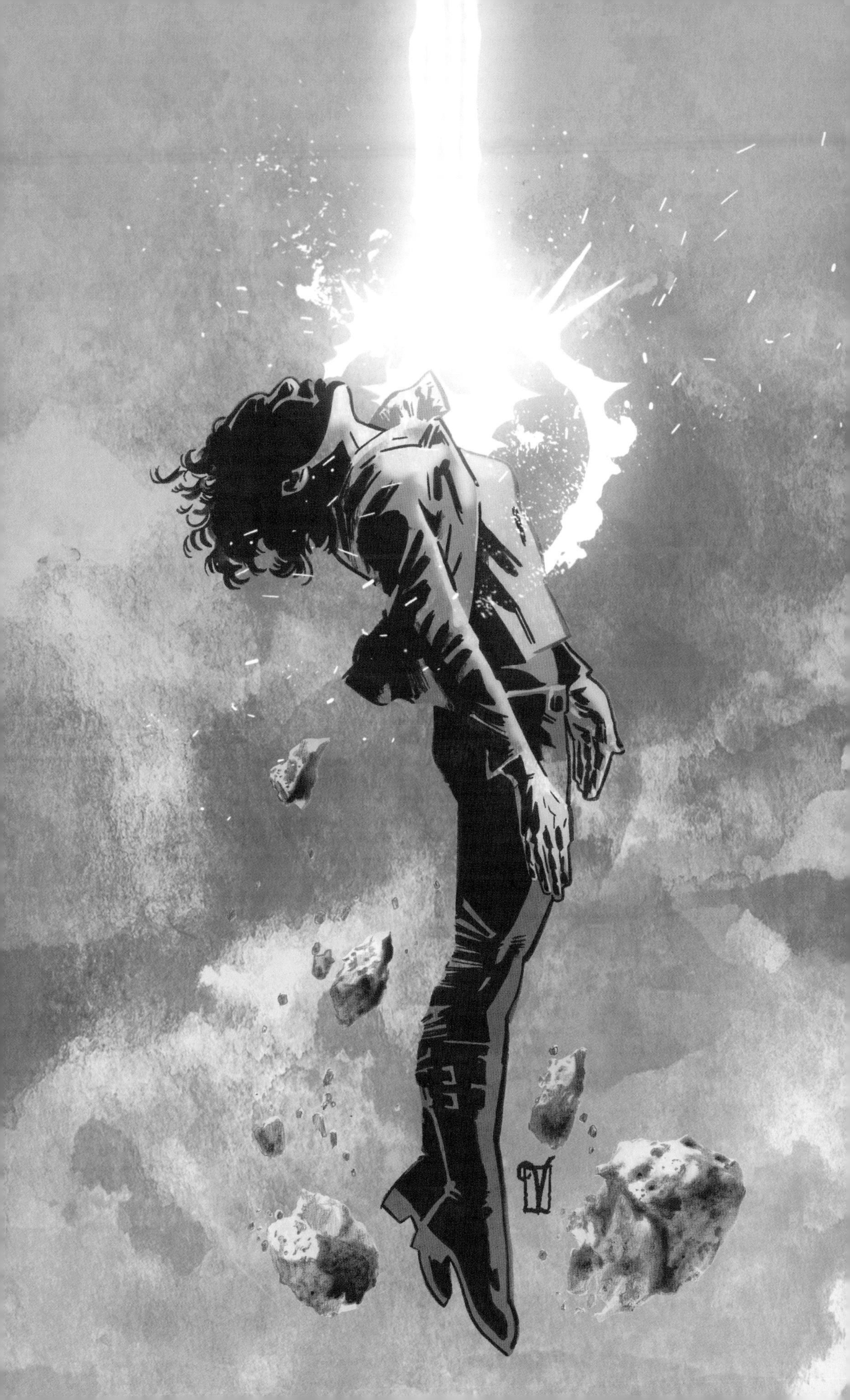

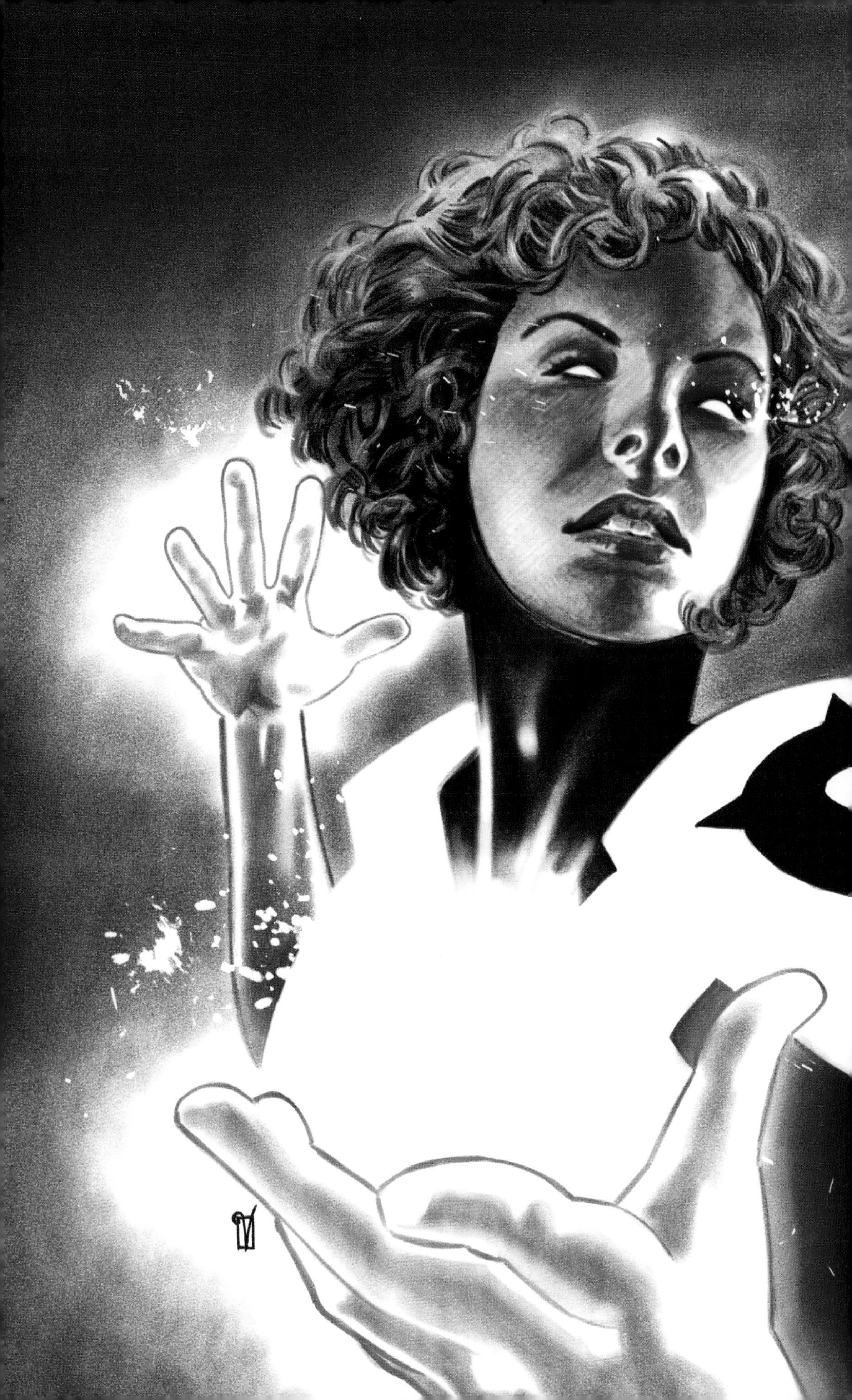

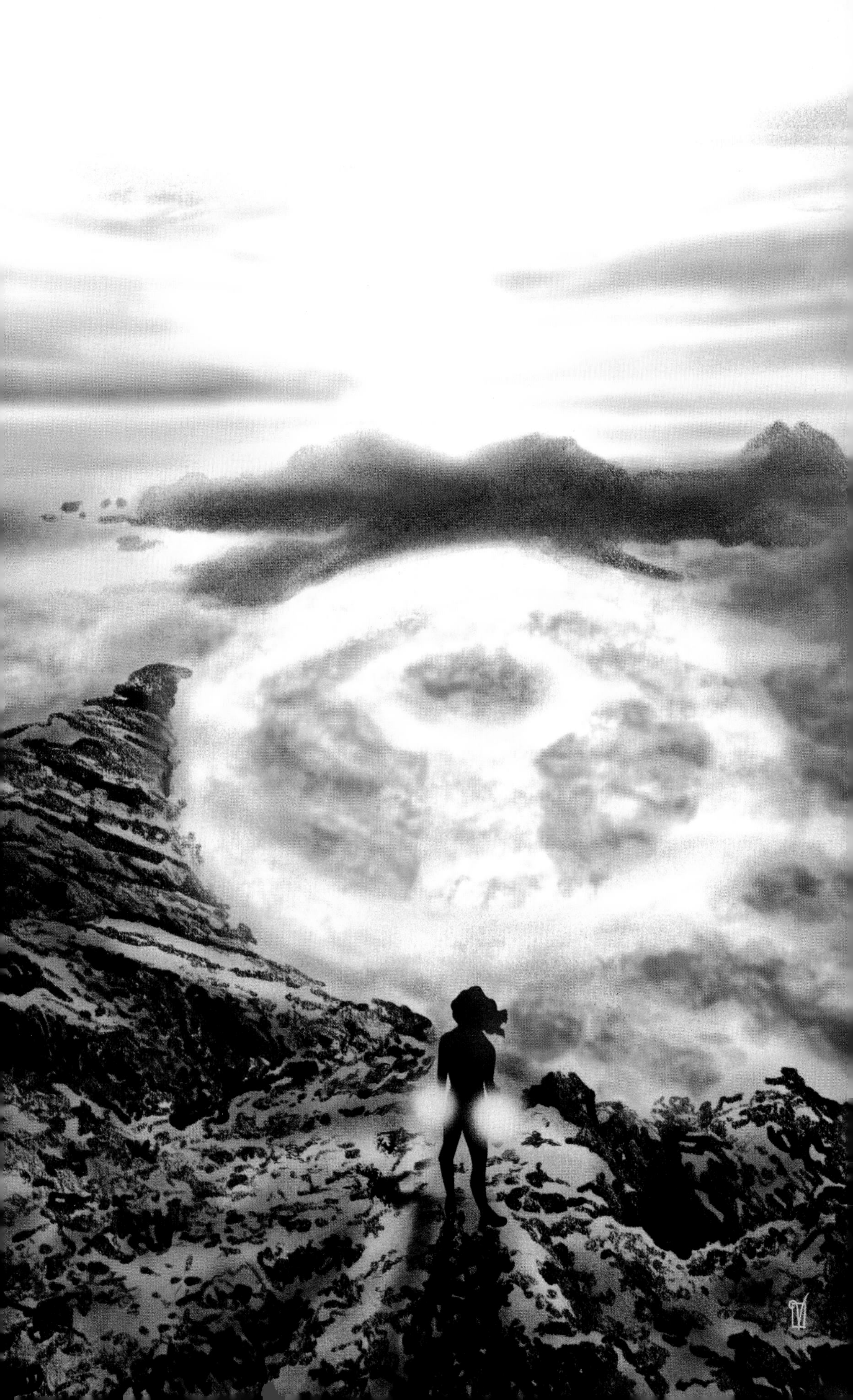

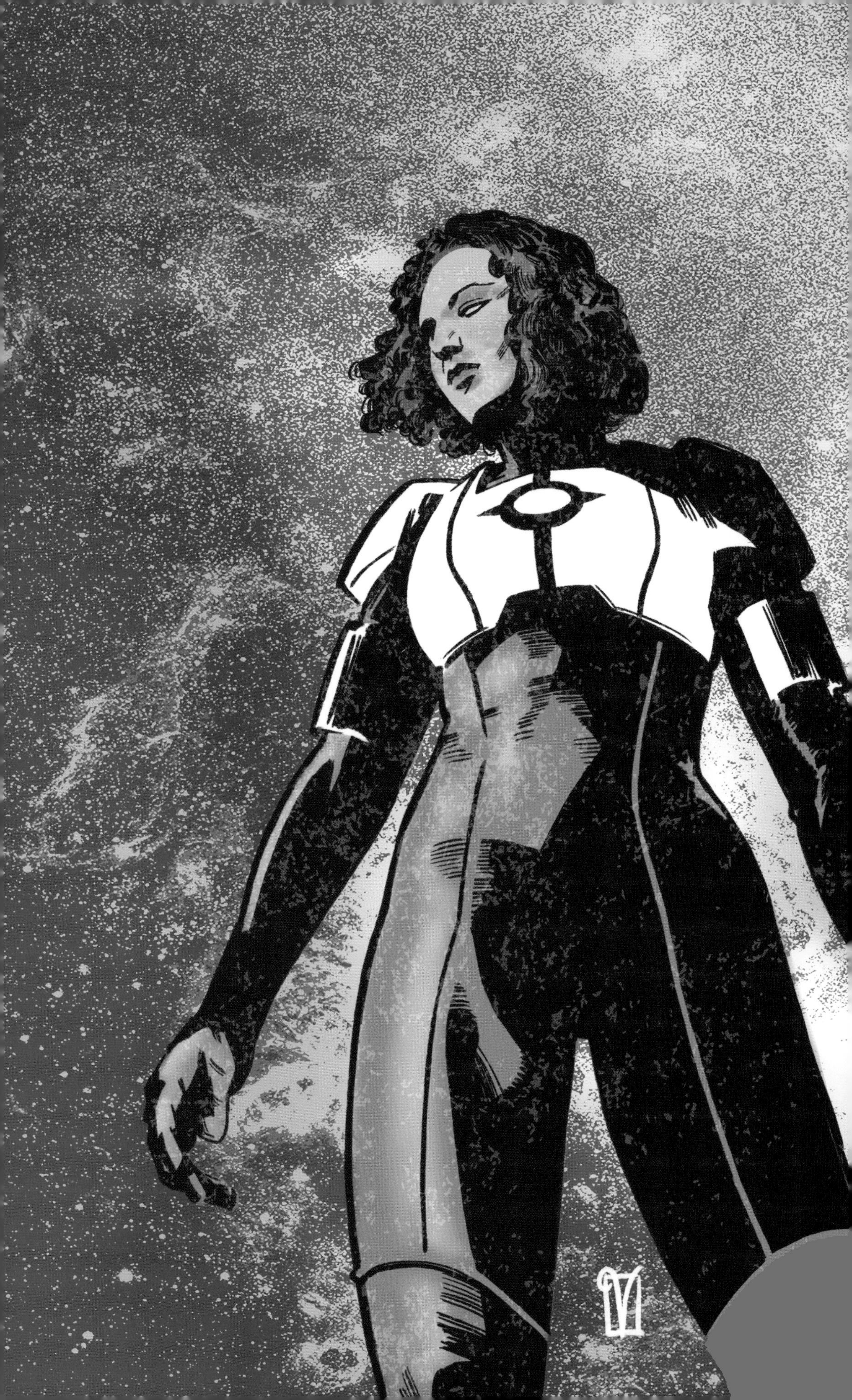

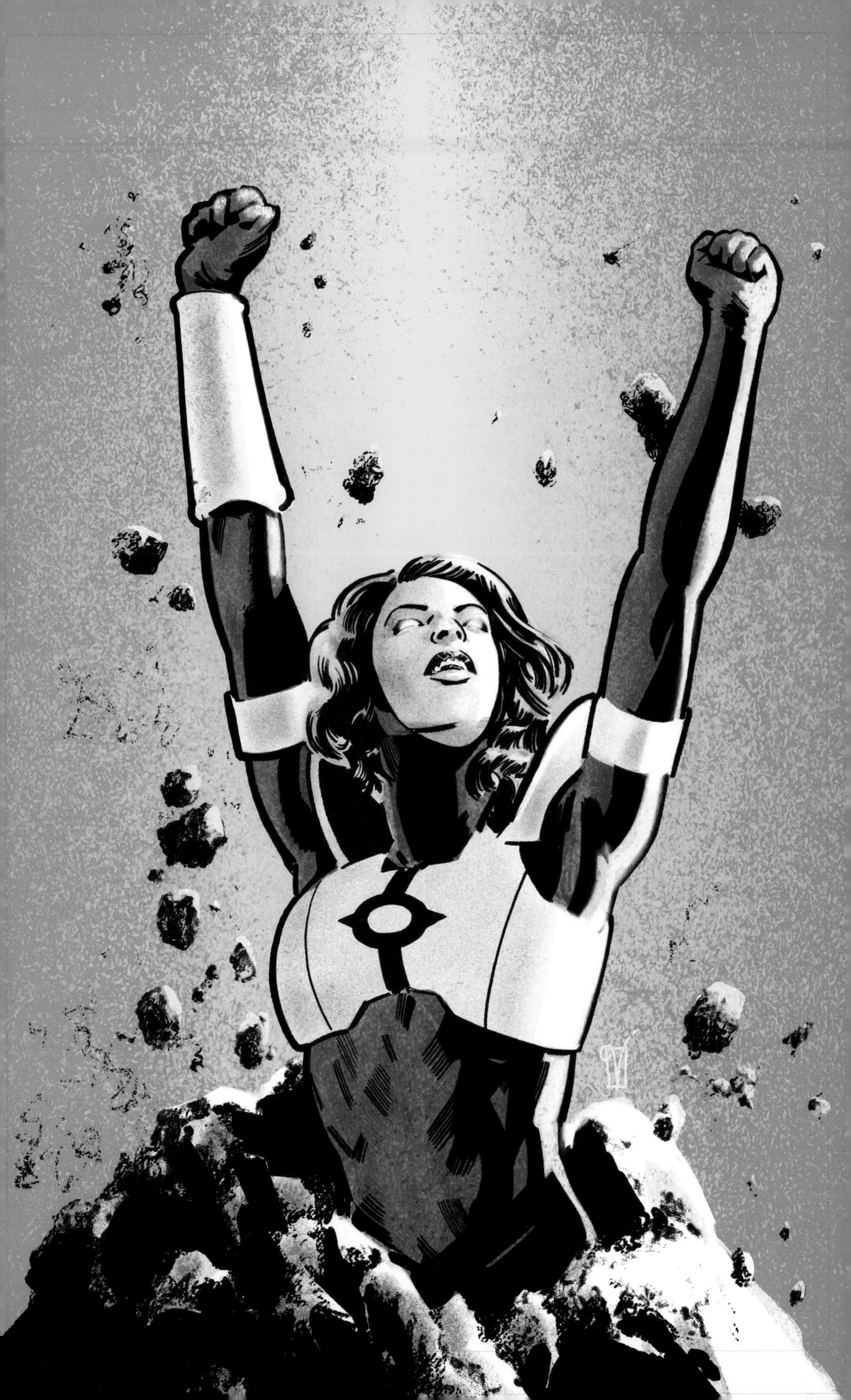

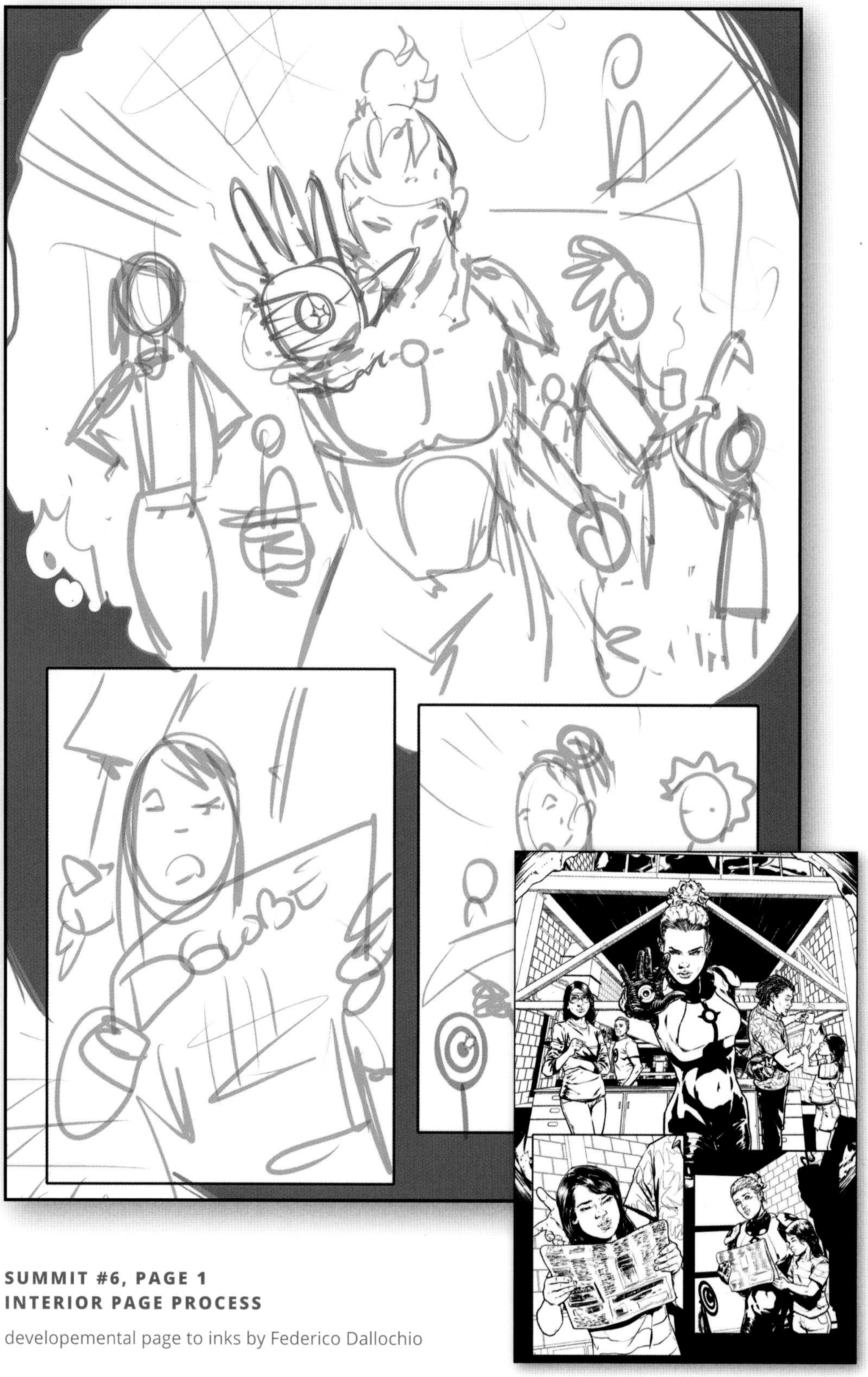

SUMMIT #6, PAGE 1
INTERIOR PAGE PROCESS

developemental page to inks by Federico Dallochio

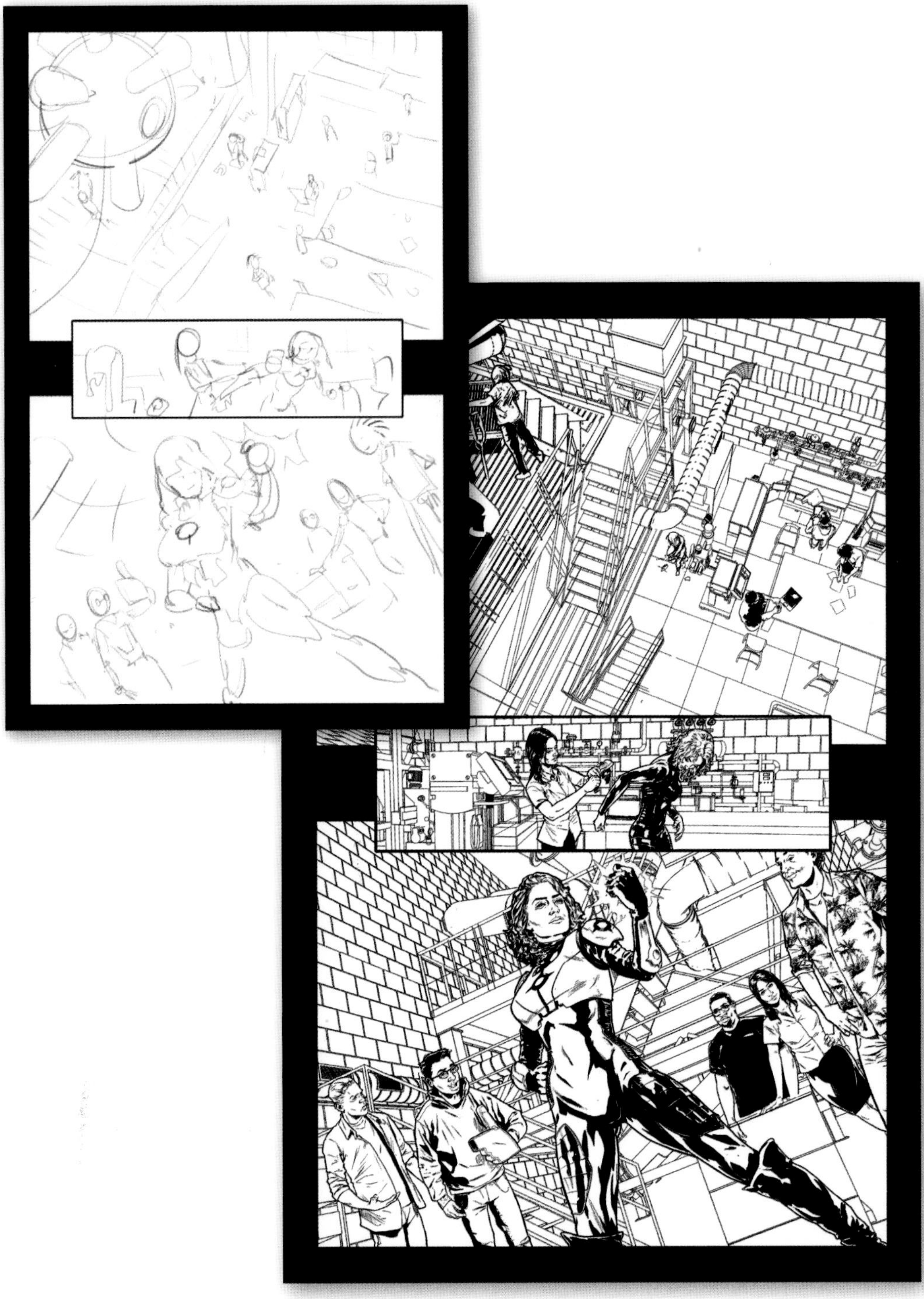

SUMMIT #7, PAGE 6
INTERIOR PAGE PROCESS

developemental page to inks by Federico Dallochio

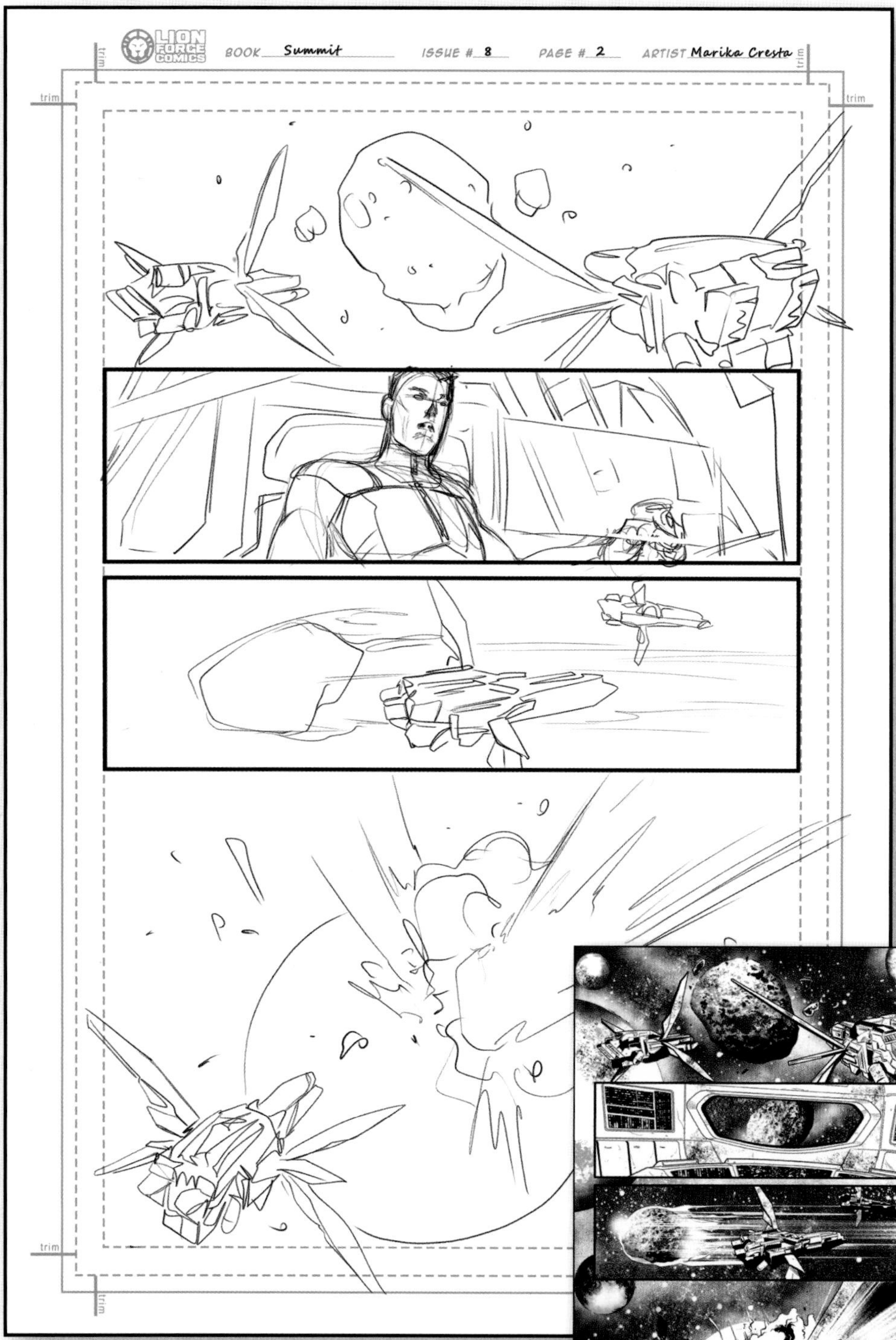
BOOK Summit
ISSUE # 8
PAGE # 2
ARTIST Marika Cresta
trim

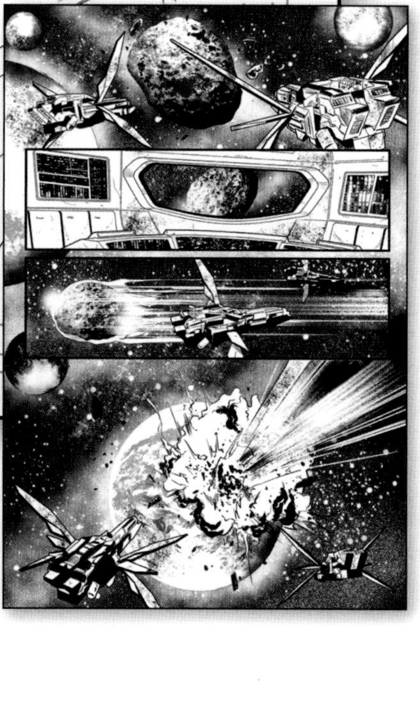

SUMMIT #8, PAGE 2
INTERIOR PAGE PROCESS

developemental page to inks by Marika Cresta

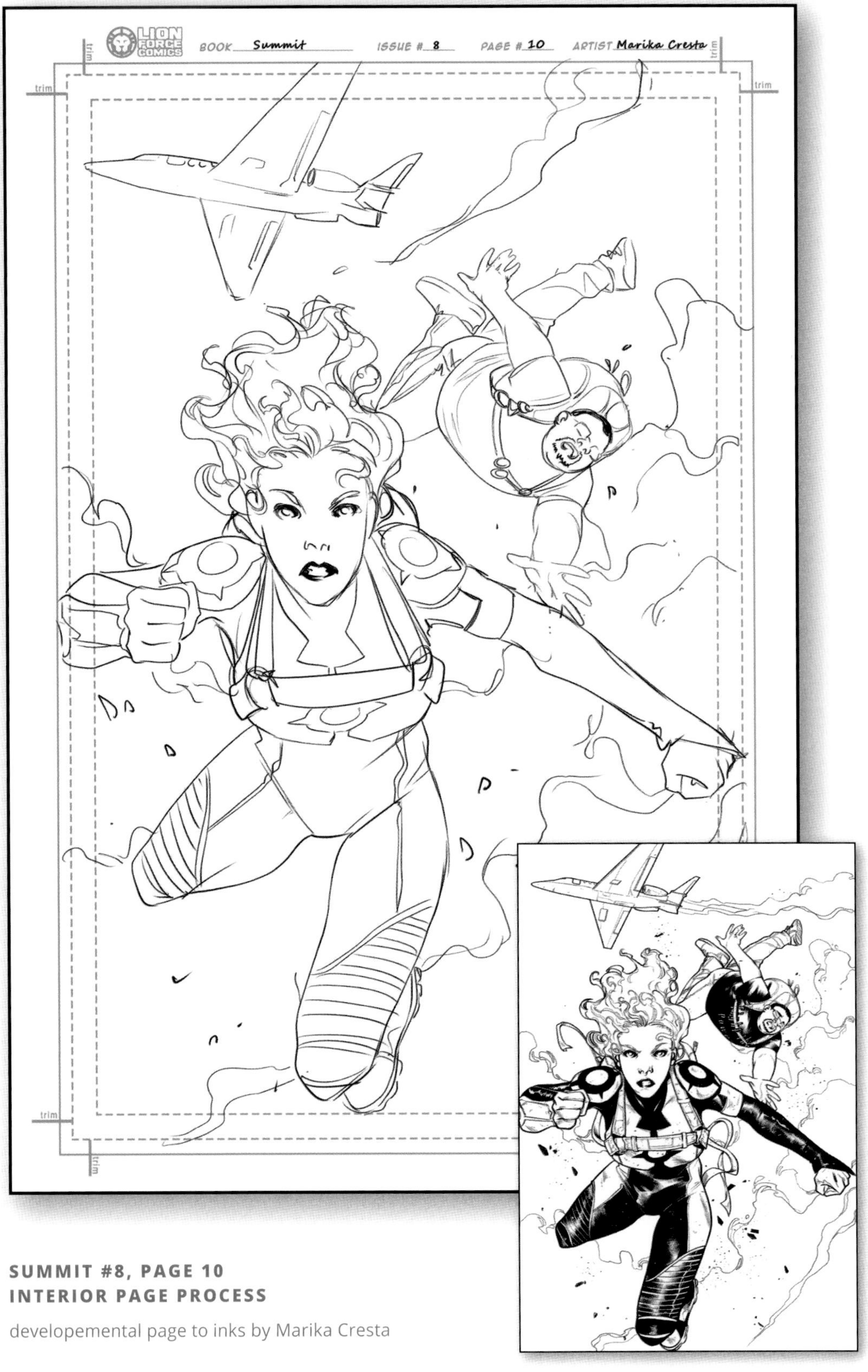
LION FORCE COMICS
BOOK Summit
ISSUE # 8
PAGE # 10
ARTIST Marika Cresta
trim

SUMMIT #8, PAGE 10
INTERIOR PAGE PROCESS

developemental page to inks by Marika Cresta

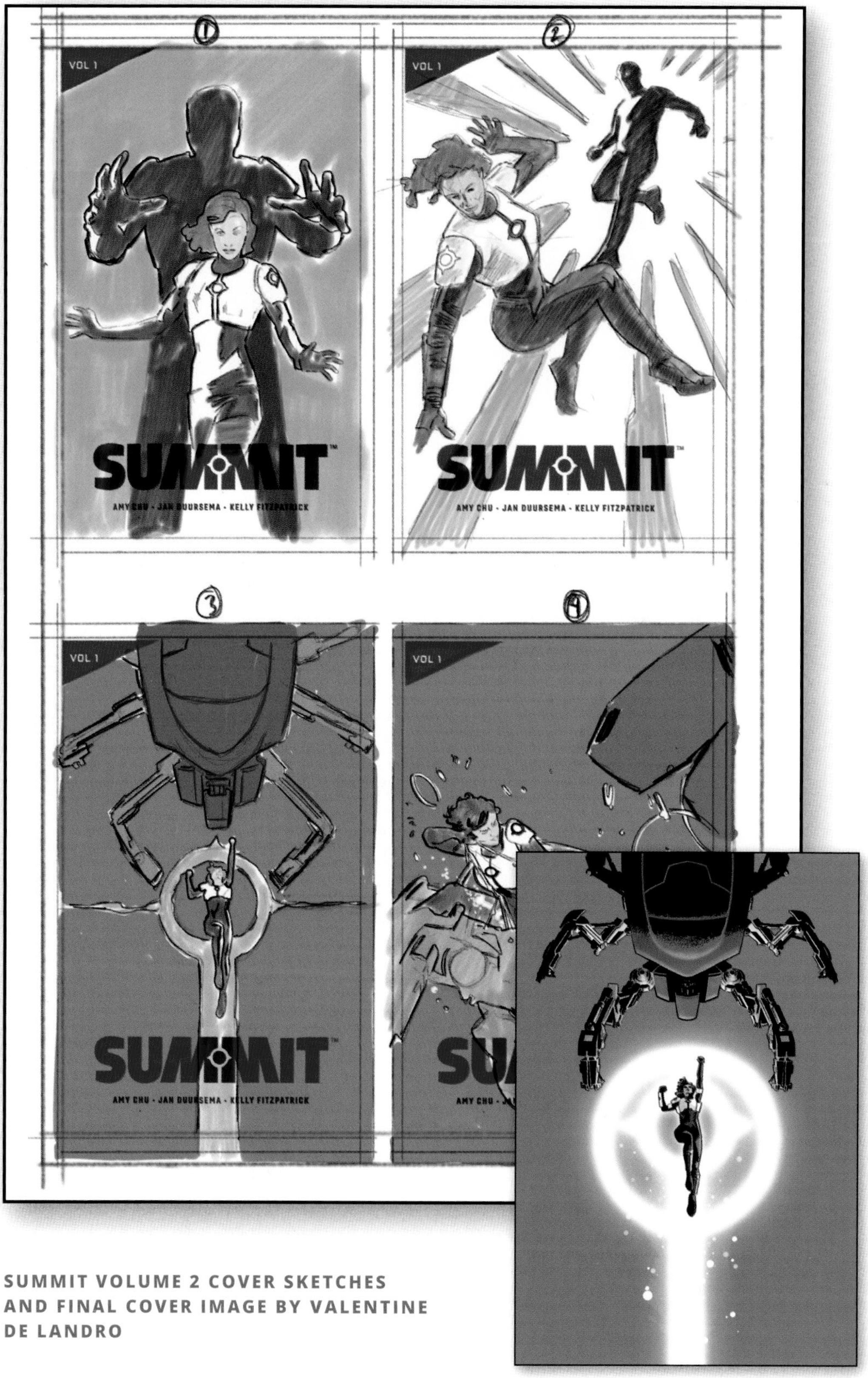
1
VOL 1
SUMMIT
AMY CHU · JAN DUURSEMA · KELLY FITZPATRICK
2
VOL 1
SUMMIT
AMY CHU · JAN DUURSEMA · KELLY FITZPATRICK
3
VOL 1
SUMMIT
AMY CHU · JAN DUURSEMA · KELLY FITZPATRICK
4
VOL 1

SUMMIT VOLUME 2 COVER SKETCHES AND FINAL COVER IMAGE BY VALENTINE DE LANDRO